Charles Marshall

An Introduction to the Knowledge and Practice of Gardening

Vol. II.

Charles Marshall

An Introduction to the Knowledge and Practice of Gardening
Vol. II.

ISBN/EAN: 9783337068165

Printed in Europe, USA, Canada, Australia, Japan

Cover: Foto ©Lupo / pixelio.de

More available books at **www.hansebooks.com**

AN
INTRODUCTION
TO THE
KNOWLEDGE AND PRACTICE
OF
GARDENING,
BY
CHARLES MARSHALL,

VICAR OF BRIXWORTH, NORTHAMPTONSHIRE.

God Almighty firſt planted a *Garden ;* and indeed it is the pureſt of human Pleaſures : It is the greateſt Refreſhment to the Spirits of Man : without which, Buildings and Palaces are but groſs handy Works.
BACON's ESSAYS.

FIRST AMERICAN FROM THE SECOND LONDON EDITION,
Conſiderably Enlarged and Improved.

TO WHICH IS ADDED,

AN ESSAY ON QUICK-LIME,
AS A
CEMENT AND AS A MANURE,
By JAMES ANDERSON, L.L.D. F.R.S. F.A.S. S.

VOL. II.

Boſton :
PRINTED BY SAMUEL ETHERIDGE,
For JOSEPH NANCREDE, NO. 49, *Marlboro'-Street.*

1799.

CONTENTS
OF VOL. II.

SECTION XVIII.

OF FLOWERS.

OF the claſſes, annuals, biennials and perennials, 3. Praiſe of flowers; of annuals in general, &c. 4. Culture of tender annuals, 6, &c. Of ſcoop trowels and watering pots; of potting plants, 9. Of watering them, 10. Of potting hardy flowers; ſecond ſowing of tender annuals; of ſowing the leſs tender ſorts, 11, &c. Of the hardy kinds, 13. Second ſowing of hardy annuals, 14. A caution; culture of biennials, 15. Of perennials. The Dutch famous for producing new flowers. Directions for raiſing bulbous and tuberous roots, 16. Of raiſing fibrous rooted ſorts 17. General culture of bulbous and tuberous roots, 18, &c. Soil ſuitable, and depth at which to plant, 19. Diſpoſition, diſtances and management, 20, &c. Of forwarding ſpring bulbs in water glaſſes, &c. Of ſtalk bulbs, 21. Of ſaving ſeed. Bulbs are yearly renewed. Propagation of flowering ſhrubs, 22, &c. Of American ſorts. Particular uſe of the hand-glaſs, 23. A uſeful obſervation, 24.

SECTION XIX.

LISTS OF TREES, SHRUBS, AND FLOWERS.

Concerning them, 24. Time of flowering, colours, names, 25. Sorts. Liſts of foreſt-trees, 26. Obſervations on ditto, 27, &c. Liſt of large deciduous ornamental trees, 30. Obſervations on ditto, 31, &c. Liſt of ſmaller deciduous ornamental trees, or large ſhrubs, 33. Obſervations on ditto, 34. Liſt of the loweſt deciduous trees, or ſhrubs, 35, &c. Obſervations on ditto, 38, &c. Liſt of evergreen

CONTENTS.

trees, 42. Obfervations on ditto, 43. Lift of evergreen fhrubs, 45. Obfervations on ditto, 47. Lift of flowers—tender annuals, 49. Obfervations on ditto, 50. Lefs tender annuals, 52. Obfervations on ditto, 54. Hardy annuals. 58. Obfervations on ditto. 61. Lift of biennial flowers, 62. Obfervations on ditto, 63. Lift of fibrous rooted perennials, 66. Obfervations on ditto, 72. Lift of bulbous, tuberous, and flefhy rooted perennials, 82. Obfervations on ditto, 86. Detached articles—auricula, 91. Carnation, 92. Geranium, 94. Pinks, 97. Polyanthus, 98. Tuberofe, 99.

SECTION XX.

A CALENDAR.

Of the general work of gardening, 101. January, the particular work of, 102. February, 104. March, 106. April, 109. May, 112. June, 114. July, 117. Auguft, 120. September, 123. October, 125. November, 128. December, 131. Clofe, 134.

⁎ In the courfe of the work, a *few* articles are referred to, which were defigned to be inferted at the clofe of the book, but are omitted in order to introduce others more important.

†₊† The neceffity of an *Index* is precluded by the above table of *contents*, the work being fo much in the *alphabetical form*.

SECTION XVIII.

OF FLOWERS.

FLOWERS, as to their cultivation, are claſſed into *annuals*, *biennials* and *perennials*. *Annuals* are thoſe that are ſown, flower, and die, within a year. *Biennials* are thoſe that are ſown one year, and flower and die the next. *Perennials* are thoſe that do not flower the year they are ſown, but the next, and continue to live years afterwards, ſome fewer, ſome more : Of this claſs there is a great variety, (perhaps fifty to one of the laſt) moſtly fibrous rooted, ſome fleſhy, ſome bulbous, and ſome tuberous, &c. Moſt of the *perennials* are annual in their ſtalks, which die down to the ground in winter, and freſh ſhoots riſe in the ſpring. But ſtrictly ſpeaking, all of each claſs are not *annual*, *biennial*, and *perennial ;* for ſome of the *annuals* come a ſecond, or a third year, as *Chineſe holyhock*, and *Indian pink*, and others would live through the winter if houſed. Of the *biennials*, the ſame may be ſaid of the *ſtock July flower*, *ſweet William*, and *wall flower ;* only theſe plants do not always live, and will not come ſo neat and ſtrong as before, and are therefore to be ſown, or propagated, as they are claſſed, in order to have a certain and fine blow. Of the *perennials*, ſome do not flower well above three or four years, as the *holyhock*, &c. for which a ſowing ſhould of courſe take place the year before they are wanted. See pages 41, 42, 56, 57, 60, 65, 66, 67, 70, 113.

Flowers, the sole luxury which Nature knew,
In *Eden*'s pure and guiltless garden grew;
Gay without toil, and lovely without art,
They sprung to cheer the sense, and glad the heart.
BARBAULD.

What sweets are these which gratefully diffuse
Their fragrance round ?————
—————————— 'Tis the *flowers*,
The incense of the garden's breath, that sheds
This balmy sweetness.————
—————————————— To the smell
How grateful, nor less pleasing to the eye
The bloom of opening flowers.—Kind Nature here
In nice proportion all her favours deals;
Those gales around the blissful *garden* pours,
Neither too strong the organs to oppress,
Nor yet so faint the senses to elude.
How often is the sated palate cloy'd
At the rich sumptuous feast, how soon offend
The loathed dishes which last moment pleas'd?
But the high relish which each sense partakes
From Nature's gifts the appetite ne'er tire,
Which please it more, the more they are enjoy'd.
E'en luxury itself, when feasting here,
Is guiltless, and esteem'd a crime no more.
See in what various tints the flowery tribes
Their several beauties shew, and court the eye
With new delight, distinguish'd each from each
By different hues—how wise the bounteous hand
Of that indulgent power! tho' perfect all
His works, who yet on all the charms bestows
Of novelty to shew 'em still more fair.
NEWCOMB.

I. OF ANNUALS.

Annual flowers are divided into three classes, i. e. *tender*, *less tender*, and *hardy*.

In

SECT. XVIII. OF FLOWERS. 5

In the lift, section 19th. the *tender* annuals are marked 1, the *lefs tender* 2, and the unmarked are *hardy*.

To this *lift* of flowers might be added others, and fome poffibly that are pretty; but many of the annuals that have been introduced for variety's fake in large gardens, plantations, &c. are weed-like, dull and rambling; and perhaps a few among thofe here mentioned may not be fufficiently *ornamental* (as, for inftance, the *whites*, where there are other colours of the fame flower) to give general fatisfaction; for a *gay appearance* is certainly the firft object in the cultivation of flowers. There are rare plants, and others admirable in their ftructure and properties, which make no fhow; but thefe are rather fubjects for the curious *botanift*, and he will think them well worthy of a place in *his* garden.

Some *flowers* are both beautiful and fragrant; but many have only one of thefe properties to recommend them. Some are cultivated cheifly for the elegance of their *leaf*, as the *ice plant*, *palma chrifti*, and the *curled mallow;* and fome that bear pretty and fweet flowers, are meanly furnifhed with leaves, as the *yellow fultan*. Others obtain a place in the garden, neither for fragrance, or flower, or leaf: but merely for the fingularity of the *fruit*, or feed veffel, as the *egg plant*, *fnails, catterpillars, hedge hogs, horns*, and others.

In the given *lift*, fome of the tender annuals may occafionally be confidered as *lefs tender;* as *Amaranthus coxcomb*, and *tricolor*, *balfams*, *double*, as well as *fingle*, and *ftramonium;* only they will not be fo forward and fine. Some of thofe alfo among the *lefs tender* may be fown as *hardy*, for a late blow, as *China after, Indian pink, love lies bleeding, marigold, French* and *African, princes feather*, ten week *ftocks, fultan,* red and *white*. Some among the *hardy* annuals may advantageoufly be treated as the *lefs tender*, to enfure their germination, or to bring them *forward*, as *belvidere*,

dere, Indian corn, (the large sort of which *must* be forwarded upon heat) *mignonette, mulberry blight, nasturtium,* and *persicaria.*

The CULTURE of each Class follows.

I. OF ANNUALS.

ABOUT *Mid-March* is a general good time to sow the TENDER (and in short, all) sorts, though the curious and skilful being well furnished with proper frames, &c. may begin a month sooner; the end of *March,* or beginning of *April* is, however, not too late, and will better suit a *young* gardener than if he sowed earlier. In order to succeed in this business, there should be provided, fine dry and rich earth, good stable dung, frames, or roomy hand-glasses, and mats.

A moderately strong *hot bed,* for a one light, must be prepared, and the violent heat being certainly over, the seeds may either be sown thinly in *drills,* two or three inches asunder, on five or six inches of mould, or less on a weak bed. May sow also in *pots,* plunged to the rims. Cover the seeds from a quarter to half an inch, or more, according to their size. Some of them will appear in a few days, and others will lie a fortnight, or more, according to the circumstances of their *nature, age,* and the *heat,* or *moisture,* they meet with.

Thin the plants a little in time, and soon after to an inch, and then again to two, asunder.

Water, just warm, must be *gently* given them, (not to beat them down) as they may appear to need it, and *air* (particularly in a full sun) as much as they can be thought to bear, a little at first, and by degrees more, for this is essential to their health and strength.

The

SECT. XVIII. OF FLOWERS.

The feeds may alfo be fown in pots, and plunged at the back part of a *cucumber* or *melon* bed. A bed may be got ready to *prick* them into, or into pots placed in the like manner; and where only a *few* are cultivated, this method is advifable, (to fave trouble) not beginning too early.

Provide *another bed* by one month from the fowing, to prick the plants out in, having fix inches depth of mould, place them five or fix inches afunder, allotting thofe to the warmeft part of the bed, which were longeft coming up, and which are of courfe the weakeft, as *globes*, &c. Let the mould be warmed through before planting. There had better be too *little*, than too much heat ; but if the bed gets cool, *line* it, or *cover* round with ftraw, as directed in the management of hot beds, page 179.

If not fown till the beginning of *April*, this fecond bed may poffibly go through the bufinefs, with proper management to keep up its heat, and covering well on nights ; but a *third* bed is commonly neceffary, in order to fucceed *well*, and bring the plants on forward and fine, which is neceffary to the credit of the gardener. In this bed, it being covered over with four or five inches of mould, the plants fhould be in fmall pots, one in each, and plunged an inch deep, clofe to one another. As the bed gets cooler, the pots are to be earthed higher, till up to the rims in mould ; but if planted without pots, the diftance fhould be about nine inches afunder.

More *water* and *air* is neceffary as the plants increafe in fize ; and every time they are fhifted, let it be carefully, with fome earth about their roots, though a warm bed will foon make them ftrike, if without mould. Let them be *fhaded* from fun a few days ; i. e. till rooted in their new habitation. As thefe tender annuals do not rightly bear the full open air till *Midfummer*, give them refolutely as much of it as poffible in the frames, (by degrees) even to taking off the

glaffes

glaffes in mild parts of the day. Keep up a heat in the third bed as long as can be, that the plants may continue in a growing ftate, and not ftunted by bottom cold. To this end a *fourth* bed, for fome of the forts, as *globes*, *coxcombs*, &c. would be a great advantage, as to fize.

It is hardly neceffary to hint that the *beds* muft be larger, and *frames* deeper, every time the plants are fhifted. As the firft frame was a *one* light, let the fecond be a *two* light, and the third a *three* light, which may be raifed upon bricks, or boarded round the bottom, as occafion may require. From the fmall *pots*, let them be tranfplanted into bigger in time, or (as foon as they can fafely be) into warm borders, where if covered with hand-glaffes, fet on bricks for a while, it would fecure them from unkind weather, till got a little hardened. In this changeable climate of *England*, there is hardly any knowing when tender plants may be expofed fafely ; yet *too* much houfing and covering is to be avoided as much as poffible. Many flowers will need *fupport*. See page 56. For the method of *fhifting* plants from pots, as into bigger, or to the open ground. See page 190.

Some tender flowers in pots may be in the ground, to keep their roots cool, and for the fake of being conveniently covered ; in which cafe, put a bit of tile below the pot to keep out worms.

Good *feed* from tender annuals will not be well had, but from *February* fown plants. Skilful gardeners, fowing early, and having plenty of dung and *drawing frames*, produce furprifing plants of the tender annual clafs, fo that the *globe amaranthus* to three, and the giant *coxcomb* and *tricolor* from three to five or fix feet high have been feen. Flowers defigned to gather *feed* from, fhould begin to have fome protection of glafs about *Mid-Auguft*, at leaft on nights, till they are fully ripened in *September*.

Scoop

SECT. XVIII.   OF FLOWERS.

Scoop trowels of two or three fizes will be found very ufeful in the fhifting of flowers in general, but particularly of the hot bed fort ; and as they fhould be clean from dirt when ufed, fo alfo fhould they be free from *ruft*, by which they will work much pleafanter, and more fuccefsfully : In fhort, *all* garden tools fhould be kept bright, as well for ufe as neatnefs. Before a trowel is ufed, in the removal of a plant, it is a proper, and fafe way, to cut ftrait down round the root, and to the bottom, with a clean, and not very blunt knife ; fo will the trowel take all up whole, and the fibres will not be lacerated, or barked.

A *fmall watering pot* (i. e. from two to three quarts) with a *finely* pierced rofe, is alfo neceffary, to give refrefhment without bending down the plants, or hardening the furface of the earth. The *form* of many a good flower is fpoiled in its infancy by *rough* watering, and particularly *capficums ;* to avoid which evil, whatever watering pot is ufed, it fhould be only half full.

The *potting* of plants is often carelefsly, but ought to be moft carefully performed, that as little check as poffible may be felt by the roots. Fill the pot one half or two thirds full, (as the cafe may require) and then make a hole in the middle, adapted in form to receive the plant, with its *ball* of earth ; and do it right at firft, fo as not to be too high, or too low, for once put in, it will not be fafe to take it out again, left the mould drop from the roots. Do not prefs the ball of earth, (as fome do) but only juft faften the loofe mould that is put round it. If the foil is light, prefs that a little which is firft put in at the bottom. If a plant that is to be potted be *without* mould about its roots, raife a *hillock* (at a proper height) in the middle of the pot, to lay the roots on and round : It muft always be avoided planting in the pots *too* deep, becaufe fo much of the pot is loft as is above. In all *tranfplantations* it is proper to fhorten fome of the roots, and the moft ftraggling are to be chofen for the purpofe ;

pose; so that when it is done with a *ball* of earth, some of the external fibres must be cut off, if it was not done by taking up, which it generally is when the plants are any thing large.

Annuals in *pots* will require water every day, in very hot weather, and in moderately so, every other; but those in the open ground will do twice as long (or more) without water being given them. Some sorts will need more water than others, as *egg plants* and *balsams*, than *coxcombs* and *tricolors*. This matter and a variety of others, will be learned by *observation*, without a good share of which, no one can possibly become a *good gardener:* The most exact directions will not take in every case, and rules will be of little avail, where the mind is not in diligent exercise.

In general, *potted plants* require *water* according to the weather, their situation as to the sun, the size of the pots, the fulness of the roots, the quantity of leaves, and the particular nature of their substance, as succulent or not: The smaller pots must have the most. The *earth* also in which plants grow makes a great difference, as some sorts of soil retain moisture much longer than others. It may be a *question* whether pots of *annual* flowers standing in *pans*, should have water constantly kept in them, or only watered (in due time) on the top, till it runs through: Both practices are followed by good gardeners; but the latter seems best, as keeping the young fibres at the bottom always sodden can hardly be right: With respect to *perennials* (except of an *aquatic* nature) it must be wrong. Let pots of flowers in the summer be placed pretty much in the *shade* and *shelter;* but not by any means be under trees, or a roof. A situation where they have only the *morning sun* till eleven or twelve o'clock is the best; and some persons are so curious in this respect as to have *awnings* for the purpose, and temporary *reed fences* to keep off the wind, to which flowers (particularly of the tender kind) should not be wholly exposed.

exposed. *Annuals,* or even a few *perennials,* may be put in covered places, when nearly in full blow, for the sake of their ornament; but the latter should not be continued longer than while the prime show lasts.

It is *advisable* not to *pot* more plants than necessary, as they occasion much trouble, if properly managed; and after all, will not be so fine as those growing in the open ground. Some things are too tender for open culture, and by potting they are conveniently protected by *frames,* or by *housing,* and sometimes simply plunging them in the ground, close against a warm wall, in winter, where a little protection may be easily given them; others it may be desirable to pot, for the sake of moving them into particular places when in *blow,* and to have some ready to put into the ground, where others are gone off, so as to keep certain favourite borders and walks always in glow; but do not have *too* much to do in this way.

A *second* sowing of *tender* annuals should take place two, three, or four weeks after the first, according as that was made, late or early; for their beauties are certainly desirable, as long as the season will permit us to behold them, and they are the *florist's* chief dependence in the *autumn.*

* * * * *

The LESS TENDER annuals should have a slight bed (about two feet thick) made for them at *Mid-March,* or a little after, being sown and managed as directed for the tender sorts, when they are one or two inches high, (according to their nature) they must be taken up with a scoop trowel, so as to keep a ball of earth about their roots, and either transplanted on another bed, about one and a half foot thick of dung, or into the cold ground; the small kinds at four or five, and the larger at six or eight inches asunder, in a *good* well broke soil. Let them be immediately watered and

and kept moift, and fhaded from fun till well fettled.
Here they may grow till their leaves begin to meet,
when they fhould be cut between their roots with a
knife, and lifted up neatly with a fcoop trowel, to be
potted or planted where they are to flower: If this
bufinefs is done *well*, they will receive but little check
in their tranfplantation. *Spindle* rooted plants (as
ftocks) fhould be moved where they are to blow, as
young as may be; but *fibrous* rooted ones may be
fhifted much older.

Plants will *flag* a little even when removed with a
large ball of earth; but as moft likely *fome* of the
fibres of the roots are either broke or cut, the effect is
natural, as a plant is chiefly fed by the youngeft and
moft *extreme* parts of the root. If poffible, let all *fummer* tranfplanted flowers be *fhaded* from fun, by garden
pots, (raifed a little) or otherwife, till they have ftruck
frefh roots, which they will foon do; but uncover on
nights. This will occafion fome trouble; yet the advantage attending it, makes it very advifable, and
efpecially the plants moved with none, or very little
mould about their roots.

A *hot bed* for thefe, as it is moderate, may be covered
with hoops and mats, and do very well, or rather better than frames and glafs; for it often happens, that
annuals are kept *too* clofe, by which they become weak,
and get ftunted when planted out in the free air, which
is made (by over nurfing) unnatural to them. Towards the end of *April*, almoft any of them will come
up under *hand-glaffes*, on a warm border, in a light and
rich foil; but they will blow late, and be not near fo
ftrong. The *Chinefe holyhock*, though it will certainly
come *up* well at this late fowing, will be hardly able
to produce flowers before winter. Thofe flowers of
this clafs, however, that have been mentioned as to be
occafionally confidered as hardy, may be thus treated
for a *fecond* blow.

Other

SECT. XVIII.   OF FLOWERS.   13

Other modes of cultivation are, that a few of the lefs tender forts may be fown in pots, and placed (not plunged) in any hot bed that is in work for other things ; but they muft not be kept clofe, or hot, which would draw them up weak : This plan may do for them a little while, and a flight heat may be got ready to prick them out upon.

Again, both this clafs of annuals, and the former, if not very early fown, do exceeding well, (or rather beft) when on *hot beds* under *hand-glaffes*, or *paper lights*, particularly *balfams*.

What was faid of *tender* annuals apply here, as to *air*, *water*, and *cover*, but more freedom in the prefent cafe fhould be taken. If any are under *mats*, the cover muft be removed on days, except the weather be bad ; or it may be only turned back, and half off, to let the fun and light in from the *fouth*. Never let the *feeds* or *plants* of annuals really want *water* when the weather is dry. See page 56.

* * * * *

The HARDY annuals have fome little difference in their temperature. Though all may be fown from the middle to the end of *March*, as the beft average feafon, fome may generally with fafety be fown at *Mid-February*, as *candy tufts*, *cornbottles*, *larkfpurs*, *hawkweed*, *lavatera*, *lobel's catchfly*, *lupines*, *dwarf lychnis*, *nigella*, *fweet peas*, *poppies*, *mulberry blight*, *oriental mallow*, *perficaria*, *fun-flower*, *annual fnap dragon*, *Venus' looking-glafs*, and *navel wort*, *virginian*, or *annual ftock*, and *winged peas*, with fome others.

But *nature* feems evidently to direct an *autumn* fowing, for *many* forts which are then fhed (fome always, and others often) come up at fpring, and thefe make the fineft *blow*, and produce the beft *feed* for propagation. A number, (all the above forts) therefore, might be fcattered on the furface of the ground at random,
not

not immediately as soon as ripe, but kept a *little* while to harden ; but this is not a common practice, as gardeners like to have their borders spring dressed before they sow their annuals.

For the *spring* sowing, the ground being deep dug, and *well* broke, make hollows (by drawing the mould aside) of from six to twelve inches diameter, or more, according to the size of the garden, as large ones should have the biggest patches. Sow thin, and cover according to the size of the seed, from a quarter to an inch. Take out mould enough to leave the patches somewhat hallow, which will serve to show where they are sown, and to receive the rain, or occasional watering. If the plants come up crowding, thin them soon, and leave a number suitable to their usual size of growth ; as one only of the *belvidere, cornbottle, persicaria,* and *sun-flower ;* two of the *lavatera, oriental mallow, mulberry blight,* &c. three *larkspurs ;* and four of less plants. Annuals are very often sown *too* thick, and suffered to stand *too* close for flowering, and that altogether not by neglect, but choice ; yet a few short strong plants with fine full flowers, are surely better than tall dangling weak ones.

A *second,* or even a *third,* sowing of hardy annuals may be made, at two or three weeks between, to continue the blow, especially of those that come early, and are soon off : *May* is not too late for the sowing of these. The *larkspur,* for instance, will make a long show with us, by *autumn* and *early,* and *late spring* plants ; in short of every flower that blows in *summer,* there may be three sowings, and two of those that come early in *autumn,* in order to a *full* succession.

Hardy annuals do not in general *transplant* well, so should be sown where they are to remain, and they must have a good soil, as well as the tender kinds, in order to succefs. Take care to sow the *tallest* sorts *behind,* and the *lowest* in *front,* and to form the patches at a sufficient distance from one another, that the ground

may

SECT. XVIII.   OF FLOWERS.   15

may be ſtirred and raked between them. A garden may be *too* full of flowers, which it certainly is, if the earth is not ſeen about them : for when that is clean and freſh, all things growing in it appear more lively : It is, as it were, the back ground of a picture.

* * * * * *

2. OF BIENNIALS.

There are but a few of theſe, and the principal ſorts will be found in the *liſt* of them, *next ſection*, where obſervations will be made on particular plants.

Theſe are to be *ſown* in drills, or in beds, at broad caſt, the latter end of *March*, or beginning of *April*, where they have only the morning ſun, and the ground ſhould be cool, or kept ſo by occaſional watering : The beginning of *May*, however, is not too late.

Thin the young plants on the ſeed beds a little, ſoon after they appear, to about an inch, and again to three or four inches aſunder, and keep them well weeded. They may either thus remain till *autumn*, to be planted out where they are to blow ; or if they grow too ſtrong and crowding, let every other be drawn in *ſummer*, (chuſing a moiſt time, if poſſible) and planted out wider into nurſery beds for uſe in autumn, or the following ſpring : The latter ſeaſon will do for final planting, though the former is beſt, as the roots get eſtabliſhed in the ground ; when if moved in the ſpring they meet with a check. It is beſt to tranſplant with earth about their roots ; but ſhorten all ſtraggling fibres, and cut off dead and rambling leaves. In *ſevere* winters, thoſe moved in *autumn* are ſometimes killed, and therefore a few may be reſerved to *ſpring*, in caſe of ſuch an accident.

* * * * * *

3. OF PERENNIALS.

This clafs (as has been obferved) is very numerous, and the plants are propagated, many of them by their *roots*, according to their nature, as fibrous, bulbous, &c. fome by *layers, fuckers, offsets, flips, cuttings,* &c. and very few by *feed* only ; though all forts (bearing feed) are occafionally propagated this way, for *new varieties*, or to produce *finer* plants, as thofe from feed generally prove, with refpect to ftrength, fymmetry, and flowers. It happens, however, when propagated from *feed*, that fometimes a better, but more frequently a lefs beautiful flower is produced of many forts ; and this is the reafon why the other modes of propagation are fo much adopted, by offsets, &c. as thus they come identically the fame with the mother plant. Another obftacle againft fome forts being *fown* is, that they are feveral years before they come to bear, as bulbous, and tuberous rooted flowers.

The *Dutch* have made themfelves famous by their patience and perfeverance in raifing bulbs and tubers, and fow every year fome of each kind, which *pays* them well, when they meet with an eminently good flower. A new fort of *anemone, auricula, carnation, ranunculus,* and even a *polyanthus* will frequently fetch a guinea, and a *tulip*, or a *hyacinth*, fometimes ten.

To *raife* bulbous and tuberous rooted flowers, they fhould be fown in boxes (fuppofe three feet long, two wide, and fix inches deep) of light rich earth, about the middle of *Auguft*, or *September*, and fetting them in a funny fheltered place (not under cover) fow *anemonies* and *ranunculufes* a quarter of an inch deep ; *irifes, colchicums,* and *cyclamens,* half an inch ; and *tulips, frittillaries,* and *hyacinths,* near an inch deep, giving water in a dry time, fo as to keep the mould fomewhat moift, but not wet. A little hay may be kept over the feeds till the plants appear, which perhaps will be fpring

with

with some. Sowings may take place also in *March*, or *April*, removing the boxes in *May*, to where they may have only the morning sun. Thin them a little, if they come up thick, and when stalks die, put on half an inch of fine mould ; and after the decay of the leaf next summer, they must be planted out in nursery beds, (latter end of *August*) two, or three inches asunder, (according to their nature) and some will blow the following year, as the *anemone* and *ranunculus*, &c. though the *hyacinth* will be four or five, and the *tulip* seven or eight first. These must be removed from the first nursery bed to another, (as soon as their tops are decayed) and planted at six inches distance ; and ever after treated as blowing plants. Keep them very clear of *weeds*, particularly the seed boxes, or borders. Protect the seedlings in severe weather from frost, or heavy rain, by mats and hoops. A reed hurdle, or something else, put up at the *N. E.* end, to break off the wind *when* it is harsh, will be proper.

Fibrous rooted, &c. *perennials*, if propagated from *seed*, are to be treated as *biennials ;* but they are mostly increased (as observed) otherways, with less trouble, and *chiefly* by parting the roots in *autumn* and *spring*, or by rooted slips or offsets. Many of them have creeping roots, and increase so fast, that it is necessary to take them up every three or four years ; and a removal of this sort is proper for most perennials, in order to greater neatness, and a superior cultivation ; for though large tufts look handsome, they may be *too* bulky, and some kinds are apt to rot (as *bachelor's buttons*) when thick, the stalks and flowers come weak, and the leaves, toward the bottom, turn yellow.

In the *next section*, is a list of the most common, ornamental, or curious *perennial* flowers, (easy of cultivation) having *fibrous* and *fleshy* roots, of which not all the sorts are named, but those only which seemed most worthy.

Many *perennial* flowers have *bulbous* and *tuberous* roots, and their *general culture* is, to take them up annually soon after they have flowered, when their leaves and stalks turn yellow and decay, then the root is at *rest*, and its fibres die. When first taken up, lay them covered in the ground for a few days, and then clean and harden them in the sun, (sparingly, if exceeding hot) when they must be stored in a *dry* place, till wanted, for damp is apt to rot them : Never put many together, for this reason.

It is not *absolutely* necessary to take bulbs and tubers up every year, as every second or third may do ; but it is the common practice, because it gives an opportunity to remove the *offsets* for propagation, and the mother bulbs are thus strengthened, as also from the renewed soil they meet with by a fresh plantation. It is not uncommon for bulbous roots to be suffered to stand *many* years without taking up ; but then they cramp and starve one another, and are apt to go off from their original beauty.

Bulbs and *tubers* may be either replanted immediately on being taken up, or kept out of ground for several months ; i. e. during their natural periods of rest. *Autumn* flowering bulbs are to be taken up in *May*, if their leaves are decayed.

Spring flowering bulbs should be replanted in *September*, or *October* ; those of the *summer* in *October*, or *November* ; and those of *autumn* in *July*, or *August*. A little before, or after, is not very material ; only when they are put in too soon, they come so forward as to be liable to be damaged in severe winters, and springs ; and when kept out of the ground too long, the bulbs spend themselves first in making roots. The *scaly* bulbs (as lilies) should not be kept out of the ground above six weeks, or two months. Those that flower in *summer*, may be put in the ground at different times, as early and late in *autumn*, and early in the new year, (not later than *February*) to obtain a succession

SECT. XVIII. OF FLOWERS. 19

ceffion of blow. This is a common practice with the *anemone* and *ranunculus* ; but when planted in *winter*, the foil fhould be a *dry* one, or made fo, by digging in a good quantity of fine fea-coal afhes, and coarfe, or drift fand ; elfe they are apt to rot, if much wet falls, efpecially when followed by fharp froft. They may be protected from wet by mats, and from froft by peas haulm.

Offsets of bulbs, and weak tubers, muft be planted a month before the full fized roots ; and as they are not expected to flower the firft year, fhould be difpofed of in *nurfery* beds, rather clofe, where they may grow a year, or two, according to their ftrength, as fome will be this time, or longer, before they flower. Thofe taken from *fcaly* bulbs, will not endure to be out of ground, and muft therefore be planted almoft immediately. *Bulbs* taken up *out of feafon*, i. e. when they have remained fo long in the ground as to have ftruck out frefh roots, fhould be removed with balls of earth ; for though they may live without this care, they will be exceeding weak ; it is therefore neceffary exactly to obferve the proper feafon for removal.

The *foil* that beft fuits bulbous and tuberous roots in general, is a fandy loam ; but moft of the forts are not very nice. The ground for them fhould be well dug, two fpades deep, that their fibres may fhoot freely, their offsets fwell eafily, and wet be completely drained from them, when much of it falls. And this work fhould be done a week before planting, that the ground may fettle. In a light foil, roots of the *ranunculus* have been found to ftrike a yard deep, which may admonifh, that in a clay bottom, it is proper to lay a body of ftones there, (fuppofe at eighteen inches) that too much moifture may not be detained.

The *depth* at which *bulbs* fhould be planted, muft be according to their fize, three or four inches deep, from their top. *Tubers* alfo according to their fize ; *anemonies* and *ranunculufes* at two, or two and a half inches,

inches, &c. Some bulbs will come up even when a foot below the ground, as *crown imperials*, and *crocuses*, at six inches, or more ; some persons have, therefore, planted them deeper than the above rule, in order to be able to stir the surface of the ground without damaging them.

The proper *disposition* of bulbous and tuberous roots, is either in *beds* (a trifle rounded) of from three to four feet and a half wide, for the *curious* sorts ; or in *patches* of the smaller sorts, to form clusters of three, four, or five, agreeable to the room they require. There should be only one in a place (generally) of the white, or orange lily, crown imperial, and such like large bulbs.

In *beds*, the fancy sorts of bulbs, and tubers, may be set in rows, eight or nine inches asunder, and from five to seven inches in the rows, according to their size. The distance of four inches apart is, however, by some florists, thought sufficient for *anemonies* and *ranunculuses ;* but certainly more were better, where a strong blow is a first object. *Hyacinths* should be planted at seven, or eight, though they are more commonly at six inches. *Tulips* should be at eight, or nine.

When *planted*, if rain does not come in about four days, beds of bulbs and tubers should be watered, to set them growing, that they may not rot.

Though bulbs may be planted by a *dibble*, (taking care that the mould does not lay hollow about the roots) a better way is, to draw *drills*, and place them in, giving them a gentle pressure into the ground, and covering neatly up. A little free *sand* should be strewed along the bottom of the drills, under *hyacinths*, *anemonies* and *ranunculuses*, if the soil is not quite a light one.

The *best way* of planting bulbs is, to draw the mould off the bed to a *sufficient* depth ; then lay the surface perfectly level ; give a watering ; and when the top is a little dry, mark it out into proper sized

squares ;

squares; then place a bulb in the middle of each, and carefully cover up, so as not to throw them on their sides.

Those bulbs and tubers in *beds*, may conveniently be *protected*, when in flower, from rain and sun, by an *awning*, which will continue them in perfection of blow much longer than if always exposed. When these flowers, in beds, first break ground, if the weather is severe, they may have an *awning* of mats, or cloth, occasionally over them; or a little peas *haulm*, or wheat *straw*, laid thinly on, just to protect their tender state a little; this regards particularly *nights*, but on *days* a cover should not remain on in tolerable weather. But *before* the shoots appear above ground, valuable beds of these flowers should be sheltered from having much wet, (even all through winter) as moisture gives *frost* so great power.

Spring flowering bulbs may be brought forward by planting them in *pots* and *water-glasses*, and setting them in warm rooms, or hot beds; and thus, even in *winter*, we may have ornaments and sweets that court our admiration. The great variety of *hyacinths* and *polyanthus narcissus*, furnish us amply in this way; but *other* early bulbs may also be thus forwarded. *Pots*, placed in a warm *kitchen* window, may be brought forward to blow in the parlour; or placed in any window, open to the *south*, will forward them. These should be potted in *October*, and have a light dry soil, occasionally giving water. Bulbs may be put in *glasses* at this time, and once a month after, to *February* for a succession. Let the bulb just touch the water, which should be soft, and replenished so often as to keep it up to the bottom of the bulbs. Let it be completely changed about once a week; and if a bit of *nitre*, the size of a pea, be put in each time, it will strengthen the blow.

Though bulbous flowers are *propagated* plentifully by *root* offsets, yet some are increased from little bulbs formed

formed on the sides or tops of the *stalks*, as the *moly* tribe, and the bulbiforous *lily*. These should be taken off in *August*, dried in the sun, and then planted in nursery beds as *offsets*.

Bulbs propagated from *offsets*, produce a flower exactly like the parent; and *varieties* are only to be obtained from *seed*, which never comes quite like the original.

Let *seed* be saved only from choice flowers, be thorough ripe, and being hardened a little in the sun, they may be sowed soon after, in pots or boxes, of good light earth. See page 16. Persons of leisure and curiosity, would do well to amuse themselves in this way, that we may not be so much indebted to *foreigners*, for a supply of new flowers of this class.

An *observation* may be here made, that the *same* bulb (as is often thought) does not always continue; for some are *renewed every* year, as the *tulip*; and others the second, third, &c. So that when taken up to remove *offsets*, the principal bulb of the tulip, &c. which is commonly esteemed the old one, is, in fact, a new formed one, though (perhaps) not less in size, and it may be bigger.

* * * * * *

As many SHRUBS (i. e. woody plants) are propagated in a view principally to their flowers, they will properly enough be considered a little here, as to their propagation. See section On Shrubs and Shrubberies.

The *deciduous shrubs* that are most usually cultivated for their ornamental nature, will be found in the lists of the *next section;* and their modes of *propagation* are denoted thus:—*b.* budding—*c.* cuttings—*g.* graff—*l.* layers—*r.* roots—*f.* seeds—*sl.* slips—*su.* suckers—by *roots,* includes *offsets.*

Of

SECT. XVIII.   OF FLOWERS.

Of the various methods of *propagating* trees and shrubs, that by *seed* is the best, where it can be adopted, (as has been observed) and the season is *autumn* or *spring*. If in *autumn*, it may be earlier, or later, as the seeds ripen; for soon after they are ripe is the most proper time to commit them to the earth, covering the smaller seeds from half to a full inch; and kernels, nuts, &c. from two to three inches, according to their size. Any sort that is doubted to stand the winter in seed beds, may be sown in *pots*, or *boxes*, and housed in severe frosts. If in *spring*, (as it is a good rule to sow a little at *both* seasons, and some tender sorts *require* the latter) the seed must be *carefully* kept from damp and vermin, and put into the ground towards the end of *February*, or early in *March*. The seeds of some of the more delicate sorts will require to be sown, at this season, on a slight *hot bed;* and if a few of *most* of the sorts were thus treated, it would be a good method, the better to insure their germination, and to forward them. Let spring sown seeds be watered occasionally, according to the weather, to keep them moist. The earth they are sown in should be moderately light, dry and rich, and formed into beds of four feet wide, either in *drills* or at *broad cast*, first drawing earth off into the alleys, to cover with. See page 70, 72.

American trees and shrubs do very well in this climate, but the young plants are generally tender, and should have some protection, one, two, or three years, till they get woody, and inured to the climate.

For *graffing* and *budding*, (as some shrubs are propagated this way) see the section *On Graffing;* and for the propagation by *suckers, cuttings, layers,* &c. see section 5, page 85, to the end; about *suckers,* see also page 114. Those trees, or shrubs, from which *cuttings* of the *same* year's growth may be had in *June,* or *July,* may be greatly helped to strike root, by covering them close with a *hand-glass;* (as directed concerning *pinks*) and if a glass were put over *layers,* which are difficult
to

to ſtrike, it would help them. See *obſervations* on the *arbutus*, liſt 5, next ſection.

This mode of *propagation* is particularly adapted to ſome ſorts of *evergreen* ſhrubs, which emit fibres more freely from the *youngeſt*. wood. If year old wood is treated thus, the cuttings may be ſet early in ſpring ; or glaſſes may be put over thoſe put out in autumn. But ſpring cuttings, potted, and ſet on a ſlight hot bed, with hand-glaſſes, is the ſureſt method to make difficult ſorts ſtrike root.

It may prove an *obſervation* of ſome uſe, that trees and ſhrubs raiſed from *ſeed* grow the largeſt, from *layers* generally prove leſs, and from *cuttings* the leaſt. Where *budding* can be practiſed, it is preferable to *graffing*.

For *planting* and *managing* ſhrubs, &c. ſee ſection 9; *On Shrubs and Shrubberies*. For *pruning*, ſee page 169.

SECTION XIX.

LISTS OF TREES, SHRUBS AND FLOWERS.

⁂ The names of the choiceſt ſorts of *fruit trees*, will be found in ſection 17.

THE *modes of cultivation* are here directed by the letters, as in laſt ſection ; adding m. for *moiſt*, w. for *wet*, and d. for *dry*. Thoſe not marked are to be underſtood as (pretty much) *indifferent* as to ſoil, and

and indeed those marked otherwise *may grow* in a contrary kind, and often do, though not so flourishingly.

The *time of flowering* is annexed to those trees and shrubs that are *thus* at all ornamental, and the more *ordinary heights* they are found to attain are denoted in the *arrangement;* a circumstance hitherto much wanted, as useful and *necessary* to be known, in order to a right disposal of them. Those of a naturally low growth have been, sometimes, planted behind in *shrubberies*, &c. and the taller forward; but yet this unfortunate circumstance must be unavoidable to every inexperienced planter, who has no other guide, than that this is a *tree*, and that is a *shrub*, &c.

The *colours* of the flowers are mentioned when opportunity permitted, as agreeable to be known, and of use in the disposal of them at planting, to diversify the scene properly.

Such *observations*, as may be thought most useful and necessary, will follow each *list;* but as neither *all* the sorts nor the *varieties* of each sort, could be enumerated in such a work as this, so also the *minutiæ* of propagation, &c. is more than could be comprehended, or expected: Folio volumes (so copious is the subject) have left a variety of plants unnoticed, and much unsaid respecting cultivation. For *ordinary* use, a greater enumeration, or more enlarged particulars, would (indeed) have made the book *less* valuable. If the *selection* and information is good, (and pains have been taken in the business) those for whom this book is designed, will have no reason to complain.

The *names* of trees, shrubs and flowers, are in many cases various, as sometimes the scientific name prevails, and at other times the trivial; and of neither is there a perfect agreement. The object therefore here has been to give *that* name by which each is supposed to be best known. Different plants are often called by the same name, and a nice discrimination is made

by

by botanists, according to *leaf* and *flower*; but these are no farther noticed than necessary; and such descriptions are given of each, as cannot (it is hoped) fail to identify the sort, when applied for to a nurseryman.

In the following *lists* of *trees*, the larger are marked with an *asterism*; and in the *lists* of *shrubs* and *flowers*, discrimination of size is made by *figures*, each being divided into four sorts, as to height; and the lowest marked No. 1. But it is ever to be understood, that the *soil*, and other circumstances will make a difference, as to stature; so that the greater *may* become the less, and the less the greater.

Where *et cetera* (i. e. *&c.*) is affixed to sorts, it means that there are others; and where it is added to the time of flowering, it signifies of more than one month's duration. It is the nature of some things to keep in blow all the summer: to encourage which, dead flowers should always be speedily taken off, as they occur.

* * * * * *

I.

List of *deciduous trees*, usually called *forest*, or *timber* trees, serving both for use and ornament:

Abele, is the white *poplar*; and *aspen* the tremulous.
* *Alder*, common hoary leaved American, &c. *c.l.f.* w.
* *Ash*, common and American white, red and black, *f.*
* *Beech*, common and American purple leaved, *f. l.* d.
 Birch, com. white, Virginian and Canadian, &c. *f.l.su.*
* *Chesnut*, edible fruited Spanish, and horse, *f.* May.
* *Cypress*, deciduous, or Virginian swamp, *l. f.* w.
* *Elm*, small and broad leaved, wych, or Scotch, &c. *f.l.fu*
 Hickery nut, smooth white, and rough barked, *f.*
 Hornbeam, common, hop, and Virginia flowering, *f.*
* *Lime*, common, red-twigged, black American, &c. *l.c.f*
* *Larch*, common red, white and black American, &c. *f.*
* *Maple*,

SECT. XIX.   LISTS OF TREES, &c.   27

* *Maple*, great, a fh leaved, opalus or Italian, *l.f.fu.* May
  ———— com. fmall, Norway, Pennfylvanian, &c. ditto
Medlar, com. German, Nottingham, & Italian, *f.l.* May
Mountain afh is fometimes a foreft tree, fee next lift
* *Nettle tree*, as next lift, grows large, and is a foreft tree
Nut tree, common hazel, or any orchard fort, *l.fu.f.*
* *Oak*, Englifh, American forts, Spanifh, Italian, &c.*f.*
* *Plane*, Eaftern, Weftern, middle, or Spanifh, *f.l.c.* May
* *Poplar*, white, black, tremulous and Carolina, *c.l.fu.* m.
* *Service tree*, the wild maple leaved, *f. l.* June
* *Sycamore*, is the great *maple*, which fee.
* *Walnut*, the common, or royal, and black Virginian, *f.*
* *Willow*, white, or filver leaved, purple and fweet, &c.

*** For *Underwood* amongft foreft trees, the ufual forts are, *alders, afh, beech, birch, hazel, hornbeam, fallow, willow,* and fometimes the *wych elm, maple, poplar,* and *fycamore.*

OBSERVATIONS ON PARTICULAR TREES.

Alders, cuttings of it may be thick truncheons of a yard long, pointed, and thruft into foft ground half way, or into a hole made with an iron bar, and will grow readily. This is the way alfo to propagate *poplars, willows,* and *fallows;* alfo *elders.*

Afh, the American forts do not grow near fo large as the common Englifh. For the *ornamental* afhes, fee next lift.

Beech was formerly much ufed for hedges about, and the divifions of, a garden, and it ferves well for this purpofe, as it bears the fhears; but it muft be regularly clipt twice a year, the latter end of *June* and *Auguft,* or it will foon get out of order.

Birch is reckoned the worft of timber, yet the wood has its ufes in feveral particular bufineffes. The *American* forts grow much larger than the *Englifh.* The tree is of that accommodating nature, that it will grow in any foil or fituation, wet or dry. It is well known, that a *wine* is made of its fap, by boring holes in full grown trees in fpring, before the leaves come out; and from a number of trees a great deal may be collected. Without being unpleafant, (if properly made) *birch* wine is relifhed by many, and is reckoned very medicinal in fcorbutic, and other complaints. For the whole procefs, fee *Family Herbal*, octavo, by *W. Meyrick*, furgeon, a book worthy of notice. There is a method of catching the liquor, by putting into the holes (deeply bored) *faucets of elder*.

Elm, the wych, is the quickeft grower, and will flourifh in any foil; but the broad leaved is reckoned the beft timber, and the fmall leaved the moft ornamental, but it muft have a good foil to flourifh. The *wych* is eafily raifed from feed (fown after it is ripe) but the other forts are propagated from fuckers, or layers, or graffing on the *wych*. In order to obtain *fuckers*, and fhoots for layers, *ftools* are to be formed by cutting down fome young trees, almoft clofe to the ground. Trees from layers are better than from fuckers. Obferve, that whatever is to be propagated by *layers*, or *fuckers*, making *ftools* is the way to procure them.

Hornbeam, the common fort will grow very large in fome foils, but the *Virginian* (flowering yellow) will hardly reach thirty feet, and the *hop* not above twenty. All the hornbeams (the *hop* moft) have been ufed much for clipt hedges, and partitions in gardens and pleafure grounds, but the *oriental* fort fuits the purpofe beft, being naturally dwarfifh. The *hornbeam* feathers down lower and thicker than any other tree, and the property of holding its decayed leaves on all winter, adapts it for a fcreen from winds.

Nut tree, as timber, will be beft propagated from nuts, either to remain where fown, or planted out while young, keeping the ftems trimmed up, free of fhoots, to about five or fix feet, (according to ftrength) and

and then to form a head, topping the leading shoot for the purpose, which will occasion several branches to proceed from the upper eyes; and this is the way to form all sorts of trees to good heads.

Oak, the *English* produces the best wood, but the *American* sorts are the fastest growers, though they do not attain to the size of the *English*. A cool strong soil produces the handsomest trees, and toughest timber. Oaks should not be above three or four years old before they are planted, for the older they are, the more check they receive, and it is a tree that does not transplant well. Hence all the care should be taken that can be in the business. See *section* 10. But oaks succeed best without removal, having a *tap*, or downright root, which is frequently broke in taking up: *All* trees would probably thus come finer, if it was convenient. The consequence of preserving the tap has been suspected; but it is certainly Nature's direction, for rather than give up the point, the tap of the oak will make its way downward, in a direct line, through the hardest soils. See page 80.

Poplar to propagate by cuttings, see *alder;* but younger and smaller cuttings for this tree do better, as those of one or two years old, and half a yard long: The black poplar does not succeed well by truncheons.

Walnut, when planted for timber, should be young, and the tap root, if possible, preserved whole. The black Virginian grows more erect, but the other makes the largest tree, and best wood. The white Virginian is the *heckery nut*. All these make the best trees, when growing from seed without transplanting.

Willow and *sallow*, to propagate by cuttings, see *alder*.

*** Of all the *forest* trees here mentioned, the *ash*, the *beech*, the *elm*, and the *oak*, are the principal; and to plant these, and others, is a work of the most commendable, and eventually of the most profitable kind. See pages 79, 115, 122.

LIST

II.

List of large *deciduous trees*, confidered chiefly as *ornamental*, for pleafure grounds, &c.

* *Acacia*, triple thorned, fewer thorned, &c. *f. l. c. fu.* July
* *Afh*, Calabrian manna, and large flowering, *f. gr.* May
—— weeping and variegated, wh. and yel. leaved, *b. gr.*
—— dwarf flowering (fmall white bunches) *f. gr.* May
Annona, cuftard apple, or papaw tree, *f.* May *d.*
* *Beech*, white and yellow ftriped leaved, *b. gr. in.*
Birch, weeping or pendulous twigged, *f. l. fu.*
Buckthorn, common purging berried, *l. fu. c.* May
* *Catalpa* (tree bignonia) or trumpet flower, *c. l. f.* Aug.
Cherry, the bird, common and Cornifh, &c. *f. b. gr.* May
—— Cornelian, male cornus, or cornel, *f. c. l. fu.* May
* *Chefnut*, fcarlet flowered and ftriped leaved, *f. b. gr.* May
Date plum, or *perfimon*, is the *pifhamin* below.
* *Elm*, pendulous twigged and variegated leaved, *l. gr.*
Frangula, alpine and berry bearing alder, *f. c. l. fu.* June
Gleditfia is the *acacia* above, which fee
* *Hornbeam*, oriental, and variegated leaved, *l. gr.*
Laburnham, com. broad and narrow leaved, *f. c. l.* May
Larch, or the deciduous *pine*, fee laft lift.
* *Lime* (or linden tree) with variegated leaves, *l. c. gr.*
Magnolia, umbrella, glaucous leaved, &c. *f. l. c.* June. *d.*
Mountain afh, or bird's fervice, pl. and ftrip. *f. l.* May
* *Nettle tree*, black and purple fruited, *f. l. fu.* May
* —————— bloach leaved of both forts, *gr.* May
* *Oak*, ftriped, and red leaved Virginian, *b. gr. f.*
Pifhamin, Indian and European, *l. f. fu.* May, *d.*
* *Piftachia nut*, or com. turpentine tree, &c. *f. l.* May
* *Poplar*, with variegated or ftriped leaves, *c. l. gr.*
* *Robinia*, com. or falfe acacia, wh. flow. *f. c. l. fu.* June
—————— for other forts, fee the following lift
* *Service tree*, or forb apple, true and baftard, *f. l.* May
Tacamahacca, or balfamic poplar tree, *c. l. fu.*
* *Tulip tree*, fometimes called lily flowered, *f. l. fu.* July

Viburnham,

Viburnham, or meally way faring tree, *f. l. c. fu.* May
———:—— American forts, and ftriped, *b. gr. in.* May
* *Willow*, weeping, fhining leaved, and yel. twigged, *c.*

*** Thefe *ornamental* trees are proper to plant at the back of fhrubberies, &c. and here and there one on the fkirts and fronts of *woods*, or *plantations* of timber, and along the *boundaries* of grounds. Here they will appear to great advantage; but more fo fingly in detached fituations: Moft of them are good wood for timber.

OBSERVATIONS ON PARTICULAR TREES.

Annona is of North America, but fomewhat tender, and therefore fhould have a favourable fituation. It muft be raifed on a hot bed in fpring, and the feedlings potted and houfed in winter for a year or two, but not nurfed too much.

Buckthorn, if raifed from feed, fow early in *autumn*, as foon as the berries can be procured, and perhaps fome may come up the following fpring, but moft of them will lay another year. This is the cafe with various feeds.

Catalpa fhould grow fingly, that it may have its natural wide fpread, and, if poffible, let it be on a plat of grafs, where it will appear to great advantage. It is very hardy, but as it comes out late, it is advifable to give it a favourable afpect.

Magnolias are to be confidered as rather tender, efpecially young plants. The glaucous leaved is of the loweft growth, (about ten feet) but all are elegantly ornamental with their white flowers: There is alfo a blue flowered one. Let them have a dry foil, as all tender plants fhould, as well as a warm fituation.

Mountain afh produces its white flowers in *May*, but they are little ornamental. Its foliage, however, is
pretty,

pretty, and its fruit of red berries is one of the greateſt ornaments of autumn, coming very early, and hanging all winter, *if* the blackbird, &c. will let them alone. As it deſerves the moſt conſpicuous ſituation, it will be proper to plant ſome near the houſe, and where birds are likely to be diſturbed from too frequent viſits.

Piſhamin or *date plum*, is chiefly cultivated here as of ornamental foliage, for its fruit is rarely reliſhed; and, like the *medlar* and *ſorb*, muſt be in a ſtate of decay before it is eatable. If propagated from layers, it muſt be done in *ſpring*, and the following *March* (juſt as they begin to ſhoot) they may be tranſplanted. If raiſed from ſeed, ſow it on a hot bed in ſpring, and houſe the young plants in pots the firſt winter: Allow this tree a dry ſoil.

Piſtachia, this is the hardieſt of three ſorts. Treat it as a tender plant, whilſt young, for three or four years, and let it have finally a ſheltered and dry ſituation.

Tulip tree is tender whilſt young, but afterwards very hardy; is uncertain in flowering, but handſome in its leaf and growth, and has been uſed to be planted ſingly on lawns, &c. It is a native of *Virginia*, where it attains to ſo vaſt a ſize, as to be from twenty to thirty feet in girth, though here it keeps pace only with an ordinary elm.

Virburnham, though a way faring tree, (found by the road ſide) is very pretty, by its hoary leaves, and white flowers, ſucceeded by fruit in autumn, in bunches of red berries. The *American* ſorts grow not near ſo high, but they rarely ripen their berries here. The *variegated* ſort does not grow ſo large as the plain, which is the caſe with all ſtriped plants.

LIST

* * * * * *

III.

List of smaller *deciduous trees*, or *shrubs* of tree growth, *ornamental* for pleasure grounds.

* *Almond tree*, sweet and bit. red and wh. flow. *f. b.* Apr.
* ——————— oriental silver leaved, *f. b.* April
Andromeda, tree sort, or Carolina sorrel tree, *l. fu. f.*
* *Apple*, Siberian and Virginian crabs, *f. gr.* May
* ——— Tartarian crab, beautiful large fruit, *gr.* May
* ——— double flow. Chinese, *(Pyrus spectabilis) gr.* May
——— American, very small or berry crab, *f. gr.* May
Aralia, thorny Virginia, or Angelica tree, *f. r.* Aug.
* *Azarole thorn*, Virginian cockspur, &c. *f. l. b. gr.* May
* *Azederach*, com. bead tree, or paternoster nut, *f.* July
Berberry, red, white, and stoneless red, *c. l. f. fu.* May
Benjamin tree, or benzion gum, yel. flow. *f. l. f.* April
Bignonia, see trumpet flower
* *Bladder nut*, five and three leaved sorts, *f. fu. l. c.* May
———— *sena*, see colutea
Buckthorn, sea, European, and Canadian, *f. c. l.* June
Caragana, or Siberian robinia, yel. flow. *c. l. f. fu.* May
* *Cashiobury bush*, or bastard cassine, wh. flow. *f. l.* Aug.
* *Cherry*, com. double white and blush flow. *b. gr.* May
———— weeping, or pendulous branched, *f. b. gr.* May
* ———— *Mahaleb*, or perfumed cherry, *f. b. gr.* May
Chinquapin, dwarf American chesnut, or oak, *f. in* May
Clematis, (a climber) see *virgin's bower*
Colutea, com. or tree bladder sena, yel. flow. *f. l.* July
* *Dogwood*, or bloody twig, com. and Virginian, *c. l. f.* June
* *Elder*, bl. wh. gr. and red berried and striped, *c. l. f.* June
Gueldre rose, often called snow-ball tree, *c. l. fu.* May
* *Hawthorn*, com. doub. scarl. berried, &c. *b. gr. l.* May
* ———— Glastonbury, blows sometime in winter, *f. b. gr.*
———— Virginian thorned and thornless, *f. l. b. gr.* May
* *Judas tree*, com. and Canadian, pur. red, wh. *f.* May
Kidney-bean tree, Carolina, blue scar. and red, *f.* July *d.*
* *Lilac*, com. purple, blue and white flow. *f. fu. l.* May

Medlar,

Medlar, woolly leaved, pur. fl. red, fruit, *f. l. b. gr.* May
* *Nettle tree*, eaſtern yel. flow. and bloached, *f. l. c. gr.* May
* *Oleaſter*, or wild olive tree, *l. c.* June *d.*
Peach, doub. bloſſ. as a ſtandard, no fruit, *b.* April
* *Pear*, doub. bloſſ. harſh baking fruit, *b. gr.* May
Plum, doub. bloſſ. and ſtriped leaved, *b. gr.* May
Privet, deciduous, plain and ſtriped *f. ſu. l. c.* June
Robinia, or roſe acacia, ſcar. flow. *f. c. l. ſu.* May
—————— ſhrubby quaternate leaved, yellow *l. f. ſu.* June
* *Spindle tree*, nar. broad, and ſtriped leaved, *f. b. c. gr.* April
Sumach, tanners, wh. fl. and ſtag's horn, red, *l. ſu. f.* June
—————— Carolina ſcarlet, and Canadia red, &c. ditto
Tamariſk, French, with pale red flowers, *c. l. f.* July
—————— Venetian, (cotinus) pur. flow. *l. ſu. f.* July
* *Trumpet flower*, (bignonia) ſcarlet and yel. *c. l. f.* July
Viburnham, variety as to leaf, white flow. *f. l. c. ſu.* July
Virgin's bower, entire leaved, doub. pur. flow. *l. c.* Aug.
—————— ſingle pur. blue, red ſtriped, *b, c.* July
—————— ſee *clematis*, in the next liſt
* *White beam*, or white leaf tree, wh. flow. *f. l. ſu.* May

*** In the above liſt, there are ſeveral plants rather too *tender* for open culture, but every thing does ſo much better abroad, than when their roots are confined in pots, and houſed, that it is very proper to *try* what may be done in this way.

OBSERVATIONS ON PARTICULAR TREES, &c.

Andromeda tree is tender, and muſt therefore have a ſituation accordingly. It is always a part of the green houſe furniture, but does well ſometimes abroad.

Apple, theſe crabs produce rather ſlender wood, and therefore to have them ſtrong and fruitful, (and conſequently beautiful) ſhould not be in a crowded, or ſhady ſituation, but rather, as much as poſſible, in detached ſingle plants. The fruit of the three firſt makes ſuperior *tarts*, and the latter an excellent *preſerve;* and the fruit of all of them may be introduced in the *deſert*,
when

when full ripe. Allow the *double flowering* apple, a good situation, to preserve its charming blow as long as possible.

Azederach consider as tender; its foliage is beautiful, flowers white, and fruit yellow.

Cashiobury bush should have a sheltered situation, particularly the young plants, which should be protected for two or three winters.

Kidney bean tree, (climbers) the two latter sorts are rather green house plants, but have done abroad.

Spindle tree (sometimes called *prickwood*) is very beautiful with its leaves in autumn, for which (as many other plants) it is chiefly considered as ornamental, its flowers making a poor appearance. The seed lies two years before it comes up.

Trumpet flower, sometimes called *scarlet jasmine*, is a trailing plant, and therefore requires training to a wall for support; or having something to climb on, it will proceed much in the way of an *honeysuckle*. It is rather tender, and must have a good situation; but when properly managed is a great beauty. Prune it to a few eyes, precisely upon the principle of a *vine*.

* * * * * *

IV.

List of the lower deciduous trees and woody plants, called *shrubs*, cultivated for ornament:

2 *Almond*, dwarf, single and double red fl. *f. fu. b. gr.* April
2 ———— dwarf, with leaves hoary underneath, ditto
3 *Allspice* tree, Carolina, or pompadore, *l.* May *d.*
1 *Allyson*, prickly and hoary leaved, white *f. fu. c.* July *d.*
4 *Althea frutex*, purple, red, white strip. fl. &c. *l. fu. f.* Sept.
3 *Amelanchier*, dwarf bl. fruited *medlar*, *f. l, fu. b. gr.* May
2 *Andromeda*, shrubby wh. yel. red and pur. fl. *f. l. fu.* July
3 *Aralea*, herbaceous Canada and Virginian, *r. f.* June
4 *Azalia*, American honeysuckle, white, red, scarlet, *l. r.* July

4 *Bladder*

4 *Bladder fena*, pocock's early deep yellow, *f. l.* June
4 ——·—— oriental, or the blood red, *f. l.* July
3 ——·— shrubby Ethiopian scarlet, *f.* August, *d.*
  ——·—— see *colutea* in the last list, and below
4 *Bramble*, doub. blossomed, and white berried, *l. fu. f.* May
4 *Briar*, sw. sing. doub. semi. pink and scar. *f. fu. l.* June
2 *Broom*, com. English, Dyer's, and dw. Portugal, *f. r.* May
3 ———— large Portugal, and upright Montpelier, *f. r.* Ju.
2 ———— wh. flowered, trailing and upright, *f. r.* June
2 *Buckthorn*, dwarf, purging berried, *f. l. c.* May
3 ———— long leaved dwarf ditto, *f. l. c.* May
4 *Button tree* (cephelanthus) American, *f. l. c.* July
2 *Clematis* (virgin's bower) upright wh. blue. *r. f.* June
4 ———— oriental climbing yel. flow. *l. c.* May, &c.
4 *Candleberry myrtle*, wh. flow. blue berried, *f. l. fu.* Ju. m.
3 ———————— dw. Carolina, br. leav. *c. l. f. fu.* Ju. m.
4 *Chaste tree*, nar. and br. leaved, pur. and wh. *l. c.* Sept.
3 *Cherry*, com. dwarf, and dw. Canada bird, *f. b. gr.* May
4 *Clethra*, alder leaved, fall of wh. flow. *f. l. fu.* July, &c.
1 *Colutea* (coronilla) joint-podded, Spanish, &c. *f.* June
3 *Cotoneaster*, (a medlar) or dw. quince, *f. l. b. gr.* May
4 *Coreopsis*, two American sorts, yel. flow. *off* July, &c.
2 *Cinquefoil shrub*, (potentilla) com. yel. flow. *fu. f. c.* June
1 ———————— grandiflorus, and silvery, yel. fl. *r. f.* June
1 ———————— wh. flow. upright and trailing, *r. f.* June
3 *Cytisus*, bl. based, and sessile leaved, *f. c. l.* June *d.*
3 *Elder*, dwarf, wh. flow. and black fruit, *f. c.* July
3 *Gale*, the sweet willow, or Dutch myrtle, *r.* June *w.*
2 *Germander tree*, wh. yel. and pur. flow. *fl. c. f.* July, *d.*
4 *Hawthorn*, gooseberry, leaved, yel. fruited, *f.* May
3 *Hamamelis* (wytch hazel) Virginian, *f. l.* flow. in wint.
4 *Honeysuckle*, climbing Eng. wh. and red, *c. l. f.* June, &c.
4 ———————— climbing Dutch red, early and late, ditto
4 ———————— climb. Italian, wh. red, and yel. *c. l. f.* May
4 ———————— erect fly, wh. flow. and red berry, ditto
3 ———————— erect alpine, red flow. and red berry ditto
3 ———————— erect acadian (diervilla) yel. *l. c. f. fu.* May

Honeysuckle,

SECT. XIX.   LISTS OF TREES, &c.   37

3 *Honeyſuckle*, there are two climbing *ſtriped* leaved ſorts.
3 *Hydrangia*, Virginian white flowering, *r. ſu.* Aug.
3 *Hypericum frutex,* br. and nar. leaved, *l. ſu. c.* June
4 *John's wort,* ſtinking, inodorous, and Canary, *ſu. ſ.* June
1 ———— large flow. ſomewhat tender, *ſu.* Aug.
4 *Itea* Virginian, full of white flowers, *l. ſ.* July, &c.
4 *Jaſmin*, wh. fl. plain, and wh. and yel. ſtrip. *l. c.* June,&c.
4 ———— trailing yellow flowered, *l. c. ſu.* June, &c.
2 ———— erect dwarf yel. flowered, *l. c. ſu.* July, &c.
4 *Ivy*, deciduous five leaved, or Virginian creeper, *c. l. ſ.*
4 *Mallow tree*, com. ſhrubby lavatera, *ſ. c.* June, &c.
3 ———— three and five lobed ſhrubby do. *ſ. c.* June
3 *Medlar*, dwarf alpine, red fruited, *ſ. l. b. gr.* May
3 ———— Canada, ſnowy, purple fruit, ditto
———— ſee *amelanchier* and *cotoneaſter*
2 *Mazereon*, wh. purp. red, and crimſon, *ſ.* Feb. &c.
2 *Orobus*, or bitter vetch, purp. and blue, *ſ. r.* April, &c.
4 *Perſian lilac*, blue and white flowering, *ſ. ſu. l.* June
2 *Poiſon oak*, common white flowered, *r. l. ſ.* July
4 ———— aſh, or varniſh tree, ditto
4 *Pomegranate*, ſing. doub. and ſtrip. flow. *l. b.* in July.
4 *Raſpberry*, common ſweet flowering, purple, *ſu.* July.
2 *Reſt harrow*, com. ſhrubby purp. flow. *ſ.* May, &c.
2 *Rhododendron*, alpine, and Mount Baldis red, *ſ. c. r.* Sep.
3 ———— ferrugineous leaved, red flow. *ſ. c. r.* Aug.
2 *Robinia*, dw. quaternate leaved, yel. flow. *ſ. c. l. ſu.* May.

Roſes : The *loweſt ſorts* are, dwarf Scotch ſingle red—dwarf common ſingle white—dwarf Pennſylvanian ſingle and double red—dwarf burnet leaved, ſingle red and ſtriped—roſe de meux—crimſon Burgundy, and dwarf bluſh Burgundy.

Middling heights.—Cinnamon ſingle and double red—common red and white, ſingle and double, and ſemi-double—monthly red, bluſh, white and ſtriped—maiden's bluſh double—virgin pale red thornleſs--moſs provence double red--roſe of the world, ſemi-double ſtriped—velvet, double and ſemi-double.

Taller ſorts are,—Provence red, bluſh and white double—damaſk white, red and bluſh ſemi-double—York and Lancaſter ſemi-double and variegated—Auſtrian ſingle, yellow, and another ſingle, red one ſide, and yellow on the other—double yellow.   *Talleſt*

Tallest sorts are,—Apple bearing, single and double red—royal red, a large double—Frankfort, purple red—great burnet leaved, single red—Carolina and Virginia single red—musk, single and double white.

4 *Scorpion sena*, com. large, yel. flow. *c. l. s.* June, &c.
2 ———— common dwarf ditto
4 *Snowdrop tree*, or fringe tree, white flow. *s. l.* June
3 *Sperea frutex*, com. willow leaved, pink, *su. l. c.* June
3 ———— downy leaved red, and wh. flow. ditto
4 ———— guelder rose leaved, wh. flow. *su. l. c.* July
3 ———— Siberian and Spanish, wh. fl. *su. l. c.* May
3 *Sumach*, myrtle leaved, white flowered, *su. l.* June
Sun-flower, tickseeded, see *coreopsis*
4 *Syringa*, large plain, and stri. leaved, wh. *c. l. su.* May
2 ———— dwarf double flowered, white, ditto
4 *Tamarisk*, German, very prettry, red fl. *c. l. s.* July, &c.
———— for other sorts, see last list
Toxicodendron, see *poison oak* and *ash*
Tree trefoil, black base, *(secundus clusii)* see *cytisus*
2 *Tutsan*, or park leaves, (like *St. John's wort*) *su. s.* July
2 *Vetch*, wood, or sylvan, wh. many flowered, *s. r.* August
4 *Virginian silk*, a variety, pur. flow. a climber, *c. l.* July
2 *Willow herb*, or French willow, pur. &c. *r. s.* July, *m.*
3 ———— see loosestrife, list XI.

*** As it is common to plant herbaceous perennial flowers in the front of shrubberies, &c. so *amongst* the shrubs, some of the loftier sorts may properly be, though annual in stalk, as the tall *aconites*, or *monkshoods*, *everlasting sun-flower*, &c.

OBSERVATIONS ON PARTICULAR SHRUBS.

Allspice tree must have a warm and dry part of the shrubbery. The whole plant is aromatic.

Aralia, thorny, is propagated by pieces of its large roots, and perhaps several plants might be so: In this way the *pyramidal campanula* succeeds.

Azalea likes cool ground, but must have a sheltered situation; and in this climate should rather have

have a dry foil, kept cool by occafional watering, except in winter: It is a very beautiful upright fhrub.

Candleberry myrtle is fo called, from the Americans procuring a wax from the berries of this plant to make candles of. It is rather tender, yet likes (as many American plants do) a moift foil; let it be fheltered from bleak winds.

Clethra is an elegant fhrub, flowering all fummer and winter; it prefers a moift foil.

Colutea is too tender to abide fevere winters, but in general will do, with a little attention: Its flowers are pretty, of a bright yellow. The other forts (three) are more tender, and are to be potted for protection from frofts, by houfing.

Cytifus, deciduous and evergreen, there is a variety of, and all very ornamental, with their yellow flowers. They are rather too tender for the open ground, and the hardier forts here mentioned, muft have a dry warm fituation. Seedlings fhould be houfed, or well protected abroad for the firft winter, but not kept too clofe.

Germander tree treat as tender, for though it will live abroad, it is moftly a green houfe plant.

Mallow tree manage as the *cytifus*, though it is not quite fo tender. All *feedlings* that can be brought up in the open air, make much finer plants; and every thing of this fort, fhould be effected as much as poffible. Of thofe plants confidered as *rather* tender, fome may be put out in nurfery beds, and *occafionally* protected by covering, and fome potted to be *occafionally* houfed.

Poifon trees, even the touch of the leaves of thefe plants will affect the fkin, but the fap is *very* (even dangeroufly) acrimonious.

Pomegranate muft have a good fouth wall, and rich foil. The double fort fhould be occafionally matted in *fevere* froft. In *very* favourable fituations (however) they have fucceeded in *efpaliers*, dwarf, half, and even full ftandards. The beft feafon for planting the pomegranate is in fpring, when juft beginning to fhoot. It is rather rude of growth, and muſt therefore have timely training. The principal pruning ſhould always be in *autumn*, and from time to time all ſtraggling, ſuperfluous growths taken off, that ſhoots may be encouraged to put out ſtrong bloſſoms, in the fulneſs of which the great merit confiſts. Theſe bearers ſhould be ſix inches, or rather more, aſunder. The mode of flowering is at the ends of the young ſhoots; and nothing equals this plant in fineneſs of blow. The double ſort is more commonly planted; but the ſingle flower is very beautiful, and its fruit, which will ripen in ſnug favourable ſituations and ſeaſons, makes a fine ſhow alſo, eſpecially when burſt. Both flowers and fruit are of a fine ſcarlet.

Roſe claims precedence of other ſhrubs. In its varieties it ſhould be planted in all ſituations, but the *Provence* more particularly. This ſhrub, in moſt (if not all its ſorts) does beſt in a cool ſtrong ſoil.

The *order* of blowing may be thus: *Cinnamon*, (ſometimes called the *May-roſe*) *monthly, damaſk, burnet, Scotch, Pennſylvanian, apple*, &c. Then the lateſt roſes we have, are thoſe of the *monthly* again, and the *muſk*. Occaſionally every ſort may bear a few *late* ones, but chiefly the *Provence*. To encourage this ſhrub to *treat* us in the latter part of the year, pulling off the firſt roſes, as ſoon as they begin to decay, is a means; but to pull off all the *buds*, at the uſual time of blow, from a few trees, is a more certain method. A more ſure way ſtill is, to top the new ſhoots towards the end of *May*, or prune down to two or three eyes; All theſe manœuvres ſhould be particularly exerciſed on the *monthly* ſorts. Tranſplanting roſes in ſpring, is a means to effect a middle blow; and if not a north border, and cool ground, this may be done late in *April*, or even in *May*, (occaſionally watering) pruning at the ſame time ſhort. Early roſes are obtained by being trained againſt a ſouth wall. The *monthly* thus planted, and having glaſs (as the light of a cucumber frame) put before it, will ſometimes come as early

early as the end of *April*, or beginning of *May*. It is a good way to put moſs round the roots of theſe wall trees in *March* to keep the ground warm, and at the ſame time moiſt, which helps us to both forward and large roſes.

To *diſpoſe* roſe trees to bear forward, the not ſuffering any flowers to blow the preſent year, and pruning ſhort in *July*, or *Auguſt*, is a means from which much may be expected, eſpecially if there is any artificial warmth uſed in the ſpring to force them. With a view to this, ſome good bruſhy rooted, low growing plants, may be potted in *autumn*, not ſuffered to bear the next *ſummer*, and being pruned down (as above) will force well the next *ſpring*. Roſe trees potted for an ordinary blow, muſt not be in too ſmall ones, nor placed in a warm ſituation, except early in *ſpring*, and muſt be kept cool by watering. As to the *propagation* of roſe trees, many will ſend forth *ſuckers* enow, and thoſe that do not, may be *layered*, by ſlitting (as carnations) or budded ; but *may* be two years before they root. See page 67. Some will come by *cuttings*, but uncertainly, as the *burgundy*, &c. The *evergreen, everblowing roſe*, takes well by cuttings ; but it will not do abroad, except in the ſummer months, and therefore is not in the liſt : It is a ſemi-double dark crimſon, and may be treated as a *geranium ;* grows low, and rather weak. The *burnet, apple*, or any other ſort, producing good ſeed, may be propagated that way ; but it is a ſlow way, the ſeed ſeldom coming up till the ſecond year. The *double yellow* roſe blows indifferently, but *when* fair, the flowers are very beautiful. Plant it againſt an eaſt wall, and in dry, but ſtrong ground.

Snow-drop tree. is conſiderably ornamental. Layers will be two years in rooting. If raiſed from ſeed, (imported) ſow it as ſoon as it arrives, in pots, or boxes, and houſe it before froſts come. If they come not up the firſt year, ſet them on a gentle heat the following

lowing spring, and they will soon appear. Shelter the seedlings the first winter in a frame, or a green house.

Tutsan grows wild in woods, and will therefore do well in the shade, as among trees. Every shrub, or plant that *will* flourish in such a situation is valuable; and a gardener's attention will be well employed to discover them, by trials, &c. The *St. John's wort*, and *St. Peter's wort*, (allied to *tutsan)* may be planted in the shade.

Willow herb, as its roots run much, should some of it be potted; and as it loves moisture, may be set in the shade, and kept well watered.

* * * * * *

V.

List of *evergreen trees*, some of which are considered as forest, or timber trees.

* *Arbor vitæ*, common American and Chinese, *f. l. c.*
* *Andrachne*, or oriental arbutus, *f. l. in* fr. in. Nov. *d.*
  Andromeda, or Carolina sorrel tree, *f. l. fu.* July *m.*
  Arbutus, com. and scar. fl. sing. and double, *f. l. in.* Nov.
  Bay tree, com. and doub. fl. and striped leaved, *l. f. fu.* d.
  Box tree, br. and nar. wh. and yel. strip. leaved, *f. l. fl. c.*
* *Cedar* of Libanus, Carolina and Virginia, *f.*
  ———— Phœnician, Lycian and Bermudian, *f.*
  Cork tree, see the article *oak*
* *Cypress*, large common upright, and male-spreading, *f.*
  ———— Portugal pendulous or *goa cedar*, *f.*
  ———— the lower upright, or pyramidal shaped, *f.*
* *Fir*, spruce, Norway, American sorts, &c. *f.*
* ———— silver, (i. e. the pitch fir) and balm of gilead, *f.*
  ———— hemlock, and variegated balm of gilead, *f.*
  Holly, several plain, and many variegated sorts, *f. l. gr. b.*
  ———— Dahoon, and Yapon, or S. sea tea tree, ditto
  Juniper, Swedish, and two Spanish sorts, *f.*
  ———— see *cedar*, Virginian, (i. e. the red) &c.
  Laurel, com. or cherry bay, and wh. and yel. str. *l. c. f. fu.*
  ———— Portugal, reddish wood, bright leaves, ditto

* *Magnolia*,

* *Magnolia*, or laurel leaved tulip tree, *l. f. c.* August
* *Oak* (ilex) common evergreen, br. nar. leaved, *f.*
* —— Montpelier, or holly leaved oak, *f.*
* —— cork tree, broad and narrow leaved, *f.*
* —— Molucca, or the American live oak, *f.*
—— scarlet-bearing, or the kermes oak, *f.*
* *Pine tree*, wild Scotch pine, commonly called fir, *f.*
* ———— pinaster, stone, mountain Siberian, *f.*
* ———— Weymouth, torch, or Virginia swamp, *f.*
* ———— Carolina swamp, or prickly coned, &c. *f.*
Privet, common evergreen, white flower, *f. fu. l.* June
* *Pyracantha*, or evergreen thorn, red berry, *f. l. c.* May
Savin, large upright, plain and variegated, *f. l. c.*
Spindle tree, American plain and striped evergr. *f. l. c.*
Strawberry tree, see *andrachne* and *arbutus*.
Yew, short, narrow, broad and striped leaved, *f.*

*** Some of these, though they attain, in a course of years, considerable height, may be occasionally considered as large *shrubs*, instead of trees, and planted accordingly: Skilful pruning may keep large shrubs down, and lead others to mount.

OBSERVATIONS ON PARTICULAR TREES.

Andromeda tree should have a dry soil, and sheltered situation.

Arbor vitæ, though both sorts are in estimation, yet the *Chinese* is most ornamental. Naturally they are of large growth, and hardy, yet sometimes the *Chinese* sort is kept in pots, as an agreeable companion (for several years) of other exotic evergreens.

Arbutus may be propagated from the first young shoots of the summer, planting them in pots, and putting them in a moderate hot bed, (rather of *bark*) covering close with a *hand-glass* that is air tight; and thus most tender shoots of woody plants, which are found difficult to strike, may (most probably) be made to grow, as the *bay, celastrus, cypress*, &c. They may be be tried on a warm border, keeping the earth cool, and the glaſſes perfectly cloſe. If the cuttings are planted juſt within the glaſs, watering well round the outſide will reach them, and thus they need not be uncovered: If the glaſſes are taking off for watering, it is not (however) material, provided they are carefully fixed cloſe again. As ſoon as the cuttings appear to *grow*, air muſt be given them, or they will run up weak.

Bay, the common plain ſort is rather tender, and requires a ſituation ſheltered from bleak winds; but the variegated and double flowered ſorts are tenderer ſtill; and as they rarely ſucceed well abroad, they are commonly conſidered as green houſe plants.

Cedar, the Bermudian, is tender whilſt young, and ſhould have a favourable ſituation afterwards.

Fir, there is a variety of each ſpecies, denominated from the number of the *leaves*, and the ſhape and colour of the *cones*. The *balm of gilead*, and *hemlock* ſorts, are the loweſt growers. To get the *ſeed* from the cones, lay them before a good fire, ſo as not to ſcorch them; and if they come not out well, after heating this way, bore a hole up the middle, and drive ſomething of iron in to ſplit them open.

Oak, the evergreen ſorts are excellent timber, and very ornamental in pleaſure grounds, page 27. The red excreſcences upon the *kermes oak*, are occaſioned by *inſects* making inſertions in the bark for depoſiting their eggs, which cauſing an extravaſation of the ſap, it there condenſes, and forms the little granulous ſubſtances, uſed for ſcarlet dying.

Pine, there are ſeveral other ſorts of leſs eſtimation. The *Weymouth* and *torch* pines are the loftieſt, and the *Carolina* ſwamp the loweſt growers. To get out the *ſeed*, obſerve what is ſaid above, as the *pine* cones are harder to open than the firs.

Pyracantha requires ſome ſupport of ſtakes, pales, or wall, though it may be trained as a ſtandard buſh, or form an hedge impregnable. It is very beautiful

when

when in *full* fruit ; but it fo often miffes being fo, (chiefly through bad pruning, page 172) that it is got too much out of repute. It does beft in a dry poor foil, and an eaftern afpect. Young *cuttings,* in *June,* will ftrike, being potted in good earth, and fet in the fhade till autumn, and then plunged in the ground under a warm wall. See *arbutus,* obfervations on.

Savin, the variegated is beautifully ornamental, and it not getting out of bounds, feldom growing above a yard high, fhould be more frequently met with than it is.

* * * * * *

VI.
List of low *evergreen trees* and *fhrubs.*

3 *Adam's needle,* common and Virginian, pur. and wh. *f. r.*
4 *Alaturnus,* large, a variety in leaf, pl. and ftr. *f. l.* Feb.
3 ———— lower growing, ditto
2 *Andromeda,* yellow flowered Virginian, *f. fu. c.* July, *m.*
1 ———— box leaved, poly, fhining, &c. ditto
4 *Box tree,* tall fort, fee the laft lift.
1 ———— dwarf, plain, and ftriped leaved, *fl. l. c. f.*
4 *Briar,* fw. evergreen double red and yellow fl. *fu. l. b.* May
2 *Butcher's broom,* common, knee holm, or holly, *f. r.*
2 ———————— broad leaved, or Alexandrian laurel, *f. r.*
1 ———————— long leaved, or Alexandrian bay, *f. r.*
3 ———————— large, or fhining leaved Alexan. bay. *f. r.*
3 *Celaftrus,* or ftaff tree, climbing and upright, *f. l.* July, *d.*
3 *Ciftus,* poplar leaved, gum, &c. feveral, wh. *f. c.* May
4 *Clematis,* evergreen, or Spanifh climber, *c. l. f.* Nov.
3 *Cytifus,* hairy evergreen, Spanifh, yel. fl. *f. c.* June, &c. *d.*
2 ———— Auftrian, ditto
2 *Furze,* common, yellow and white flowered, *f.* April
3 ———— French, yellow flowered, ditto
4 *Groundfel tree,* ivy leaved, oleander, &c. wh. fl. *f. l. c.*
1 *Heath,* com. Englifh pur. wh. and yel. flow. *l. r. f.* July
1 *Hyffop,* blue and red fl. and ftriped leaved, *f. fl. c.* June
3 *Jerufalem fage,* yellow and purple flow. *r. l. c.* June
4 *Jafmine,* trailing yellow flowered, *l. c.* July
5 ———— dwarf upright, ditto

4 *Ivy*, tall plain, wh. and yel. ſtrip. *c. l. ſ.* fl. Sep. fr. Jan.
2 ⸺ com. dwarf bl. berried, and yel. berried, ditto
1 *Germander tree,* yel. white and purple flow. *ſ. ſl. c.* July, *d.*
1 *Horſe tail,* ſhrubby, the greater and leſs, *ſu. r.* July
4 *Juniper,* common ſhrubby Engliſh, yel. flow. *J.* April
4 *Honeyſuckle,* evergreen ſcarlet trumpet, *c. l. ſ.* June
4 *Kalmia,* broad leaved, pale red flower, *ſ. ſu. l.* July
3 ⸺ narrow leaved, bright red flower, ditto
2 ⸺ hairy leaved, reddiſh purple flower, ditto
1 ⸺ glaucous leaved, pink flower, ditto
1 *Lavender cotton,* com. and roſemary leaved, yel. *r. ſ.* Ju.
1 ⸺⸺⸺ ſea, com. and ſhrubby Siberian, bl. *r. ſl. c.*
2 ⸺⸺⸺ French, (ſtæchas) yel. flow. *r. ſl. c.* June
3 *Lauruſtinus,* com. br. and nar. leaved, *l. ſ. c.* Aug. &c.
3 ⸺⸺⸺ hairy, ſhining, and ſtriped leaved, ditto
4 *Moon-trefoil,* (medicago) ſhrubby, yel. flow. May, &c.
4 *Phillyrea,* mock privet, or privet leaved, *J. l.* March
⸺⸺ ſtriped, box leaved, bay, roſemary, &c. do.
1 *Periwinkle,* trailing and upright, blue fl. *l. c. ſu.* Feb. &c.
1 ⸺⸺ doub. fl. and white and yel. ſtriped, ditto
2 *Purſlain tree,* ſea, ſilvery leaves, com. and Spaniſh, *c.*
2 *Ragwort,* common ſea, hoary leaved, *ſ. c.* June, &c. *d.*
4 *Rhododendron,* large, or laurel leaved, red fl. *ſ. l.* Aug.
3 ⸺⸺⸺ dwarf, or the Pontic *roſe bay, ſ. l.* Aug.
4 *Roſe,* common muſk evergreen, wh. flow. *l. ſu.* Aug.
4 *Roſemary,* com. plain, and variegated, *c. l. ſl.* June, *d.*
3 *Rue,* broad, narrow and ſtriped leaved, *c. l. ſl.* June
3 ⸺ Aleppo, broad and narrow leaved, ditto, *d.*
3 *Savin,* common plain ſpreading, and variegated, *ſ. l. c.*
4 *Smilax,* or rough bind-weed, wh. fl. red fr. *l. r. ſ.* June
1 *Widow-wail,* (cneorum) a trailer, pl. fl. *c. l. ſ.* May, &c.
1 *Wormwood,* ſea, or lavender leaved, and Roman, *ſl. r.*

⁂ If the *tenderer* ſorts of theſe ſhrubs are judiciouſly planted, they may ſucceed abroad, and are worth the trial, as their place may, at any time, be eaſily ſupplied by ſome ſhrub from the nurſery. While young, for a winter or two, in ſevere weather, a few buſhes laid round, and a little peas haulm on the top, would ſave many a curious exotic, when they are nearly hardy enough to endure our climate.

OBSERVATIONS

OBSERVATIONS ON PARTICULAR SHRUBS.

Adam's needle (yacca) is somewhat tender, and should be out of the way of cutting winds.

Andromeda tree is too tender for the open ground in general, but has survived abroad, our ordinary winters, being in a favourable situation. It naturally likes a moist soil, but the roots should be kept dry in winter.

Celastrus, the upright, or Virginian studded, is somewhat tender, and must be planted accordingly: It is the prettiest of the two, bearing white flowers, and scarlet fruit.

Cistus, all the sorts are rather tender, but if brought up as hardy from the sowing as may be, and planted in a dry soil, shelter and sun, will stand ordinary winters abroad in the shrubbery, and prove delightful ornaments: Cuttings do not make so fine plants as seedlings, but are hardier.

Cytisus, Spanish, must have a dry warm situation.

Germander tree, though generally considered as a green house plant, it is asserted, by some, will endure ordinary winters abroad, with proper management. Risk of experiment in these cases, or the trouble attending, should not be minded, for if a shrub *will* live abroad, it is surely much better there; and it has been found that several things will do so, which have been used to be housed, even in stoves.

Groundsel tree, or ploughman's spikenard, must have a snug situation abroad, as hard frosts are apt to cut it; and if it is potted and housed, it must have a great deal of air, as it only needs protection in severe weather. This is an argument for trying all things abroad, of which there is a chance of living there, for they cannot have the air they require in a *green house*, where are so many plants of a tenderer nature.

Honeysuckle, evergreen, allow it a sheltered situation, and let it be as much as possible in sight.

Moon-trefoil is a very beautiful evergreen, flowering from May to October; but as it is tender, must have a dry warm situation, and then a little attention in severe frosts may secure it.

Phillyrea in all its varieties, though rather a rambling grower, is considered as one of the standing ornaments of our shrubberies; yet it has beauty in neither flower, nor fruit, as is the case with some other plants, (particularly evergreens) being retained only for their foliage. The *striped* sort should have a sheltered situation, as indeed is, in a measure, necessary to all variegated plants, as their ornamental nature, in this respect, is the consequence of hereditary weakness.

Periwinkle is a pretty under shrubby evergreen, if properly kept up to the lower part of pales, or a wall, or the larger sort may be trained to a low stake, or even kept as a little bush. It is very well to confine the roots (being apt to run) by slaty stones, or tiles: It succeeds well in shade and moisture.

Purslain tree, the Spanish is not so hardy as the common sort, but will generally survive our winters, in good situations.

Ragwort, this sort (as all the others) used to be housed in winter; but will stand abroad in a warm, sheltered, dry situation, and its hoary leaves are very ornamental, though there is no great beauty in its flowers. When raised from seed, it is apt to get greener in leaf, and therefore it will be best raised from cuttings, which should be taken from the whitest plants. A likeness to the original is frequently lost from seed, but is assuredly maintained from cuttings and layers, though the former method is generally to be recommended, where no inconvenience attends it.

Rose, this sort will need support, being rather trailing.

Rosemary will not do in all situations. See page 261.

Smilax, as it is trailing, or climbing, is commonly planted to run up the trunks of trees, &c. It may be trained to tall stakes, and should be planted in sight, as in the front of plantations. There are several sorts of it, and the bay leaved Virginian has black fruit.

VII.

The flowers in the following *list of annuals* are numbered (as the shrubs were) agreeable to their most usual heights. The time of flowering is not mentioned, because that will vary, according to the time of sowing, management, and season; very few before, or after *June* and *July*. Many continue longer in flower than a month.

TENDER ANNUALS.

4 *Amaranthus* tree, tricolor and bicolor
3 ——————— globe, purple, red, white and striped
4 ——————— coxcomb, com. large red, scarlet, yellow, &c.
2 ——————— common dwarf of colours as ditto
3 ——————— spike flowered coxcombs, a variety
3 *Balsams*, double, red, scarlet and purple striped
3 *Browallia*, spreading and upright, blue flowered
2 *Calceolaria*, or slipper-wort, winged leaved
4 *Capsicums*, red, yellow and white podded
3 *Cleome*, prickly stalked, and five leaved
4 *Colutea*, or scarlet African bladder sena
4 *Convolvulus*, scarlet, (ipomæa quamoclit) a climber
3 *Egg plant*, white, yellow, red, and prickly fruited
2 *Humble*, or spreading branching *sensitive plant*
1 *Ice plant*, or diamond ficoidas, white and yellow flowered
4 *Pentapates phænicia*, scarlet flowered
3 *Physalis*, or winter cherry, angular and downy
  Sensitive, see *humble plant* and *observation*
4 *Sida*, or Indian mallow, heart leaved, pink
4 *Stramonium*, or thorn apple, double purple, &c.

*** Some persons cultivate the *serpentine cucumber*, or *melon*, as a curiosity of the summer, the fruit being produced from one to two yards long, under good management; but it is to be remembered it will take up much room.

As

As to the *spirting* (or wild) *cucumber*, though it may be mentioned here, it is very hardy, so as to sow itself in autumn, come up in spring, and will abide as a perennial. Sow in *March*, and allow it two yards square. This is merely propagated for *diversion*, as a *noli me tangere*; for if the fruit is touched when ripe, it bursts, and throws its *fœted* contents to some distance, perhaps over the clothes of the adventurer.

In order to have *gigantic* flowers of the taller sorts of this class, (particularly *coxcombs*, *tricolors*, and *stramoniums*) drawing, or multiplying frames are used by some. These are made of boards about five or six inches broad, to put under the top frame, for it to rest upon; and two, or three of these are used, as the plants increase in height. But this business may be effected, by strong stakes at the corners, with holes, to put iron pins in to rest the frame on, nailing matting, or cloth, round the bottom.

OBSERVATIONS ON PARTICULAR FLOWERS.

Amaranthus, the *tree* sort, grows larger than the others, and bears purple flowers. The *tricolor* and *bicolor* are so called, from the former having the *leaves* of three colours; i. e. a bright red, yellow and green; and the latter of two, a deep red and purple; and it is for these, and not the flower, that they are cultivated. The flowers of the *globe* sorts have the peculiar property of retaining their form and colour a long time (years) when gathered, and have therefore the denomination of *everlasting*. Clear the seed of this flower from its downy covering before sowing, as a means of forwarding the germination.

Balsam, when double and well marked, is a very fine flower. The plain coloured red and white, semi-double and single ones, are not of much account with the curious, but may be put out in ordinary borders to make a shew. The *seed* of this flower should be

nicely

nicely saved from the fullest blossomed, and distinctly striped sorts, that have not grown near small, or self coloured ones. The plants elected for seed, should be protected from the wet and cold, after *Mid-August*, by putting them under lights, or in a green house window, where they may have the full sun.

Calceolaria, the flower of, is esteemed only for the curiosity of its slipper shape. The blow may be continued all summer, by planting cuttings at different times.

Capsicums are usually ranked in the less tender class, and though they are in nature so, yet to have them fine, and to fruit in time, they should be brought forward, by being treated as balsams, &c. at least in situations far north of London. They are grown only for the beauty and use of their *pods*, and these are variously shaped, as long, heart, cherry, &c.

Cleome is a very tender annual, (has been long considered as a *stove* plant) but may come under the cultivation of the ordinary florist, by continuing it longer in a frame, as suppose to *Mid-July*, or later, if the season is then unkind; and then plunging the pots in a warm border. When autumn approaches, a hand glass may be set on forked sticks over this, or any tender plant, and thus preserve it abroad longer.

Colutea is a perennial shrub of somewhat tender nature; and though the seed will come up on cold ground in high spring, yet by sowing it as one of this class, it may be brought forward enough to produce its beautiful flowers the same autumn. See *lists* IV. and X.

Egg plant must have a dry soil, and warm situation, but yet plenty of water in hot weather. The blossom is not striking, but the fruit is often as large as a swan's egg, and with common management will be as big as a hen's. This plant requires, however, to be sown forward, and should be brought on by a third hot bed, if it might be.

Humble plant is one of the *sensitive plants*, the property of which is to close its leaves, or drop them upon being touched. The common sensitive plant will grow erectly to eight feet, in a *hot house*, (which is its proper place) but the humble plant is spreading, and seldom reaches more than a stature of two feet ; for its lower growth it is therefore more proper for our purpose here. It is called *humble* from its receding and dropping so completely when touched, footstalk and all, as it were making a bow. The humble plants are distinguished from the common upright growing sensitives, as the latter only closes the leaf, without dropping the stalk.

Ice plant trails and spreads wide on the ground, makes no shew in its flower, but is beautifully covered with chrystal drops, shining like *diamonds* when the sun is on it ; or as the frozen drops of *icicles*. It is not nice in its culture, or weather, though it should not be put out too young. The best way is to plant one in a pot of six or seven inches diameter, without any thing at bottom over the hole ; and keeping it in the frame till it gets too big for the pot, plunge it in the ground a little over the rims. Thus the plant will not be *too* luxuriant, but yet sufficiently nourished, (for it has small roots) and will flower sooner, and ripen the seed better for this treatment.

* * * * * *

VIII.

LESS TENDER ANNUALS.

3 *Alkekengi*, or winter cherry, angular and downy
3 *Amaranthus*, trailing, or pendulous flowered, red
3 ——————— bloody leaved, with erect flowers, purple
3 ——————— upright, reddish purple flowered
3 *Aster, China*, double, white, red, purple, brown, strip. &c.
2 *Balsam*, yellow, *noli me tangere*, or touch me not

2 *Basil*,

2 *Basil*, common sweet, red and purple flowered
1 ———— dwarf, or bush, a variety in leaf
  Capsicums, see the last list
2 *Carthamus*, or common bastard saffron, yellow
2 ———————— woolly, or distaff flower, yellow
2 *Cerinthe*, or honeywort, great and small, purple and yel.
4 *Chrysanthemum*, double, white and yel. plain and quilled
4 *Convolvulus major*, pink, purple, and deep purple
1 *Geranium*, African trailing, variegated flower
4 *Hollyhock*, Chinese, single and double variegated
1 *India*, or *Chinese pink*, single and double, striped variously
  Love apple, or *tomatum*, see page 264
  Love lies bleeding, see *amaranthus trailing*
  Mignonette, see observation, next list
4 *Marigold, African*, pale and deep yellow, plain and quilled
3 ———— French, yellow and crimson striped, velvety
2 ———— dwarf sorts of both African and French
4 *Marvel of Peru*, white, yellow, red, purple and variegated
  Nasturtium, yellow and orange flower, July, see observation
1 *Nolana*, Peruvian dwarf, a trailer, blue flower
4 *Palma Christi*, large and small, a variety in stalk
  Persicaria, see next list
2 *Poppy*, Mexican, or prickly poppy, yellow flower
  Prince's feather, see *amaranthus upright*
  Scabious, sometimes made an annual, see *biennials*
2 *Stock*, com. ten week, red, scarlet, purple and white
1 ——— dwarf French fine scarlet, and ditto
2 ——— Prussian, or wall flower leaved, ditto
2 *Sweet sultan*, yellow, purple, red and white flowered
4 *Tobacco*, common broad and narrow leaved Virginian
3 *Xeranthemum*, or eternal flower, white violet and purple
3 *Zinnia*, yellow flowered, and red many flowered.

⁂ The seeds of most of these flowers will come up very well in cold ground, (if not sown too early) but are forwarded by a little heat, so as to have them much earlier, and a finer blow, producing seed, which late plants will not. The sorts of these that *naturally* require heat are, *aster, basil, geranium, love-apple, marvel of Peru, palma Christi, yellow sultan*, and *zinnia*

The *gourd* may be added to this class; but to succeed *well*, it should have a good south wall to be trained against, and it will take up a good deal of room there. Sorts numerous, as to size, shape and colour. The common *pumpion* (see page 243) is the hardiest; and the warted *orange gourd* is commonly thought the prettiest.

OBSERVATIONS ON PARTICULAR FLOWERS.

Aster, to have it forward and fine, should have a second slight hot bed to prick a few out upon, and indeed this would be a great advantage to any of the other sorts. Those not thus forwarded, will make a second blow. The *striped* sorts are much the prettiest, yet the plain ones make a good shew, and do very well for shrubberies, &c. particularly the *superb* white and red. It is a good way to plant a few *asters*, or any flowers designed for seed, in beds by themselves, in a way of nursery, as in the best borders it is much neater to have all flowers pulled off regularly, when their beauty is over: Pull up all bad flowers (as soon as discovered) from amongst such seeding plants.

Balsam, yellow, is more frequently sown in cold ground, (as others of this list, *carthamus, cerinthe, poppy, prince's feather,* and *xeranthemum*) but it is worth while to afford the assistance of a little heat. This flower is sufficiently ornamental to merit a place in the garden; but is chiefly curious for the elastic property of its seed pods bursting with force, when just pressed between the fingers, throwing the seeds to a distance.

Chinese hollyhock should be brought forward (especially northwards) to insure a timely blow. See page 12, vol. 2.

Chrysanthemum, to preserve some of the finest *doubles*, plant cuttings, or slips, in *September*, in pots, and house them before *November*, or the frost comes; and they will survive the winter, and flower much earlier, though not so strong as those sown in spring.

Convolvulus.

Convolvulus major will need support by a wall, stake, or otherwise, to be trained, or run up, as a scarlet bean. The deep blue is called *convolvulus nil*, or *anil*. The major convolvulus makes a good shew, and may be sown in *April*, in the places designed to flower; but it is the best way to sow three or four seeds in a small pot, which being placed on a gentle heat, will be much forwarder and finer, and may be turned out whole (when about three inches high) into open ground; for this flower, (as many other annuals) does not transplant well : *Nil* will not do without heat to bring it up.

India pink is now brought to blow much more double and variegated than formerly, and it is a very neat, engaging flower, blowing a long time. Prick them out when quite small, (for they readily strike) that they may not be drawn up weak, and let them grow in single detached plants, in a dry light soil, and they will be strong. If cut down as soon as the principal blow is over, they will stand another year.

Marigold the *African*, grows strongly erect. There is a variety in the form of the flower, and the quilled sorts are mostly admired. The *French* grows weakly spreading, and there are beautiful varieties of it from seed, which should be carefully saved from the most double flowers, having had no single ones growing near them. The smell of these flowers is unpleasant; but there are sweet scented sorts of each.

Marvel of Peru is considered as an annual, yet is naturally perennial in root—our climate makes it annual. If the *roots* of those growing abroad are taken up in *October*, and dried a few days, they may be packed in dry sand, and kept in a dry place (from frost) till spring ; when potted and placed on a gentle heat, they will shoot, and come forward. Or if the *plants* are housed in *autumn* (before the leaves are damaged by frost) and the pots stand till the mould gets very dry, they may be cut down, and the roots (probably) live, having no moisture to rot them.

Palma Christi, the *large leaved* (often half a yard broad) will grow from seven to ten feet high, according to culture, as early sown, &c. As it is valued for its noble stature, and ample foliage, some gardeners bring it forward as a tender annual, in order to produce a *giant;* but it is not advisable. The *small leaved* grows to about four feet high, and is an agreeable plant in the leaf, in other respects than size.

Nasturtium seed comes up well on natural ground, but a little frost kills the plants, hence it has been considered in this class, to have it flower early. Late sown plants, if potted and housed, will blow in winter, and live round to spring. Cuttings of it will grow. The spreading, rambling nature of this shewy annual, makes some people object to it; but the evil may be remedied, by growing it in a poor dry soil, or treating it as directed for the *ice plant,* in last list. The dwarf sort is preferred by some for flower borders, but is not so floriferous as the large. See page 259.

Stock, ten week, (as beautiful and fragrant) is the most important annual flower we have. Every one admires it, and its absence is always felt. It therefore merits every attention, to raise fine double flowers, to have them early, a continued succession, and as late as possible.

There should be *four* sowings of this flower in the year. Let the *first* be in the spring, (as at the end of *February,* or beginning of *March)* on a gentle heat; and being soon thinned a little, they should be pricked out in about a fortnight upon another moderate hot bed, at four inches asunder, where they may grow till this distance is thought too crowding; but the best rule is, to give them their final station as soon as they have acquired eight leaves.

The *second* sowing should take place on a little heat, when the first plants are pricked out; and let this sowing

SECT. XIX.   LISTS OF TREES, &c.   57

sowing be presently thinned to an inch asunder; prick the plants out in the full ground, (or on a moderate hot bed, if you wish to forward them) at six inches asunder. Here they may grow till either put out with eight leaves, or stand till their *flower buds* appear, which shew plainly whether they will be double or single; the double having round buds, and the single long ones. But if every other is drawn with eight leaves, the rest will do the better, and may be taken up with large balls of earth; concerning the method of doing which, see page 9, vol. 2. Or, every other being taken up from the bed, the rest may remain to make a grand shew in flower. Let as many single ones as are not wanted for seed, be pulled, or cut up.

The *third* sowing is to be upon cold ground, in a warm border, or rather under a hand-glass, some time, between the first and tenth of *May*. Let the plants be thinned in time, so as not to draw one another up weak, and pricked out at four inches, as soon as may be, in showery weather, for stocks will transplant very young; and when they have eight leaves, let them be planted where they are to blow. It is a good way (in furnishing borders) to plant three or four stocks together, about four inches from one another, and those that prove single, may be *cut* out as soon as discovered.

The *fourth* sowing is designed for plants to be preserved through the winter for a *spring* blow, and should be made either the last week in *July*, or the first in *August*. Plant some close under a south wall, and pot others for housing; but let them not be sheltered before, or more than necessary. If two or three plants are put in a pot, the single may be *cut* away from the double as soon as discovered.

The *French* stock is very floriferous, and there generally comes more double of this than the others. The *Prussian* is sometimes called the *sea-green* stock,

I0

to distinguish it from the others, which are somewhat hoary leaved.

To save *seed* that is most promising for double, mark those flowers which have five or six leaves, by tying a bit of thread round them. A single flowering plant that has double ones growing near it, produces good seed; but those single flowers that come out before the double ones appear, it is proper to take off, as also all the late flowers, which if they ripen their seeds at all, would be weak; and a plant having but few pods to ripen, will certainly produce the boldest seed, and of course the largest plants and flowers may be expected from it. Be sure that the seed is ripe before gathered, and that it is kept dry, which will be best in their pods, close tied in paper bags.

Sultan, the yellow is the finest flower, and has a very agreeable musky scent; but it is the tenderest, and will hardly do without the assistance of heat to bring the seeds up: It has a chance, however, if sown under a small hand-glass, that is air tight, on a warm border. The yellow will produce many fine flowers, if pricked out upon a second slight hot-bed.

Zinnia, the colours of this flower are dingy, but yet agreeable. Some gardeners chuse to treat it as the balsam; but a moderate hot bed will produce the plants large and forward enough to ripen their seeds. Zinnia is, however, rather more impatient of cold than others of this class.

* * * * * *

IX.

HARDY ANNUALS.

2 *Adonis*, pheasant's eye, or bird's eye, red and yellow
1 *Amethystea*, the flower is a pretty amethyst blue one
1 *Alysson*, sweet scented, white flowering
2 *Balm*, Moldavian, blue and red flowered

Balsam,

SECT. XIX.   LISTS OF TREES, &c.   59

   Balsam, yellow, see last list, and observation
2 *Belvidere*, annual, summer or *mock cypress*
2 *Borage*, variegated leaved, purple and red, see page 253
1 *Campion*, dwarf, viscous, or *dwarf lychnils*, purple
1 *Candy tuft*, white, red, crimson and purple
1 —————— bitter, and sweet scented white
1 *Caterpillar plant*, four sorts yellow, see page 5, vol. 2
2 *Catchfly*, *Lobel's* red, purple and white
   Cerinthe, or honey wort, see last list
2 *Clary*, annual pink, purple and white topped
1 *Convolvulus minor*, blue, white and striped
4 *Cyanus*, or corn bottles, blue, red, purple, white and strip.
   Devil in a bush, see *nigella*
1 *Geranium*, annual red musk, and a showy blue and purple
1 *Erigeron*, or Canada flea wort, white
2 *Hawkweed*, (bastard) red, pale and deep yellow
1 *Heart's ease*, or pansey, large Dutch, &c. a variety
4 *Indian corn*, dwarf, or *maize*, yellow flower, red fruit
2 *Ketmia bladder*, or flower of an hour, yellow
4 *Larkspur*, tall, unbranched, branching and rocket
2 —————— dwarf rocket, as of ditto, a variety
3 —————— Neapolitan, branched and spotted
2 *Lathyrus*, joint podded, blue flowered
3 *Lavatera*, or cretan mallow, red, white and purple
2 —————— three month's Syrian, pale red flower
1 *Lupine*, sweet scented, yellow flowered
3 —————— common, two blue sorts, and a white
4 —————— hairy giant blue, and rose coloured
   —————— scarlet, see *pea*, Tangier
   Lychnis, dwarf annual, see *campion*
4 *Mallow*, curled leaved Syrian, and Chinese, pink
   —————— Venetian, see *ketmia*
   —————— Cretan and a Syrian, see *lavatera*
3 *Marigold*, giant, or large common double
2 —————— large cape, hybrid, or mongrel
1 —————— dwarf cape, leafy, and naked stalked
1 *Mignonette*, (trailing) or sweet scented reseda

                                                3 *Mulberry*

3 *Mulberry blight*, or strawberry spinach, red fruit
1 ——————— dwarf plain and variegated leaved
  Nasturtium, see observation, last list
2 *Nigilla*, blue, white and yellow, single and double
  Normandy tuft ; i. e. red *candy tuft*, which see
4 *Pea*, sweet, purple, scar. wh. pink and wh. or painted lady
4 —— Tangier, sometimes called *scarlet lupine*
2 —— blue flowered, or cultivated lathyrus
4 —— crown, rose, or cape horn, pink and white
1 —— winged, or winged podded *lotus*, red flower
4 *Persicaria*, oriental, red flowered, see pages 6, 13, vol. 2.
4 *Poppy*, tall, double purple, scarlet, carnation, &c.
2 —— dwarf, or corn poppy, double, a variety
2 —— prickly Mexican, or yellow flowered
3 —— chelidonium, or horned scarlet
  Scabious, see next list
1 *Snails*, hedge hogs and horns, yellow, see page 5, vol. 2
2 *Snapdragon*, annual Sicilian, white flowered
1 *Stock*, (maritime) dwarf annual, or Virginian
4 *Sunflower*, large double, pale and full yellow
3 —— —— dwarf double ditto
2 *Toad flax*, or three leaved antirhinum, yellow, blue, &c.
1 *Whitlow grass*, white and yellow flowered
1 *Venus's looking glass*, blue, white and purple
1 ——— navel wort, common and Portugal, white
  Xeranthemum, or eternal flower, see last list.

*** There will not need many observations on the flowers of this class. Directions respecting their cultivation will be found in the last section. It was there said, that *May* was not too late for sowing those annuals that come quick into flower ;—the season may be extended (for late blows) to some, through *June*, or even the beginning of *July*, as *annual stock, candy tuft, convolvulus minor, corn bottles, heart's ease, yellow lupine, mignonette, sweet pea,* and *pheasant's eye.* But, if dry weather, the seeds must be watered to bring them up, and the plants also to bring them forward.

OBSERVATIONS

OBSERVATIONS ON PARTICULAR FLOWERS.

Belvidere is of a beautiful regular growth. The autumn sown seed make far the finest plants, and as self sown ones often come up, they should be preserved. This flower is adapted for potting, in which situation it looks well. See pages 5, 14, vol. 2.

Ketmia, the flower fades in a short time, when the sun is out; but the plant produces a great number, in long succession.

Larkspur is seldom permitted to attain its utmost perfection, not allowing it room enough. The large sorts *should* be from a foot to eighteen inches asunder, and the dwarf half this distance: A first rate florist directs two feet for the branching larkspur. See page 14.

Mignonette is often sown on heat, early in the spring, to obtain forward plants for pricking out into pots, boxes, or baskets, to be housed in windows, &c. But, as it does not transplant well, take it up with a little earth about the roots; and, if convenient, put the pots, &c. on a little heat, till well rooted.

Mulberry blight or more properly *blite*, i. e. the herb *blitum*, whose fruit resembles a red unripe *mulberry*. It is also called *strawberry spinach*, from the leaves being like those of the prickly *spinach*, and the fruit like a scarlet *strawberry*. The branches of this plant must be supported by a wall, pales, or sticks, or the weight of the fruit (not eatable) will bring them to the ground. It looks best, and is very handsome, when trained to a wall, which it should be, just as a fruit tree, suffering no side shoots to remain on. The seed is near a month coming up, which makes autumn sown plants valuable, in order to have the fruit forward and fine. Some persons sow it in spring upon a slight hot bed, and prick the plants out where they are to grow; but to sow forward, in their proper place, (not to be transplanted) generally does very well; as

it

it will then decorate the autumn, when other things begin to fail.

Stock, annual, if sown about *Mid-August*, for an edging, or in little patches, will make a pretty early spring blow, as it is very hardy: A light soil suits it best. This little flower is commonly spoiled by being suffered to grow thick, which makes it trail, and ramble too much. Four in a patch, about four inches asunder, is sufficient.

* * * * * *

X.

List of *biennial flowers*.

2 *Campion, rose*, single red, white and striped and doub. crimf.
3 *Canterbury bells*, blue, purple and white flower, June
2 ——————— variegated, and double flower, June
2 *Carnation*, (or gilliflower) a great variety, see obfervation
2 *Chelone*, forking, penciled, American, purple, September
2 *Clary*, garden, a variety in leaf, purple, see p. 254, June
   Colutea, see *sena, bladder*, below
3 *Honeysuckle French*, red, white and striped flower, June, *d*.
3 *Honesty*, satin flower, or moonwort, purple and white May
2 *Lion's tale* Virginian, or monarda punctata, yellow July
4 *Mallow tree*, (proving sometimes biennial) purple, June, *d*.
2 ——————— vervain, ditto, red and white, June, *d*.
2 *Milk vetch*, fox tail, (often biennial) yellow, *f*. June, *d*.
4 *Mullein*, branching, phlomoide and sinuated, yellow, June
2 *Penstemon*, (a biennial perennial) violet and pl. *f*. Sept.
2 *Poppey*, common, horned podded, yellow flower, July
4 *Primrose tree*, com. hairy and smooth stemed, yellow, June
2 *Rampion*, (see page 261) a large blue bell flower, June
4 *Rudbeckia*, three lobed Virginian, yellow flower, July, *d*.
3 *Scabious*, purple, black, red, white and striped, flow. June
3 ——————— hen and chicken flowered, purple, June
3 ——————— stary, Spanish and Montpelier, purple, July
4 *Sena, bladder*, (colutea) Ethiopian scarlet, August

Snapdragon,

SECT. XIX. LISTS OF TREES, &c.   63

2 *Snapdragon*, red, purp. white, yellow and variegated, June
2 ——————— red, &c. with variegated leaves, June, *d*.
3 *Stock*, Brompton, scarlet, blush and white, May
3 —— queen, red, blush and white, May
3 —— Twickenham, purple flowered, May
3 —— shrubby, white, tinged and spotted, May
4 —— large red Dutch and Patagonian, May
2 *Sweet William*, single and double, a variety, June
2 ——————— mule, or sweet Wil. pink, doub. red, June
2 ——————— broad leaved, striped and red flower, June
2 *Wallflower*, large, yellow and bloody, single and double
1 ——————— white, and dw. yellow, single and double, May
2 ——————— winter and early spring, single yellow

*** Several *biennial flowers*, if sown early, or brought forward upon a little heat, will blow the same year, only later, as *French honeysuckle, honesty, scabious, senna*, and *stocks;* but it is not generally desirable to attempt this, as they do not come so fine and strong, when made annuals of. Those just named, of course, though sown late the preceding year, will blow the next; but some of the biennials, in this case, will not blow the next year, as has been particularly experienced with *Canterbury bells*, a few of which, though sown at their proper season, may stand over for another year.

OBSERVATIONS ON PARTICULAR FLOWERS.

Campion, though a perennial, should be considered as biennial, in order to a timely supply, as it sometimes is of no longer duration. The *double* (as bearing no seed) is propagated by *slips* from the roots.

Carnation is seldom considered as a *biennial*, though in fact it is so, as much as several others, usually denominated of this class; for, after the first blow, the plants become straggling, and flower weakly; it is, therefore, that they are always *layered*, &c. to continue them. The plain, deep red, or *clove* scented carnation, is the original, and an established cultivated sort.

fort. The reft are claffed under the heads, *flakes*, *bizarres*, *picquetees*, and *painted ladies*, according to their colours, ftripes, fpots, and pouncings. For *layering*, and *raifing* carnations, fee the end of this fection.

Chelone, the feed of this flower is beft fown as foon as ripe, in autumn ; and coming up in the fpring, they may be planted in the borders, in *June* and *July*, and will flower the fame feafon.

Primrofe tree, produces fo immenfe a quantity of feed, that it becomes rather a troublefome weed to fome people. Cut the flower ftems off, or pull up the plant, juft before the feed pods are ripe enough to fhed their contents.

Rudbeckia, or Ameriean fun-flower, this biennial fort is called hardy, but fhould neverthelefs have a dry fheltered fituation. The narrow leaved dwarf *perennial* (about three feet) fometimes proves *biennial*, and may be fown as fuch, a little every year, by thofe who would extend their work in the culture of flowers.

Scabious has been noticed in the two laft lifts as an *annual*, which it becomes, if fown early ; and fome gardeners make a point of doing it on a little heat to forward them. As a *biennial*, it fhould not be fown too foon ; but if forward plants are tranfplanted in *June*, it will prevent their flowering till next year, when they will come very fine and ftrong.

Sena, *bladder*, or *colutea*, Ethiopian fcarlet, is rather tender, and the feedling plants muft be potted and houfed, or fheltered by a frame from fharp frofts. This flower is a *perennial*, (fee lift IV.) but as it is apt to be cut off in fevere weather, it is here confidered as *biennial*, and may take its chance after the firft flowering. It is fometimes made an annual. See *colutea*, lift VII.

Snapdragon we confider as biennial, it not blowing fo handfome afterwards. The variegated (as all ftripes are) is tenderifh ; this muft be propagated from *cuttings*, as indeed the plain may be, though the fineft

plants

plants come from seed. This flower is of longest continuance in a poor soil, and will grow out of cracks in walls.

Stock, or stock gilliflower, is apt to get too rampant (in some seasons) before winter, and when killed by frost, it is chiefly owing to this circumstance; for nothing stands severe weather well, that has grown very freely. Hence it used to be the custom of florists to transplant them several times in the summer; (even at every full *moon*) but to keep them down, and hardy, by this means, tends directly to weaken the blow, if not to kill the plant. The most reasonable method in this business is, not to sow *too* early, (or before the first week in *April*) to *thin* them, and to *prick* them out in time, that they may not be drawn up long legged; and by no means to let them have a dungy soil to grow in, or a very rich one. Prick them out the first cool weather after they have six leaves, at six or eight inches asunder, where let them remain till *August*, chusing a showery time, (rather about the middle) to plant them out where they are to blow; but let not this be into a moist soil, or damp situation. It is a good way to mix half sand in the mould that lies about the shanks above the roots; and when wet and frost comes, to lay coarse, or drift sand, round about them, two or three inches high, which remove at spring. Some plants may remain in the nursery bed till spring, to put out in cooler or moister ground, for in such a soil they blow best, though they do not stand the winter well in it: Stocks blow much finer in a showery summer than in a hot one. It will be a great advantage to those moved at spring, to have balls of earth to the roots, though they do not well retain it. To dispose them to it, and make them fitter to transplant, they may be cut round in autumn, with a long knife, five or six inches deep, and three inches from the stem, making one slanting cut under the root, at six inches depth, to cut those asunder that strike

directly

directly down. This is a practice that would answer
in most things that are to be removed at spring; and
if not, it would generally be of service, as the cutting
off the end of a root, occasions it to throw out several
others of a more fibrous nature.

Sweet William (or bearded pink) is distinguished
into broad and narrow leaved sorts. This flower
comes very diversified from seed, many plain, others
beautifully striped, and a *few* double, perhaps one in
thirty or forty. But the single ones are generally so
ornamental, that the want of doubles is not much la-
mented. The *double* sorts are propagated from *layers*,
as carnations. The *sweet William* is perennial, but
as the plants cease to be handsome (and in some cases
die) after the first blow, it is necessary to raise some
every year.

Wall-flowers, raised from seed, produce some doubles; but the chance is not great for fine ones, which
are to be continued from slips in *May, June*, or *July*,
planting them in a rich soil and shade till rooted. The
double *white* wall-flower is tender, and should be potted for housing, as indeed other good sorts should be,
and generally are.

* * * * * *

XI.

List of *fibrous rooted perennial flowers*.

2 *Adonis*, or perennial pheasant's eye, yellow, r. f. August, *m*.
3 *Acanthus*, smooth and prickly, white and pink, f. r. July, *d*.
3 *Agrimony*, the large, or odoriferous, yellow, f. r. July
3 ————— hemp, common wild, red, f. r. August, *m*.
2 ————— spotted stalked American, purple, ditto
3 ————— lower Pennsylvanian and Virginian wh. ditto
4 ————— Canada or tall purple flowered, ditto
4 ————— tallest Pennsylvanian, white flowered, ditto
2 *Alkekengi*, com. winter cherry, red fr. wh. fl. r. f. June
1 *Alysson*, rock, Cretan, and prickly, yel. and wh. f. r. May
1 *Anthemis*, or sea camomile, a trailer, white, f. July

3 *Anthemis*,

SECT. XIX. LISTS OF TREES, &c.

3 *Anthemis*, ox eye fort, yellow, white and red, r. June
1 *Anthyllis*, double, purple and fcarlet trailing, f. r. June
1 *Arum*, com. fpotted leaved, wh. fl. red berry, r. June
1 ——— white ftriped leaved, and friar's cowl, r. May
4 ——— dragon, common fpotted ftalked, purple, r. June
1 *Afarabacca*, Virginian vein leaved, &c. purp. r. May
2 *Afphodel*, or king's fpear, yellow and white, f. r. June
 After, a variety, fee *ftarwort*
1 *Auricula*, or bear's ear, fee *obfervation*
1 *Avens*, com. alp. yel. and marfh, pur. &c. f. r. May, m.
3 *Bachelor's button*, fing. and double, red and wh. f. r. May
  ——————————— blue, fee *cyanus*
1 *Balm*, grandiflorus, purple, red and white, r. June
1 *Barrenwort*, alpine (epimedium) red, r. May, *fhade*
 Bear's breech, fee *acanthus*
1 *Bear's ear fanicle*, of Matthiolus, fine red, r. June, d.
1 *Bear's foot*, or hellebore, greenifh flower, f. r. Feb.
2 *Betony*, com. Danifh, oriental, pur. red, wh. f. r. July, m.
2 *Birthwort*, upright yel. and trailing purple, f. Auguft, d.
4 *Bee larkfpur*, common, and great flow. blue, f. r. July
2 *Bloodwort*, or bloody ftalked dock, white, f. April
2 *Borage*, oriental perennial, blue flower, f. r. May, d.
1 *Bugle*, com. pyramidal blue, red and wh. r. May, m.
1 *Buglofs*, com. (fee p. 253) blue wh. and red, f. June
1 ——— oriental trailing and Virginian yellow, f. May
2 *Burnet*, com. (253) and agrimony leav. red, f. r. June
4 *Bryony*, common white flowered, red berried, f. May
2 *Cacalia*, alpine purple, a variety in leaf, f. r. June
 Calamint, Hetrurian, fee *balm* grandiflorus
4 *Campanula*, pyramidal, or fteeple flow. blue, f. fl. Auguft
1 ——————— grandiflora, and Carpathian, purp. f. r. July
 Campion, rofe, fee *biennials*, laft lift
3 *Cardinal flower*, fcarlet, blue and violet, f. r. c. Aug. d.
 Carnation, fee *biennials*, laft lift
2 *Catchfly*, or vifcous campion, doub. red and wh. r. June
4 *Centaury*, great pur. and woad leayed yel. f. r. June
2 *Chelone*, Virginian, &c. wh. blue, red and purple, r. Sep.
4 *Chervil*, perennial, or *fweet fern*, white, f. June
1 *Chriftmas rofe*, or black hellebore, white, r. January

4 *Clary*, Indian blue, and glutinous yellow, *f. r.* June
3 *Columbine*, com. plain, striped and spotted, *f. r.* June
3 ———— feathered, (thalictrum) wh. and pur. ditto
2 ———— mountain, or alpine, large blue, *f. r.* May
1 ———— Canada dwarf early, red with yel. *f. r.*
Cookoo flower, or *meadow pink*, see *ragged robin*
4 *Coreopsis*, verticillate, yellow, a long blow, *r.* July
1 *Cowslip*, double yellow, and double scarlet, *r.* May
1 ———— American, or *Meadia* purple, *f. r.* May
2 *Crowfoot*, meadow, double yellow flowered, *r.* May
1 ———— mountain, double white flowered, *r.* May
2 *Cyanus*, mountain, or perennial blue bottle, *f. r.* June
1 *Daisy*, wh. red, scar. variegated, coxcomb, &c. *r.* Apr.
1 ——— globe, (globularia) a fine blue flower, *r.* June
3 ——— ox eye, American and Montpelier, wh. *f. r.* July
——— Michaelmas, see *starwort tradescants*
Dittany, see *fraxinella*
2 *Dodartia*, oriental, deep purple flower, *r.* May
2 *Dog's bane*, willow leaved, purple and white, &c. *r.* July
3 *Dragon's head*, Virginian purple flowered, *f. r.* August
2 ———————— hyssop leaved, blue flowered, *f.* June
3 *Eryngo*, or sea holly, Amethystine and Russian, *f.* July
2 ———— maratime English, and aquatic American, ditto
2 *Eternal flower*, pearly, or white everlasting, *r.* June
3 *Feverfew*, two doub. fl. and a curled leav. wh. *f. r. c.* June
4 *Figwort*, Spanish, elder leaved, red and gr. *f. r. fl. c.* July
4 ———— aquatic variegated leaved, ditto
4 *Flax*, perennial Siberian blue flowered, *f.* June
3 *Foxglove*, pur. red, wh. and iron coloured, *f. r.* June
2 ———— great and less yel. and Spanish purple, ditto
———— American, see *monkey flower*
3 *Fraxinella*, wh. and purple flowered, *f. r.* June
3 *French honeysuckle*, Canadian red, wh. pur. *f.* June, *d.*
3 ———————— sensitive branched, yellow, ditto
1 *Fumatory*, diffused branching, yel. and wh. *f.* June
2 ———— upright American purple, ditto
3 *Gentian*, great yellow, and purple flowering, *f.* July
1 ———— asclepias leav. and crosswort, blue, *f. r.* May
1 *Gentianella*, fine azure blue flower, *f. r.* May
1 *Geranium*, *(English)* blue, purple, red, black, *r.* May

1 *Geraniums*

SECT. XIX. LISTS OF TREES, &c. 69

1 *Geranium, African,* or tender sorts, see *observation*
2 *Globe flower,* European and Asiatic, yellow, *s. r.* May, *m.*
4 *Globe thistle,* great, blue, and white flowered, *s.* June
2 ————— less, deep blue, and white flowered, ditto
3 *Golden Rod,* common Mexican and American, *r.* August
4 ————— tall late blowing American, *r.* September
4 ————— New-York, fleshy leaved, evergreen, *r.* Octo.
1 ————— lowest, or dwarf Pyrenean, *r.* August
2 *Goldylocks,* German, a bright yellow flower, *r. c.* July
1 *Hawkweed,* (or grim the collier) orange colour, *s. r.* July
1 ————— great yellow or French goat's beard, *s.* June
  Hedge mustard, single and double, see *rocket* yellow
4 *Hellebore,* (veratrum) white, black and yellow, *s. r.* May
2 *Helonias,* two sorts, white and cream coloured, *s. off.* July
1 *Hepatica,* red, blue, white and str. sing. and doub. *r.* Mar.
1 *Heart's ease,* or tricolor violet, yel. pur. wh. *r.* April
  Herb bennet, (geum) see *avens*
4 *Herb Christopher,* com. and long spiked, white, *s.* June
4 *Hollyhock,* com. doub. wh. yel. pink, red, sca. &c. *s.* Aug.
4 ————— fig leaved, or palmated, a variety, ditto
  ————— Chinese, or painted lady, see list VIII.
1 *Ladies' mantle,* common fringed, Alpine, &c. *r. s.* May
1 *Ladies' smock,* double, purple and double wh. *r.* May, *m.*
1 *Ladies' slippers,* yellows, purples, red, &c. *s. r.* May, *m.*
1 *Lavendersea,* great, &c. white and blues, *r. st. c.* July
1 *Lily of the valley,* wh. red, str. sing. and doub. *r.* May, *m.*
2 *Lion's foot,* single and double, blue flow. *s. r.* June, *d.*
2 *Lion's tail,* scar. and pur. fl. pl. and strip. leaf, *r. st. c.* July
1 *London pride,* or none so pretty, spotted flow. *r.* May
3 *Loosestrife,* common great yellow flowered, *r.* June
3 ————— willow leaved white Spanish, ditto
1 ————— ciliated Canadian yellow, ditto
1 ————— moneywort, or herb two pence, yellow ditto
  ————— see *willow herb,* list IV.
2 *Lupine,* perennial Virginian blue flowered, *s.* June
1 *Lungwort,* blue, purple, red and white, *r. s.* April
3 *Lychnis,* single and double scar. pink and white, *s. r. c.* July
3 ————— Chinese, fine orange coloured flower, ditto, *d.*
2 *Lychnidea,* red, purple, blue and wh. sw. scented, *r. c.* July
  Madwort, see *Alysson*
2 *Mallow,* Virginia smooth and rough leaved, wh. *s. r.* June

1 *Marsh*

1 *Marsh marigold*, double flowered yellow, *r.* April, *m.*
2 *Masterwort*, great black rooted, yellow, *r.* June
4 *Meadow rue*, common and Montpelier, yel. *r. s.* June, *m.*
, *Michaelmas daisy*, is *starwort, tradescants*, which see
1 *Milkwort*, com. and bitter, blue, red, wh. &c. *s.* June, *d.*
3 *Milk vetch*, goats rue leaved, and oriental, yellow, *s.* July
2 *Monkey flower*, or American fox glove, blue, *r. s.* July
3 *Morina*, purple, white, pale and deep red, *s. off.* June
4 *Mullein*, yellow, purple and iron coloured, *r. s.* June
1 ———— myconic borage leaved, trailing, blue, ditto
1 *Navelwort*, perennial trailing, blue flowered, *r. c.* April
 Orobus, see vetch
 Orchis, biennial, see next list
 Orobus, see vetch, bitter
2 *Orpine*, the greater, purple and white, *fl. c.* July, *d.*
1 ———— the lesser, (anacampseros) a trailer, pur. ditto
1 ———— true, (telephium) white flowered, *s. r. fl. c.* July
4 *Ox eye daisy*, American and Montpelier, white, *r.* July
2 ———— corymbous flowering, white, ditto
 Pasque flower, see next list
4 *Passion flower*, com. palmated blue rayed, *c. l. s. su.* July
4 *Pea*, everlasting, red, scar. purple and large fl. *s. r.* June
 Paeony, being tuberous rooted, see next list
1 *Pink*, com, red, white, plain and fringed, damask
1 ——— red cob, white cob, painted lady
1 ——— maiden, or matted, and grey leaved mountain
1 ——— pheasant's eye, &c. a great variety
3 *Plumbago*, or European leadwort, blue, purp. wh. *r.* Oct.
1 *Polyanthus*, a great variety in flower, *s. r.* April
2 *Poppy*, oriental scarlet, and Welsh yellow, *s. r.* June
1 *Primrose*, white, red, scarlet, double yel. &c. *r.* March
3 ———— tree, the larger, (perennial) yel. *s. r.* June
2 *Ragged robin*, or meadow pink, double red, *s. r.* May
4 *Reed*, Portugal, or Spanish, and variegated, *offsets*
2 *Rest harrow*, common purple with red flowers, *s.* May
3 *Rhubarb*, com. and waved leaved Chinese, wh. *s.* June
4 ———— palmated Chinese, and large Tartarian, &c.
2 *Rocket*, sing. and double wh. pur. and red, *s. c. r.* June
2 ———— double yellow, or double erysimum, *r.* June
4 *Rudbeckia*, jagged leaved Virginian, orange, *r. s.* July
2 ———— dwarf hairy, yellow, purple, &c. ditto
           4 *Rush*,

SECT. XIX.   LISTS OF TREES, &c.   71

4 *Rush*, sweet flowering, pink, white and purple, r. July, w.
1 *Sanguinarea*, Canada, (puccoon) sing. and double, wh. r.
2 *Sarracena*, or side saddle flower, purple and yel. f. r. July
4 *Saw wort*, New-York and Maryland, pur. flow. r. June
3 *Saxifrage*, pyramidal, often called *sedum*, wh. off. June.
2 ———— spotted hairy, and strawberry, wh. ditto
1 ———— ladies' cushion, a low trailer, wh. off. May
1 ———— golden, two sorts as to leaf, yellow, r. July
  ———— double flowered, see next list
4 *Scabious*, perennial Alpine blue flowered, fl. c. r. July
2 ———— oriental silvery, and grass leaved, f. July
3 *Scullcap*, tallest, or nettle leaved, purple, f. June, d.
2 ———— Alpine violet, and white flowered, ditto
2 ———— eastern, germander leaved yellow, ditto
Sea pink, see *lavender* and *thrift*
3 *Sena*, wild, or Marilandic, (caffia) r. f. July, d.
1 *Sisyrinchium*, Virginian and Bermudian, blue, r. f. June
  ———— see *iris*, next list
2 *Sneezewort*, double flowered white, r. f. July, m.
1 ———— hoary yel. and silvery leaved wh. r. f. July
3 *Soapwort*, double flowered purple and scarlet, r. July
1 *Soldanella*, purp. blue, wh. and fringed, r. March, m.
3 *Soloman's seal*, many flow. sweet scented, &c. r. May, m.
3 *Sophora*, oriental, fox tail like, blue, r. f. July
4 ———— four winged podded, yellow, r. June
1 ———— tinctorious Virginian, trailing yellow, r. f. July
Speedwell, see *veronica*
Spiderwort, see next list
1 *Starwort*, dwarf alpine, purple flowered, r. June
2 ———— sea, or tripolium after, blue, r. July
3 ———— flax leaved, blue flowered, r. August
4 ———— New England, violet coloured, r. September
4 ———— tradescants, a pale blue flower, r. October
3 ———— Catesby's pyramidal Virginian, blue, r. Nov.
2 ———— Italian, large bright blue flower, r. Nov.
1 *Stock*, dwarf shrubby, or window flow. red, f. June
1 *Stonecrop*, small and great, trailing, yellow, c. r. July
1 ———— poplar leaved, upright, pinkish, ditto
4 *Sunflower*, many flowered, com. double, &c. r. July
3 *Swallow-wort*, common, wh. black and yellow, f. r. June

1 *Thrift*,

1 *Thrift*, greater and smaller, red, scar. and wh. *fl. r.* June
3 *Throatwort*, great, double, white, blue and purple, *r.* June
4 ———— giant, blue, white, red, and striped, ditto
2 ———— dwarf, small fine blue flower, *f.* June
2 *Toadflax*, a variety, yellow, purple and white, *fl. c. r.* July
1 ———— dwarf Alpine purple flowered, ditto
2 *Toothwort*, five, and nine lobed, blush and pl. *f. r.* June
3 *Valerian*, common red and white mountain red, *f. r.* June
2 ———— Greek pur, wh. and variegated, *f. r.* May
4 *Veronica*, a variety, blue, white and blush, *r. f.* June
1 ———— dwarf blue and wh. and Welsh blue, ditto
3 *Vervain*, common, and spear leaved, blue, *f. r.* June
4 *Vetch*, white wood, and tufted blue, *f. r.* July
3 —— bitter, (orobus) a variety, blue and pur. *f. r.* May
2 —— Siberian, unbranching orobus, yel. *f. r.* April
 —— see *orobus*, next list
1 *Violet*, com. blue, purple and white, sin. and doub. *r.* Mar.
1 ———— Austrian purple, and Canissian blue, *r.* April
1 ———— Alpine, double red, and purple, *r.* March
1 ———— yellow, and grandiflorus yellow, &c. *r.* April
Wake robin, see *arum*
Willow herb, see *loosestrife*
1 *Wood sorrel*, common white and purple, *f.* June, *m.*
1 *Worm grass*, Maryland, (spigelia) red flower, *r.* July
2 *Yarrow*, or *milfoil*, the purple flowered, August
 ———— see *maudlin* and *sneezewort*.

OBSERVATIONS ON PARTICULAR FLOWERS.

Acanthus, or *bear's breech*, is admired for the elegance of its leaf, and was so much so by the ancients, that they introduced it into the capital of the *Corinthian* order. It spreads wide, and should have room allowed it, in a warm light soil, and sheltered situation; but still rather a shady, than a sunny one.

Alkekengi roots run much, and are sometimes kept in pots, or boxes, to confine them. It is not a pretty plant; but has been long admitted into gardens for the show of its red berries in winter, when there are few ornaments to adorn the ground. *Alyssons*

Alyssons do best in a dry hungry soil, but should have a favourable situation, where they will blow long and prettily.

Avens will grow in any cold moist shady ground.

Auricula, from the great and elegant variety of its flower and leaf, arising perpetually from seed, is one of the *florist's* chief delights, and to which he pays much attention in the culture. It is one of the first flowers, and ranks in nature with the *primrose* and *polyanthus*. The sorts admitted in the present collections, are about four hundred. The *auricula*, the *carnation*, *tulip*, *hyacinth*, *ranunculus*, *anemone*, &c. are called *fancy flowers*. For the *propagation* and *culture* of the *auricula*, see the end of this section.

Bear's ear sanicle is very hardy, but is a proper plant to *pot*. It may be planted in any cold place, and should have a dry lean soil, but be duly watered in summer; and most things that a poor soil suits, must still have water freely in warm weather. This sanicle is about six inches high; that of *Gmelin* only four, and is not so pretty.

Betony, as it is a native of the woods, is proper to plant in shrubberies, and shady places.

Birthwort is tender, and seedlings of it must be sheltered by a frame in winter.

Bryony is a climber, and will grow in plantations to run up trees, &c.

Campanula, pyramidal, may be propagated (as well as from seeds and slips) by pieces of its *root*, planted about an inch and half in the ground, in a shady, but not moist border. The finest plants are produced from *seed*; but will be three or four years before they blow. Sow a few every year in *April*, in a light fresh soil, where the morning sun only comes. As much wet in the cold seasons is apt to rot this root, it will be proper to guard against it, by some occasional covering, when there is a continuance of rain, or snow.

A few

A few *potted* may be removed under shelter. A *mat* set *high* over is a proper covering for a bed of them. In the *summer* they must never want water, especially when spindling, or in blow. There is a *white* sort.

Cardinal flower must have a dry soil and a warm situation; occasionally also a little protection. They are commonly potted, and some should at least be so, lest those in the open ground be cut off. This flower is very ornamental, but the scarlet much more so than the blue, and is not tall of growth.

Christmas rose is very hardy, but a dry warm situation may be allotted it; and when in flower, a little protection to preserve it in beauty, as a *hand-glass*, may be advisable. A plant or two potted (large pots as it spreads) is agreeable enough, to house when in blow.

Columbine, when sown in spring, is rather apt to miss. Autumn is therefore preferable; and these plants will also be much stronger, as they do not blow the next, but following year. The plants should not stand above two years, as afterwards they get unsightly, and plain in flower.

Cowslip American is commonly potted, as indeed some plants should be, as it thus appears to advantage; but it is hardy, and grows best in borders that are somewhat shady, or have not the afternoon sun.

Dragon's head should have a moist shady situation.

Figwort, the plants are somewhat tender, and may only be expected to stand through ordinary winters, in a warm soil and situation. Let some be *potted*, for housing, lest those abroad be cut off. The *pilewort* is sometimes called *figwort*; but this is a different plant, whose proper name is *scrophularia*, whereas the *pilewort* is *ranunculus ficaria*;—this has a red flower, that a yellow;—this a fibrous, that a tuberous root—this grows to about five feet, that attains only to so many inches.

Foxgloves

Fox gloves do best in a somewhat strong soil, and shady situation, and will be found a useful flower in shrubberies, &c. in all its varieties.

Geranium, or *crane's bill*, (so called from the shape of the seed vessel) the *exotic* sorts are tender, *Africa* being their native climate. As favourite flowers, the different sorts are cultivated by all descriptions of people, as opportunity affords to preserve them in winter: They are properly *green house* plants. The principal kinds are as follow, classed according to their ordinary height of growth:

1. Flaming, or Vervain mallow leaved, scarlet. Three coloured; i. e. red, black and white. Ladies mantle leaved, whitish and bluish. Sweet scented mallow leaved, white. Gooseberry leaved, reddish. Caraway leaved, or variable geranium, red, crimson, purple, white, &c. Vine leaved, red and white. Night smelling, yellowish with dark spots, three sorts. Pinnated, or proliferous, of different colours.

2. Spear leaved, white. Fleshy stalked, or celandine leaved, white. Square stalked, flesh coloured.

3. Birch leaved, reddish. Sorrel leaved blush, plain and stripe flowered, and variegated leaved. Three gouty stalked, or columbine leaved, purple. Rose-scented, a purplish blue. Glutinous vine leaved, reddish purple and white. Horseshoe, green leaved, variegated, silver edged, silver striped, gold striped, pink, two scarlets and a purple, and one large scarlet, or grandiflorum.

4. Vine leaved, balm scented, blue. Shining, and mallow leaved, scarlet and deep scarlet. Butterfly, or variegated flowered, with a pointed mallow leaf. Marsh mallow, or hood leaved, purplish; and a variety of this with angular leaves. Rasp leaved, flesh colour, spotted red. Two coloured, purple and white. See the end of this section.

Gentianella likes a cool loamy soil, and eastern situation, and should not be often removed, or in too small pieces.

Globe flower, or *globe ranunculus*, is very ornamental. The *European* is sometimes called *locker gowlans*. They both do well in a cool soil, and *north* border; though the name *Asiatic* seems to direct to a dry soil, and warm situation. The case is, they are natives of moist, shady places; and whenever this is the case, we may conclude such plants are organized accordingly, and that they must be accommodated by us agreeable to their nature. The *constitution* of plants is necessary to be known, in order to their proper culture; and a *gardener* cannot direct his attention more to his credit, than to make *observations* and *experiments* to discover it.

Golden rod will grow in shade, and particularly the evergreen sort; but being late blowers, this circumstance rather directs to an open, or forward situation.

Hellebore, the white flowered, is the common officinal plant. A light soil and dry situation, not subject to snails, suits it best.

Helonias is a very elegant and ornamental plant, worthy of the most conspicuous part of the pleasure garden. It requires only the ordinary culture of perennials. Seeds are imported from *North America*, as it does not ripen them here.

Hepatica is found to transplant best when in flower; but it must not be in small portions, lest it wither away; and they never look well in small patches, as is the case with all dwarf blowers. Situation and soil as *gentianella*.

Ladies smock, and *ladies slipper*, do best in a moist soil and shade, as in a *north* border, where not many things do well.

Lily of the valley should have a cool situation, and if not in a moist soil, give it at least an *east* border, or where it has only a little of the morning sun.

Lion's foot is somewhat tender, and to do well must have a favourable place in the garden, as to sun and shelter; and it does best in a light, or sandy soil. Let some be potted, for it is pretty, and blows all summer.

London

London pride (a saxifrage) used to be planted much as an edging; but it does not answer this purpose well. A few plants here and there in patches is best; and by no means allow it a good border, for it is not very handsome, though it has such fine names: It prefers a moist soil and cold situation.

Loosestrife, the common, is found wild; but it is a showy plant, and where a variety is wanted is very admissable. It grows in shady moist places, and should be planted accordingly, in the borders of a shrubbery, &c. The smallest is a trailer.

Lupine will be best raised from seed, without transplanting, as the roots strike down deep: If they are transplanted, let it therefore be while quite young.

Lungworts prefer a shady situation; but the *Virginian* (an elegnt little plant) rather one dry and sheltered

Lychnis, the double scarlet is a beautiful flower, but not apt to increase much at root; recourse is therefore to be had to *cuttings*, which also are not certain in striking root. In *June*, or *July*, take cuttings from the side shoots, (without flower) and let the pieces planted have three, or at the most four eyes. Put them into a good soil, fine and rich, but not dungy, as deep as half way between the second and third joint, in an *east* border; and keep them cool, but not wet. A *hand-glass* will greatly assist in this business. See *pink* at the end of this section. The *Chinese lychnis* is rather too tender for open culture; but in a choice situation may abide moderate winters. It makes a good potted plant among myrtles and geraniums.

Lychnidea, take the cuttings off close to the ground, and discharge the tops; and plant them in pots, or borders, in a place not of much sun.

Masterwort (a medicinal plant) is of no great ornament; but is commonly cultivated for borders of shrubberies, &c. as being of low growth, and hardy nature. There is an *alpine* sort about a foot high.

Marsh

Marsh marigold is a flower, (as its name imports) that will flourish in a wet soil; but yet it does not do much amiss in a dry one. In default of a moist soil, any plant that requires one, should at least be accommodated with a shady situation, and never want water in summer.

Milk vetch is somewhat tender, particularly the seedlings, which should be protected by a garden frame in winter. *Fox tail* sort, see *biennials*.

Monkey flower is very ornamental, and of easy culture, not difficult in situation.

Monk's hood is a poisonous plant in every part, but very ornamental, and commonly cultivated. Shade suits it, and it will even grow under trees, or in any damp place, where few other things will.

Morina is worthy of a conspicuous place in the garden. It has a strong taproot, and should be transplanted whilst young, that it may not be damaged; but sowing in the place where it is to grow (as directed for the *lupine*) is the best way.

Mulleins prefer a light soil, but like a north border; and the borage leaved being very low, is proper for an edging in a cool shady situation.

Orpine, this, as all succulent plants, should have a dry soil and situation, and not often watered.

Passion flower should be planted against a warm wall, where it may have room to spread, as it is a *very* free shooter. The sorts are numerous, (for *green house* and *stove*) but only this well suits open culture. In fine situations, and the *southern* parts of *England*, there are two more, however, that may do abroad. Prune it about *Michaelmas*, leaving the shoots from two to four feet long, as the strength of the plants, or room, dictates, and a foot asunder. Before the frosts come, cover the roots, a yard round, with dry litter; and renew it with dry, when afterwards it gets much and long wet. The branches also should be covered with a mat (a thin one, and not over close) before *severe frost*

frost sets in; but uncover as soon in spring as may be, or, in short, in mild weather, on *days* through the winter, if not too much trouble. This flower has been sometimes trained to a stake, in which case, shorter pruning must take place to keep it down. It bears upon the young shoots, which should be regularly trained in, and the flowers are the glory only of a day, but generally a great number are produced in succession. This flower takes readily from cutting, of about seven or eight inches long, taken off in March, and planted in a good soil, kept cool by water, and shaded from much sun.

Pink, the sorts are numerous, for *seed* is constantly producing new varieties, occasionally one that vies with its predecessors in beauty, and whose superior excellence is not neglected by the *florist*. He gives it a name as fancy directs, and it is enrolled in the *nurserymen's* catalogues of worthies. *Maddocks* mentions in his, an *ever blooming* pink, price 2s. 6d. The *pink* (as the carnation was) might be considered biennially, the good sorts being regularly layered, &c. every year for increase: They do, however, stand on for older plants, better than carnations. For *propagation*, &c. see the end of this section.

Polyanthus produces an infinity of sorts from seed, and the *florist* pursues his object of obtaining *prize* flowers of this kind. The polyanthus delights in a loamy soil, and shady situation. It is an excellent edging flower for shrubberies; though fine blows are not to be expected under trees, or in much wet. An *east* border is the place for producing the best flowers. For *raising* them, &c. see the end of this section.

Plumbago, though it be a native of *Italy*, is hardy enough to abide our ordinary winters in the open ground. Afford it a dry, sunny, sheltered situation, which will be a means of preserving it, and also tend to forward the blow, as it is so late: All plants that produce their flowers towards the end of autumn,

(however

(however hardy) ſhould have a favourable aſpect, as to ſun, left winter overtake them.

Poppy, allow the *eaſtern* ſort a light dry ſoil.

Reed, Portugal, is curious for its lofty and ample growth, but rarely flowers with us. It attains to ten or twelve feet high, and its ſtems are ſtrong enough for walking ſticks. The *variegated* ſorts come only to half the ſize, and more frequently flowers.

Rhubarb, the common ſerves for ſhow, and the ribs of the leaves for tarts; but the *Chineſe* principally, and then the *Tartarian* for medical uſes of the root: The *Chineſe* is deemed the true officinal rhubarb.

Rocket, (ſometimes called *dame's violet*, and *queen's gilliflower*) the ſingle is raiſed from ſeed, and the double from rooted ſlips and cuttings. The double is rather uncertain in continuance, and requires ſome attention. Cut the ſtems down as ſoon as off their principal ſhow and time of flowering, which is a means to help them to increaſe, and get ſtrong at root, as it is from offsets formed in the preſent year, that they flower in the next. If weak, or ſmall roots are planted, they ſhould not be ſuffered to blow the firſt year. To *propagate* by *cuttings*, do it when the ſtems are about eight or nine inches long, (i. e. before flowering) making each into two; and plant them a little more than half way deep in an *eaſt* border, in good freſh undunged ſoil. Keep them cool by occaſional watering, and if the cuttings attempt to flower, nip the buds off. Cuttings of ſtems that have flowered, will ſometimes grow, but they make weak plants. A *hand-glaſs* would be of ſervice over them. See *pink* at the end of this ſection.

Rudbeckia, or *American ſunflower*, is a little tender, and muſt be accommodated accordingly. Like the *rocket*, it is rather (ſome ſorts at leaſt) unapt to form *offsets*; and therefore to encourage the putting them forth, (without which the plant dies) the ſtems may be cut down to prevent flowering: That is, when plants are more deſired flowering.

Ruſh

Rush will be proper only for places that are constantly wet, by standing water; and whoever has such a situation for them, they will prove ornamental.

Sarracena is a native of the boggs of *North America*. It requires therefore a moist situation; but is found to need protection from our sharp frosts. The whole plant is of curious formation. It is not apt to ripen its seeds here, or to make offsets; so that both are frequently imported.

Saxifrage plants are usually *potted* to move into the house when in flower, as indeed the *pyramidal* in particular should be; but they are all very hardy, except the *strawberry* sort, (not very handsome) which is too tender to endure much wet and cold.

Senna, of Maryland, must have a dry soil and warm situation. It is annual in stalk, and therefore the roots may be well protected in winter: This flower makes a very handsome show.

Solomon's seal is in greater variety, and one with double flowers. They all suit well in shady moist places.

Starworts are in general of that hardy nature, that they will flower almost any where, and increase apace from the least slip. They are apt, however, to lose their lower leaves, in proportion to the shade, cold, and wet, they grow in; and the *Alpine* sort will require an open situation, though, like the others, a stiff moist soil suits it. There are other sorts, as a *Philadelphian purple*, eight feet, and two *whites* of rather low growth, &c. The two last, as blowing late, and not rampant, may be planted near the house.

Stock, this plant is rather of a biennial nature, but is commonly of longer duration. It is proper to *pot* and place in a window, on account of its size, rising only a few inches. It is sweet and floriferous, and altogether very proper for an edging.

Sisyrinchum, allow it an *east* border, but dry soil; and as it is a small flower, *pot* some.

Throatwort,

Throatwort, the two firſt ſorts are claſſed with *campanulas*. The latter, which is the proper, or *mountain blue throatwort*, likes the ſhade, but muſt have a light dry ſoil. This, as the *ſnapdragon*, and ſome others, will grow in the crack of walls, &c. and continue longer in ſuch a ſituation, than a better: In moſt ſoils it proves often biennial.

Toothwort, as it delights in ſhade, is proper for the borders of walks in plantations; though it will grow any where.

Whitlow graſs is a wild (medicinal) herb, that grows on roofs and walls of old houſes, and rubbiſh heaps; but makes a pretty dwarf ſpring flower as an edging, &c. in a poor ſoil.

Worm graſs is a very neat little plant, with a flower bright red without, and a deep orange within.

* * * * * *

XII.

LIST of *bulbous, tuberous*, and *fleſhy rooted perennials*.

1 *Aconite*, or winter wolf's bane, yellow flower, Feb.
2 *Albuca*, or baſtard ſtar of Bethlehem, (leaſt) yellow, June
3 ——— greater, or ſpear leaved, red flowered, June
4 ——— talleſt, with ſpiked cluſters of wh. flow. June
2 *Anemone*, double broad and narrow leaved, variety, May
2 ——— common wood, dou. wh. purp. blue, red, March
2 ——— Appenine wood, doub. blue, purp. wh. April
2 ——— yellow wood, or ranunculus anemone, April
——— pulſatilla, ſee *paſque flower*
1 *Bulbocodium*, or ſpring colchicum, violet, April
1 *Colchicum*, com. ſing. and double, purp. pink, wh. &c. Sep.
1 ——— variegated flow. and a ſtriped leaved, Sep.
1 ——— mountain, (Spaniſh) red and ſtrip. red, Aug.
1 ——— eaſtern, variegated leaf, checquered flow. Aug.
4 *Comfrey*, oriental, blue (April) and German, yel. June
4 *Cornflag*, or ſword lily, crimſ. red, purple and white, June
1 *Crocus*, ſpring, yellows, a variety, plain and ſtrip. March
1 ——— ditto, blues, purples, white, plain and ſtrip. March

1 *Crocus*,

SECT. XIX.   LISTS OF TREES, &c.   83

1 *Crocus*, autumnal, or saffron, pur. blue, white, yel. Oct.
3 *Crowfoot*, Alpine plantain leaved, white, April
—————— see *crowfoot*, last list
3 —————— Pyrenean grass leaved, yellow, May
4 *Crown imperial*, single and double reds and yellows, May
4 ———————————— double crowned, triple crowned, May
4 ———————————— gold and silver striped leaved, May
1 *Cyclamen*, European, spring and autumn, pur. wh. April
3 *Daffodil*, a variety of yellows, single and double, April
3 —————— double yellow, with cup in cup, April
3 —————— yel. with white cup, and wh. with yel. cup, April
4 —————— tradescants, large double, yellow, April
2 —————— dwarf, or short-stalked yellow, March
1 —————— hoop petticoat, or rush-leaved yellow, April
3 —————— odorous, or sweet-scented starry, yellow, April
—————— white, see *narcissus*
—————— sea, see *pancratium*
1 *Dog's tooth violet*, purples, red and white, April
1 ———————————— narrow leaved, colours ditto, April
4 *Dog's bane*, (tuberous asclepias) orange, July
2 *Dropwort*, doub. flow. and varieg. leaved, white, June
3 *Fritillary*, common and Pyrenean, a variety, April
1 *Fumatory*, solid, and hollow rooted, red, pur. wh. April
  Garlick, (the flowery kinds) see *moly*
1 *Herb true love*, nodding and sessile flower, purple, April
2 *Hyacinth*, a great variety, white, red, blue, &c. May
3 —————— tufted, (or fair-haired) bl. pur. and white, April
1 —————— Spanish nodding flowered, red, April
3 —————— amethystine, a deep blue colour, March
3 —————— musk scented, purple and yellow, April
4 —————— monstrous flowered, or feathered, blue, April
1 —————— grape sorts, blue, white and grey, April
2 —————— lily, (yellow rooted) a blue star flower, June
1 —————— Peruvian starry, blue and white, May
2 —————— Italian and Byzantine starry, blue, April
1 —————— English starry, (autumn squill) blue, Sept.
1 —————— bell flowered starry, white with purple, May
—————— *Indian tuberous*, see *tuberose*   3 *Jonquil,*

3 *Jonquil*, single, semi and double yellow, April
4 *Iris*, or flag, a variety, pur. blue, yel. wh. &c. June
4 —— striped leaved stinking gladwin, purple, July
4 —— Siberian narrow leaved, blue with white, July
1 —— dwarf Austrian, purp. blue, red and white, May
1 —— vernal, or dwarf Virginian, blue, May
3 —— snake's head, or tuberous iris, purple, May
3 —— *Xiphium*, or Spanish bulbous, a variety, June
1 —— *Persian* bulbous, finely variegated, March
1 —— bulbous *Sisyrinchium*, blue and yellow, June
1 —— *Ixia*, large flowered, or crocus leaved, variety, June
1 —— Chinese sword leaved, yellow with red, July
4 *Lily*, com. sing. and doub. wh. orange and fiery, June
3 —— striped flowered, purple and white, June
3 —— striped leaved, of white and orange sorts, June
3 —— dwarf stalked, orange, or red flowered, June
4 —— Constantinople, dependent flowered, June
4 —— proliferous, or many flowered ditto, June
4 —— com. martagon, or Turk's cap, purple, June
4 —— ditto, wh. red, imperial and double, June, July
4 —— pompony martagons, several colours, June
4 —— Chalcedonian martagons, scarlet and purp. July
4 —— superb pyramidal, martagon, variegated, July
4 —— Canadian martagon, plain, and spotted yel. Aug.
4 —— day, or lily asphodel, yel. and tawney red, June
1 —— daffodil, or autumnal narcissus, yellow, September
1 —— *atamasco* amaryllis, carnation coloured, July
3 —— *Guernsey* scarlet, and *belladonna* purple, September
3 —— *pancratium* common, and Illyrian, wh. August, July
Martagons, see *lily* above
Meadow saffron, see *colchicum*
2 *Moly*, (flowering garlick) yel. wh. pur. and red, June
4 —— magicum, victorialis, and descendens, purple, July
3 *Narcissus*, poet's daffodil, variety in cup, wh. May
3 ———— peerless, or two coloured, wh. and yel. April
3 ———— polyanthus, or multiflorous, ditto
2 ———— late flowering, yellow cup, white, August

2 *Orchis*,

SECT. XIX.   LISTS OF TREES, &c.   85

2 *Orchis*, perennial, purples, reds and white, June, *d.*
2 ——— biennial, bee, or gnat orchis, red, June, *d.*
1 *Orobus*, tuberous, or wood pea, red flower, May
　——— fibrous rooted, fee laſt liſt
4 *Pæony*, com. ſing. doub. reds, purple, black, white, May
4 ——— Conſtantinople, large flower, blood red, June
4 ——— Portugal ſweet ſcented, deep red, May
3 ——— ſmall narrow leaved, red flowered, May
3 ——— dwarf, with a white flower, May
2 *Paſque flower*, common blue, red and white, April
2 ——————— Siberian, or *alpine* yellow, April
　Pilewort, ſee *ranunculus ficaria*
2 *Ranunculus*, plantain leaved Alpine, white, April
2 ——————— graſs leaved Pyrenean, ſtraw col. May
3 ——————— grandiflorous, or oriental great yel. May
1 ——————— ficaria, or *pilewort*, double yellow, April
2 ——————— Turkey, or turban, red, ſcar. yel. black, May
1 ——————— Perſian, a great variety, fine colours, May
　——————— ſee *crowfoot*, laſt liſt
2 *Saxifrage*, granulous rooted, double white, May
1 *Snowdrop*, ſingle, ſemidouble and double, white, Feb.
3 ——— great, ſpring, ſummer and autumn ſorts
4 *Spiderwort*, ſavoy, *(Bruno's lily)* and others, wh. June, *m.*
4 ——————— Virginia, *(tradeſcants)* blue, purp. &c. ditto
4 *Squill*, or common ſea onion, white flower, June, *d.*
4 *Star of Bethlehem*, pyramidal Portugal, white, June
4 ——————— Arabian, or Alexandrian lily, ditto
1 ——————— common wild, greeniſh white, May
1 ——————— ditto, with yellow flower, April
3 *Toothwort*, bulbiferous, ſeven lobed, purple, June
4 *Tuberoſe*, ſingle and double flowered, white, July
4 *Tulip*, double, a variety, yel. and red ſtriped, &c. June
4 ——— parrot, or hooked leaved, ditto, June
4 ——— Turkey ſorts, ſtriped, great variety, May
2 ——— ditto, early dwarfs, a variety, April
2 ——— wild European, ſmall yellow flower, April

　※ The *propagation* of flowers in this liſt, is generally by *offsets*, or pieces of roots, having an eye, or bud to it. Moſt
of

of them may be raifed alfo from *feed;* but this is a tedious method, and not ordinarily practifed, except by curious florifts. See page 16, vol. 2.

Some of this lift, as moft of the *bulbous* and *tuberous* roots, may be kept out of ground a long time, others a fhorter; (fee page 18, vol. 2) but thofe denominated *flefhy* roots, muft either be planted immediately, or at leaft in a few days. It is common to them all to be taken out of ground for removal, as foon as their leaves decay, the roots then being in a ftate of *reft*, which is naturally longer, or fhorter, in different plants; and if they ftay in the ground till new fibres are fhot, they are always removed with damage.

OBSERVATIONS ON PARTICULAR FLOWERS.

Albuca is too tender a bulb to endure much wet and froft, and therefore is ufually planted in pots, for putting under fhelter (as in a frame, &c.) in winter; but *may* be protected in the open ground, by covering with a glafs, or garden pot, towards the end of autumn, to keep the roots dry; and before fharp frofts come, covering round with litter. By fuch a practice, many tender things that die down to the ground, may be preferved abroad.

Anemone, the garden (in contradiftinction to the wood) is in great variety of very fine forts, divided generally into two kinds; i. e. narrow and broad leaved; the latter is reckoned the hardier. The full doubles only are efteemed choice flowers; but the femidoubles, and fingles, are fhowy enough for ordinary borders. The *fingle,* or *poppy* anemonies, (fo called from their form) frequently blow as early as *February,* or fooner; and thus become valuable, for decorating the ground at fo dreary a feafon. The *wood* kinds bear large flowers, and are very ufeful ornaments for the borders of *fhrubberies,* &c. at an early feafon, for which reafon, they fhould be planted in the moft frequented fhady places.

Colchicum, or meadow faffaron flowers about *Michaelmas,* and may be kept out of ground from *May* (or decay of the *leaf)* to *Mid-Auguft.* It is a remarkable property of this flower, (not however peculiar to it it alone) that it makes its appearance before the leaves, which grow all winter and fpring. The *colchicums* are pretty plants for the end of the flowery feafon, *(October)* which makes them eftimable objects near the houfe, where they may be often feen.

Cyclamen, the forts flowering in *winter* (Perfian) are too tender for open culture ; but clofe under a warm wall, with occafional protection of a *hand-glafs,* they have fucceeded. A culture of this nature is rather to be *attempted,* as houfing (except in places where they have much air) does not fuit them ; the roots often moulding and rotting when kept too clofe. The *colours* of the *Perfian* forts are red, purple and white. Let them have a light, and deeply dug dry foil, not too much water, and none at all after the leaves begin to decay ; for the roots now ceafing to act, would fuffer by abforbing much wet, the leaves not performing their accuftomed office of drawing it up, and difcharging it. This obfervation applies to all bulbs and tubers (in a degree) though few are fo liable to rot as thefe.

Fritillary is of feveral colours, plain, chequered and fpotted, white, purple, black, red and yellow. The kinds are broad and narrow leaved ; and there is a large double fort, a tall *Perfian,* (a yard high) and a dwarf *Perfian* about half fize, both having deep purple flowers.

Jonquil, or *rufhleaved daffodil,* has been always juftly admired for a very neat fweet flower ; but we do not fo often meet with it, as might be expected. The fingle kinds are the moft fragrant, and the large double is quite fcentlefs. It is proper always to *pot* fome, in order to bring them into the houfe when in flower, for their perfume.

Iris, the four firft forts rather prefer a fhady moift fituation ; but will grow any where, and are commonly planted in odd fpare corners of ground.

Ixias are generally *green houfe* and *ftove* plants ; but thefe two are found hardy enough to do ordinarily in open borders, in a light dry foil, and warm situation, a little protection being afforded them in severe weather.

Lily is a very ornamental and hardy flower in all its varieties increasing abundantly, and needing only to be removed every three or four years, for the purpose of taking away the offsets, and renewing the soil, for a superior blow. The *whites* will not keep out of ground above one month, but the *orange* for several. The *white* will flower tolerably in shade, but the *orange* much better: and as it is a gay flower, it serves well to enliven plantations. The *martagons* are generally not nice as to soil and situation; but the *scarlet* and *yellow* sorts, and *striped lily*, should have a light dry soil, and some sun. The *single* white lilies are very sweet; but the doubles have no smell, as is the case with some other flowers, the fragrance arising from the *stamina* and *antheræ*, which are smothered by the numerous petals. The *Atamasco Guernsey*, *belladonna*, and *pancratium lilies*, are tender, and should have a warm, or a good *auricula* soil, a full sunny border, and well sheltered situation; with protection also from much wet in cold seasons, and security from frost. These are very elegant and noble flowers, and the *Guernsey lily* is equal to, if not beyond, any competitor in the flowery creation: This is, however, the tenderest of the four; then the *belladonna* and *pancratium lily*, or *sea daffodil*, and the *atamasco* is the hardiest. All of them are usually potted for removing into shelter; but they *may* be managed so as to do abroad, except in the more *northern* and bleak parts of this island: They blow much the finer in open ground, (all things going on well) the roots having a free scope to draw nourishment, &c.

Orchis is rather difficult of culture: It likes a dry barren soil, and the *roots* should be taken up (from the places it grows wild) *just* as the leaves decay after flowering; and, if with a ball of earth about them, the

the chance of succeeding is much greater. Upon removal, let them be planted directly. If raised from *seed*, (as the *biennial*, though it is not always so) let it be sown as soon as gathered; and the plants being thinned, let them *remain*, as more likely to do well, than when transplanted. It is evidently not proper to move these bulbs (as others) often, but should stand for several years.

Pæony, the single kinds are showy, but the doubles are nobly ornamental. Let this flower have room, as it will spread (when in full sized bunches) a yard round : and let it be planted out of the way of the full sun, and of much wind. It need not be removed for many years, and will grow in any soil and situation, even among trees, which adapts it for *shrubberies*, &c. The sorts are divided into *male* and *female ;* and the former, having lost its flower, produces pods, containing rich crimson grains, interspersed with black berries of seed, that look very pretty when burst; and may be gathered as soon, or rather just before they open, and brought into the house as curiosities. Let this root be removed early in *September,* or at least before the month is out, before new fibres are formed to the knobs of the roots.

Pilewort, (the double) prefers a shady moist situation; and is a pretty wild plant, though an humble trailer. It is called sometimes the *lesser celadine*, and also *figwort*.

Ranunculus, in all its sorts, is very ornamental; but the *Persian* kinds are beautiful, and of infinite variety. This flower is left too much to the culture of professed florists; for why should not every garden be adorned with it, seeing, that not much skill is necessary in the management, and that it is hardy, and increases freely?

Saxifrage roots are like so many small peas, and should be planted five or six together, in order to form a full tuft of its flowers, which are double, and white like a stock. The stems, being slender, will need the
support

support of a light stick, which it is best to fix in the middle at the time of planting, as putting one in afterwards might injure the roots. All solid rooted plants are liable to be hurt by pushing in a stick too near for tying to, and more care should be taken in the business than usually is: The practice of placing a stick at the time of planting is the best way, when it may be fixed close; and it would serve to show where the roots are, that they may not be disturbed before they appear above ground. This *saxifrage* is usually and properly *potted*, though it does very well in borders, and makes a good show.

Spiderwort likes shade and moisture.

Star of Bethlehem, the two last sorts, are proper for the edges of borders in plantations; and the pyramidal sort is a proper flower to *pot*, mixing with others very ornamentally: The two first should have a light dry soil.

Squill will need a little protection from hard frosts; but is sufficiently ornamental to reward the trouble.

Toothwort thrives best in shade and moisture.

Tuberose, there is a dwarf stalked, and a variegated leaf sort of, but they are not so worthy of cultivation as the common single and double; of which two the *single* is preferable, as it blows better, and is more fragrant. See the end of this section.

Tulip (the *Turkey*) is classed into two sorts; the taller, called *serotines*, or late blowers; and the shorter, *præcoces*, or early blowers; some have made another distinction, *medias*, but it is not necessary. The *plain* tulips (as they generally are when they first blow from seed) are called *whole blowers*, or *breeders*; and according as they *break* into other colours, stripes, and variegations, are denominated and classed into *baguettes*, *bybloemens*, *verports*, and *bizarres*. As the *dwarf* sorts blow so early as *March* and *April*, (the *duke van tol* earlier) allow them a warm border and soil, to preserve them from frost and wet, which they are

rather

rather impatient of. These are often *potted* and *forced* on a hot bed, &c. or brought forward by water-glasses, in a warm room; but an increase is only to be expected from open ground culture, and there these early sorts do it sparingly. Take them up every year to remove the offsets, and renew the soil; and keep each sort separate, and *plant* them so, for then they will blow together, and be all of one height. There are about fifty of the early sorts; but the number of *fancy* tulips in *Maddock's* catalogue is more than eight hundred, besides breeders, &c.

* * * * * *

The following articles are detached as most conveniently inserted here:

Auricula is increased by parting the roots, or slipping rooted offsets from them; but offsets without roots will sometimes strike, if well managed, by setting them in a good soil, (in pots best) where they have but little sun, and keeping them *cool* by occasional watering. When the roots are *divided*, (in autumn) let it be with a sharp knife; and cutting off any cankered part, shorten also their ends, and let not the *tap* part of the root be too long.

The *soil* for auriculus should be a good fresh light loamy *maiden* one, to which is added one third of *wood pile*, or *willow* earth, one of sea, or any sharp, or drift *sand*; and a quantity, equal to the whole, of rotted *cow* dung, or in lieu of this, *horse* dung. This mixture should be well incorporated, at least a year before, by frequent turning over, which ought to be repeated once a month.

Dress the pots towards the end of *January*, for then the plants begin to push for flower, and must be attended to, and assisted. Take as much of the top mould off as can be, without disturbing, or bruising the roots; and fill up with the compost, a little pressed down. If the pots are dry from the shelter afforded them, give a little soft water in mild weather, about ten o'clock.

Shift, or transplant auriculas every *second* year, and that as soon as they are out of blow; those, however, that produce many offsets, or are luxuriant growers, may be shifted every year. The more common practice is to move all in *August*.

To *raise* auriculas from the seed, in *February*, fill boxes, or pots, with fine sifted middling compost; smooth the top perfectly level; scatter the seeds evenly, and cover not more than the thickness of a shilling. Set the pots, &c. on tiles, or boards, under a warm wall, and keep the surface moist. It is a good way to mix the seed with a like quantity (or a little more) of *fine* wood ashes; and to lay some small pieces of *furze*, or light *thorns* over. Remove them (as occasion dictates) to shelter, or protect them from much frost, or heavy rain, &c. and by *May* expect them to appear, when take the furze off; after which set them where they have only the *morning sun*, and when they have got six leaves, prick them out three inches asunder, in boxes, or pots; and early in the next spring, plant them again at six inches asunder, and protect them from wet and frost.

Much might be advanced respecting this flower; and the most satisfaction will probably be obtained from a little tract on its " *Culture and Management*," printed for BULL, at *Bath*, and sold by WALLIS, in *Ludgate Street*, 1782. Something more will occur in the *calendar*.

Carnation is usually propagated by *layers*, (sometimes by *pipings* or *cuttings*, as *pinks*) about *Midsummer*, or as soon after in the season as they will admit of it, by their length and strength, and the work is thus: Strip off the leaves from the lower part of the shoot; at the middle of it, close below the joint, cut it half
through

through by an upward direction, with a thin, narrow, sharp knife, and continue the slit exactly up the middle from half to three-fourths of an inch ; peg the shoot down into the earth (being before well loosened) as low as it will bear bending, setting the layer upright. This business must be done with a nice hand, and much care, lest the layer should snap off. Now, or rather before, cut off the ends of the longest of the top leaves, that the worms may not draw them in, and disturb the layer. The soil should be *fine* and *good*, and may be raised about the layers as occasion requires. *Water* them to set the earth close, and always keep it cool. In six weeks, or two months, they will be rooted, fit for *transplanting;* cut them from the old plant (at the peg) with a sharp knife, and take them up carefully, that their very tender roots may not be broken off, keeping a little mould about them, if possible : but plant them not deep, as they are then liable to decay.

The *soil* proper for carnations, is a hazelly, or sandy loam, procured from a pasture, by a spit of about eight inches depth, the turf being well broke, frequently turned, and laid so long together, as to be nearly consumed ; then add a little *lime*, (or not) and one-third, or one-fourth of very rotten dung, *(cow's* best) and let this be well mixed, and turned over, till *thoroughly* incorporated, which will be some months first ; then screen it, or sift through a coarse sieve. The soil for carnations must be *rich;* but yet *dung* is found so injurious to carnations, that some florists depend upon a good fresh soil alone ; carnations are also (except in summer) impatient of much *wet*. Turf *ashes*, or those of any vegetable, may be mixed with a fresh maiden soil, but not too freely : A *small* quantity of fine *soot*, or *wood ashes*, may me also used, to avoid dung.

To *raise* carnations from *seed*, sow thin in boxes, or pots, (in a soil as above) early in *April*, and let them have only the morning sun. When advanced a little in growth, (as about *Midsummer)* take the first opportunity

opportunity of moist weather, and prick them out at three or four inches asunder, and give a little water. If dry weather, contrive to *shade* them ten days, or a fortnight, with mats hooped over, which remove in shady or showery weather. When they have grown here a month, or six weeks, (or before *August* is out) plant them at nine or ten inches distance, and shade, if necessary. Protect them in hard frosts by mats, or hoops, set high. *Seed* is best saved from good seedling plants, rather than those long propagated from layers, &c.

Geranium (the African sorts) are propagated by *seeds* and *cuttings*. The former produces the most free growing plants; but as luxuriance is not desirable in things confined to pots, (as *geraniums* must be) and as the propagation by *cuttings* is so easy and expeditious, it is the mode of culture that generally prevails. The young plants from *cuttings* are also hardier than those from *seed*. If raised from *seed*, sow in *April*, in a light and good soil, warm border, and under a hand-glass, keeping the earth somewhat moist; but it is best to make use of a gentle *hot bed*, giving plenty of air to the plants, when they appear, which on natural ground will be five or six weeks in coming up, and on a moderate heat about three. If raised from *cuttings*, use shoots of the last year's growth, strait and short jointed. Plant them in a fine rich soil, two or three inches or at the most four deep and eight or nine inches asunder, or less, if more convenient. Or the rule may be, to plant the shorter cuttings in two thirds of their length, and the longer one half; but it is an error to put them in the ground so deep as some people do. Those raised on a little heat will be sufficiently rooted in two months to transplant into small pots; (shortening the longer roots a little) and those in the cold ground will be ready in three months, and sometimes less. A *hand-glass* set over *geranium* cuttings (or any other) will greatly facilitate the business, as is directed for *pinks*. If the
cuttings

cuttings are *raw*, or *long*, take the upper part off down to an eye. In general it may be proper to keep the cuttings out of ground a day, or two; but the soft and succulent ones should by all means, in order to dry the ends, and so heal the wound, which, if put directly in the ground, might decay and rot.

The proper *season* for planting is from *Mid-May* to *Mid-July*; a little earlier, or later, may however do: Some chuse to forward them on *heat*, in *March* and *April*; but they must not be kept close. It is advisable, to take cuttings from towards the top, in order to keep the plants down; but where they can be best spared for maintaining a good form, is the general rule.

The *management* of geraniums is, to keep them from *frost*, and as much as may be from *harsh winds*, particularly in the *spring*; as after being housed all winter, they are then tender, and far less able to bear unkind weather, than in *autumn*; when having been used to the external air, and the colder weather coming on by degrees, they are seldom hurt much, but by absolute frost. In the *spring*, they must be brought to bear air by degrees, and the more carefully, according as the *winter* has occasioned them to be more or less deprived of the external air, being let in upon them. When the weather is mild in *April*, let them be taken out in the day, (if convenient) and put in on nights; and venture them not wholly abroad till *Mid-May*, or after. In the *summer*, they should be placed in *shelter* and *shade*; but not under trees, or any roof: The morning sun is all they should have, for more of it dries the mould in the pots too fast, and fades the flowers. They will want frequent *watering*, see page 10, vol. 2. They may take up their *summer* residence about *Mid-May*, (as directed) but the *season* must govern; and it will not do to bring them out in a harsh one, which would pinch up the leaves, and deprive them of their beauty. If put close under a
south

south wall for a week or two at first, it would be proper; or an awning of mats might be used for nights.

Shifting geraniums should generally take place once a year, from smaller pots into others *one* size bigger: This may be in the first mild weather in *April*, or *May*. Loosen and take off the top mould down to the roots, (without damaging them) then turn the pot up, and shake it out. If the roots adhere to the sides of the pot, give the edge a tap upon the knee, or something, and a little pressure at the hole, with the thumb, or finger, at the same time, which will help to discharge it. Pare off the matted roots round the sides and bottom, with a *sharp* knife; and plant it in a fresh pot, (or the same again may sometimes do) putting in as much fine light rich mould, or compost, at the bottom, as will raise the ball of earth, which is about the roots, within an inch of the top of the pot; then fill round the sides, putting the mould gently in, and pressing it down a little, make all level to the top within half an inch; finally, give a watering that shall soak to the bottom, and sprinkle some dry mould over. All shifted plants should be kept rather in the *shade* for a week or two.

If any *sticks* are to the plants, they must be taken away first, and replaced (if necessary) again before watering, or rather the next day, if the plants will stand up without. This may be a proper time to *trim* off all dangling, or too crowding shoots; but if *cuttings* are wanted for increase, they should not be *trimmed* till these are to be planted. At any rate, dead leaves, or unsightly crooked parts, should be discharged, and *symmetry*, in a snug round head, provided for. Geraniums are free growers, and it is always advisable to take off *some* shoots to keep them down. A few of the plants, that most need it, (as least handsome or healthy) should be *severely* cut, for a late blow, which generally proves a *fine* one in consequence. A
judicious

judicious regular use of neat slender *sticks* is of much advantage to *geraniums*, or other potted plants.

What has been said of *geraniums*, applies to *all exotics*; in the management of which, it is a material thing not to shift into too large pots, as the roots run directly to the outsides, and so would be too hastily brought to require the biggest pots. Another thing is, to take off some of the top soil, not only as directed in *spring*, but once or twice in the *summer*; and always before housing in *autumn*, and replacing it with a rich *compost*, as one of almost all rotten *cow* dung, which being *black*, is the most suitable soil for the purpose; and it is cool and nourishing.

It is material to *neatness*, and the end of *ornament*, (for which plants are chiefly potted) that the pots should be occasionally washed, or scoured, and by no means suffered to get mouldy. This is a point so little attended to, that we often see a beautiful plant in a disgusting habitation. It is equally offensive, and is also injurious to suffer the surface earth to get mossy, or caked hard by the necessary waterings; to prevent which, often stir it a little depth, and lay it smooth, which makes all look neat and creditable.

Pinks are sometimes *layered*, or more usually propagated by *cuttings*, or *pipings*, about *Midsummer;* and may be also by *slips*, set in *March*, *April*, or *May*, with, or without roots, four inches asunder. *Cuttings* should be young strong shoots of three or four inches long, taken off just below a joint; from which stripping the lower leaves, and cutting the top ones short, plant them in a fine good soil, about two inches asunder, and in depth full half of their length. They will strike root, so as to be fit to move, in seven or eight weeks, with a little earth about their roots; or may be left to an early time in the spring; but where this is designed, they will be best six inches asunder. They may be either put in *pots*, or *borders*, where they are to blow, or rather into a nursery bed, to grow a year

at

at six inches distance. *Pipings* are obtained by drawing the heads of the young shoots out of their sockets, of the length of cuttings. In both methods, push the shoots carefully into the earth, gently press the mould about them, and give a watering; shade also from much sun. They will strike more certainly, and much sooner by being covered *close*, with a *hand-glass*, as much as possible air tight. They must be kept cool, by occasional watering; but when under glass, they will not need so much shading, or may do without any; for though the inclosed air is warmer, it is always more humid, which refreshes the cuttings with answerable supply for their support; and it is this moisture and warmth that facilitates the growth. When they appear to be growing, the glasses must be raised, and in a short time removed. To *raise* pinks from *seed*, follow the directions given for *carnations*.

Polyanthus is propagated by parting the roots in autumn, or (for new varieties) by *seed* sown and managed (nearly) as directed for *auriculus*: But as this flower is not so delicate in the cultivation, it may be sown in borders, where there is only the morning sun, any time from *August* to *April*; and as soon as the plants are at all big enough to prick out, set them four inches asunder; and sometime in *August*, plant at six inches, where they are to remain for their first blow; which should be attended to, in order to mark the best flowers, dividing these into two sorts, prime and midling; and the rest may be either planted into ordinary ground in plantations, &c. or cast away: There will be but few *good* ones in a great many; but the culture of this plant is so easy, that it is worth while to try for them. Some sow in *pots*, and *boxes*, in *December*, placing them in the sun, and housing them in severe weather; and when the plants appear, set them in an *east* aspect, lest much sun destroy the young plants; *early* in autumn, or spring, is however better: The *seed* may be covered a little less than a quarter of an inch.

inch. Both feeds and feedling plants fhould have occafional watering, (except in winter) as moifture fuits them.

A *compoft* for the polyanthus is fimply a light *loam*, (as the firft fpit from the pafture rotted down with the *turf*) and about one fourth part *cow dung*, or *wood pile* earth. If the loam is ftrong, a little drift fand amongft it will be proper. The polyanthus grows any where, but a cool foil and fituation fuits it beft; and the above *compoft*, and an *eaft border*, is neceffary for a capital blow.

Tuberofe is beft blown in a *hot houfe*; but if planted in pots, and plunged at the back of a *hot bed* frame, it will fucceed very well. This will be beft done about *Mid-April*, as fooner they are apt to get too tall before they can fafely be expofed abroad. Provide a good *frefh* light earth, and ufe no dung, except a little rich and dungy, to lay an inch below the bottom of the bulb; fill the pots only three parts, and place the root only half way, or a little more, in it. Let the mould be fomewhat moift, but give no water till the fhoot appears, and then moderately; at which time, fill up the pot, juft to cover the bulb, which fhould be but barely hid, when the pot is full. The beft fhaped pots for bulbous roots is, when the bottoms are as wide as the top; and the fize for the *tuberofe* fhould be thofe of eight or nine inches diameter at top, according as the bottom is for width; for the more fpace below, the lefs is required above.

As the *fhoots* advance in growth, the more air muft be given; and as freely as poffible on mild days, fhutting clofe on cold nights, and almoft fo on moderate ones. When they get too high for the frames, and the feafon is forward, with kind weather, they may be plunged in the ground, clofe under a warm wall; and a covering of mat contrived to protect them a while on nights, or may do if left to take their chance. If the weather is foul, they may be houfed in a good window,

window, for a week or a fortnight, and then put in the ground as directed above. Here let them remain, giving occasional *watering*, (and that freely in dry weather) till in flower, when the *house* (allowing them light and sun) will be their proper residence, to enjoy their fine powerful scent, and to protect the blow, that it may the longer continue. In their flowering state, they will want much water.

The *heat* on which this flower is forwarded, should be *moderate*, otherwise it will run up too fast. If planted under a *south wall* in *May*, covering the root about an inch, and guarding against much wet till it is growing, it will do for a late blow : A *hand-glass* of course would be serviceable, both to assist it in shooting, and shelter it from unkind weather ; but close covering is as much as possible to be avoided. Fresh *roots* are imported every year ;—the double never flowers twice with us, but the single may, if kept in a dry warm room.

SECTION

SECTION XX.

A CALENDAR.

THE *general* work of gardening has been pretty fully spoken of, in the parts concerning the *formation, cultivation,* and *management* of a *garden, propagation,* &c. The *particular* culture of *esculents, herbs, fruits,* and *flowers,* has been treated in the sections appropriated to each. It therefore remains to give *here* little more than short *hints,* by way of assisting recollection, and to make proper *references* to the pages, where *farther instructions* may be found of those that need, or chuse to consult them.

What is said concerning *seeds* and *sowing,* page 58 to 65, must be attended to. It need only be farther observed, that as to the *season* proper to do the several works of gardening, it is not the same (exactly) every where, as *soil* and *situation* make a difference. The *time* mentioned in this *calendar* is, that which the author judges will be found most *generally* right in the midland counties, as the extremes of *north* and *south* necessarily make a difference in this business.

The *work* of gardening being very multifarious, it would be a practice not unworthy, even the skilful gardener, to make it a *rule,* once a week, to consider what *is* to be done the following week; and to make *memorandums* accordingly, numbering them in the *order* he would have them performed. Thus he would never be at a loss, what to set, himself or his labourers about, and the mortification of omissions, or appearance

ance of neglect, would be avoided: This *calendar*, it is presumed, will be found a ready and sufficient assistant upon such an occasion, the author having endeavoured to make it as plain and comprehensive as it is concise.

* * * * *

JANUARY.

LET every thing be done now, that the weather and circumstances will permit, (though not absolutely necessary) in order to lessen the work of *next month*, which when it happens to be an open season, is a very important one in the way of gardening, in which the loss of a single fine day is of consequence. Many things might be prepared in the *winter*, in readiness for *spring*, which are but too often neglected.

MISCELLANEOUS WORK.

Dung for *hot beds* should be duly attended to, 176.
Manure and *compost* heaps turn frequently over.
Espaliers, garden frames, and such things, rectify.
Tools, make, repair, sharpen and brighten, 9, vol. 2.
Brush wood, prepare ready for sticking peas, &c. 237.
Planting, trench and prepare ground for, 29, 98, &c.
New planted trees, protect and tie to stakes, 102.
Prune espalier trees, standards and shrubs, 164, 166, 171.
Moss, clear trees and shrubs from, as convenient.
Webs and *nests* of caterpillars, slugs, snails, destroy.
Beds and *borders,* weed, stir the ground, and rake.
Cauliflowers and *lettuces* in frames, &c. attend, 220, 232.
Endive, tie up, when dry, to blanch; and protect it, 226.
Cions, procure for graffing, except apples, 83, 86.
Hot beds, prepare for, or make, cucumbers, &c. 174, 181.
Drain ground, scour ditches, plash hedges, &c.

SOW

SOW

Cucumbers, 181. *Melons*, 197. *Peas*, 236. *Beans*, 213. *Spinach*, 249. *Radishes*, 244. *Lettuces*, 231. *Cress*, 255. *Mustard*, 259. *Carrots*, 218. The five last on *heat*; to which may be added, *rape* and *lap lettuce*, 233, as sallading; towards the end of the month, however, they may be sown on warm borders, the sallading being under hand-glasses.

PLANT

Mint on heat, 259. *Cabbages* at distances, as 217. *Trees* and *shrubs* of the deciduous kinds, *grape vines*, *currants*, *gooseberries* and *raspberries*, if mild weather, so that the ground will work loose. Layers may be removed; but rather prepare the ground now for planting next month, 98, &c.

PROPAGATE

Trees and *shrubs* by suckers, layers, cuttings, 65, &c.

FLOWERS.

Pots of, see December *tulips*, *anemonies*, *ranunculuses*, *hyacinths*, *narcissuses*, &c. protect, 21, vol. 2.

Bulbous and *tuberous* roots out of ground, now plant for a late blow, or in the next month, 18, vol. 2; preserve choice sorts from much wet, lest they rot.

Auriculas, if disturbed by frost, immediately earth up; or if not, yet do it for assisting the blow, 91, vol. 2; and let them be protected from snow and wet, by frames, &c. or set the pots close under a south wall, where, in severe weather, they may be covered, tho' frost rarely hurts the plants, if kept tolerably dry: The *pots* will be safer, if plunged in the ground, see *November*. Some persons lay the pots on their sides, to keep them dry, and to cover them; but, in this

this position, they should not remain long, as it gives the bud a twist.

Carnations, and all hardy plants, in pots, placed under any cover, must have as much *air* and *sun* as can be given them; *wet* is now peculiarly injurious to carnations, which those in pots, at least, may be easily protected from, by frames or mats.

Flowering shrubs may be planted, if open weather, covering the roots well; but it is better done next month, getting the ground ready now, 110, &c.

NURSERY.

Vermin, guard against in time, on seed beds, &c. 73.
Dig beds for *sowing*, next month tree seeds, &c. 72.
Protect seedling trees (particular *exotics*) from frost.
Plant, or *transplant*, hardy things, cover the roots.
Prepare ground for next month's *planting* out seedlings, or stocks for graffing another year, 73.

* * * * * *

FEBRUARY.

WHEN the ground can be conveniently worked, this is a very busy month, and no time must be lost, nor hands spared, that every thing may be done in its proper, or earliest season.

The *last* week is the principal, in which *many* things are to be done, and some *full* crops sown: The *skilful* gardener is aware of this, but ordinarily this season is lost.

MISCELLANEOUS WORK.

Ground, prepare for *planting* and *sowing*, by digging, trenching, manuring, levelling, &c.
Borders should be stirred, dug, or dressed, 29, 141.
Gravel walks, weed, put in order, and roll firm.

Grass

SECT. XX. FEBRUARY. 105

Grafs plats, &c. clean up, cut the edges, or lay *turf.*
Compofts and *manures,* turn over, and break well.
Hot beds, attend regularly, and no neglect, 184, &c.
Stable dung, for hot beds, manage properly, 176.
Cauliflowers and *lettuces,* fee laft month, and ftir the furface of the mould a little about them.
Earth up and *protect* plants from froft and wind.
Stick peas, when about five inches high, 237.
Weed and *thin* crops, as winter onions, radifhes, &c. 49.
Endive, attend to blanch and ridge when quite dry, 276.
Vermin and *infects,* fee to, as mice, fnails, flugs, &c. 238.
Prune wall and other trees, but firft grape vines, 132.
Cions for graffing, provide, 83, and ufe then, 84, &c.
Edgings of box, thrift, &c. make and repair, 55.

SOW

Cucumbers, 181, 224. *Melons,* 197, 233. *Peas* fmall, 237, large, 238. *Beans,* the broad forts, or the *mazagons,* if wanted early, 214. *Radifhes* on heat, or not, 244. *Lettuces* on heat, or not. 231. *Small fallading* on heat, or on a warm border under glafs, 255. *Cabbages,* the fugar loaf forts, 217; or if *early* ones are wanted, fow the *York-fhire* on a little heat. *Savoys,* 247. *Onions,* 234. *Leeks,* 231. *Parfley,* 260. *Spinach,* 249. *Carrots* on heat or not, 218. *Parfneps,* 235. *Celery,* 222. *Kidney beans* on heat, 229. *Turnips* on heat, 250. *Cauliflowers* on heat, 221.

PLANT.

Cucumbers, 189. *Melons,* 200. *Cauliflowers,* 220. *Cabbages,* 217. *Horferadifh,* 227. *Garlick,* 227. *Rocombole,* 261. *Shalots,* 249. *Cives,* 254. *Mint* on heat, 259. *Potatoes,* early forts, on heat, and warm borders, 241. *Vines, wall, efpalier,* and *ftandard fruit trees, foreft trees,* and *deciduous fhrubs,* 30, 98, 111, 115.

PROPAGATE

PROPAGATE

Trees and *shrubs* by graffing, 84, by suckers, layers, and cuttings, 65. *Sow* kernels, stones, and seeds of fruit, &c. on fine well broke earth, allowing *exotics* a little heat, 72.

FLOWERS.

See last month. Hardy *biennials* and *perennials* should now be planted, before they shoot, 15, 16, vol. 2.
Shrubs, protect, &c. 112 ; prune and dig about them, 114.
Auricula and *polyanthus* seed should be sown now.
Bulbs and *tubers*, plant by the middle of the month ; and for variety, a few may be potted, 18, vol. 2.
Annuals, all sorts, may be sown about last week, 6, vol. 2, some of the latter may be sown in pots, 13, vol. 2.

NURSERY.

See last month. *Sow* hardy trees and shrubs, 72. *Transplant* hardy seedlings of last year, and stocks for graffing next year, or the following, 73.

* * * * * *

MARCH.

THE *first* week in this, like the last in *February*, is very valuable to the good gardener, and *must* be made the best use of by those who would have things in season. It is therefore proper to have no regard to the charge of necessary assistance : Nature now waits for us, let us not neglect to attend upon her. See *management*, page 57.

MISCEL.

MISCELLANEOUS WORK.

Order and *neatness* are now principal objects, 54.
Vacant ground, dig and apply manure where wanted.
Borders, dress by weeding, digging, &c. see last month.
Gravel walks, clean, relay, or make new ones, rolling them repeatedly after rain, 55.
Edgings of box, thrift, &c. clip, repair or make.
Grass plats and walks, cleanse, mow, and cut the edges.
Herb beds, weed and dress, see article *balm*, 252.
Asparagus beds, weed, carefully fork, and dress, 212.
Strawberry beds, weed, stir the mould, and dress, 171.
Artichokes, dress at the end of the month, 209.
Composts and *mould* heaps, turn over, and screen, or sift some ready for dressing pots of flowers, &c.
Vermin, insects, and destructive *birds*, see to, 238.
Earth up peas, beans, and whatever else needs it.
Stick peas in time, and stop them, or not, 237, 239.
Graff now, but apples towards the end of month, 81.
Prune wall trees without delay, but first vines, 152.
Blossoms of choice wall tree fruit, defend, 148.
Dig, dress, prune, shrubberies and plantations, 111.
Hot beds must be very carefully attended to, 184, &c. and new ones made in due time, 188.
Dung heaps for future hot beds, manage, 176.
Cauliflowers, &c, under glass, give air freely to, 220.

SOW.

See last month. *Radishes*, the spindle rooted, and *lettuces* of sorts once a fortnight; *small sallads* every week. The following ten things in the first week: *Alexanders*, 208. *Asparagus*, 211. *Beets*, 215. *Hamburgh Parsley*, 235. *Salsafy*, 246. *Scorzonera*, 247. *Skirrets*, 249. *Finochio*, 256. *Red cabbage*, 218. *Turnip radishes*, 245. Second week: *Turnips* on a gentle heat, and in open ground, 250; and *kidney beans* on heat, or in a warm dry border under hand-

hand-glasses, or not, 229. Last week: *Broccoli* of the purple autumn sorts, 216. *Nasturtiums*, 259. *Capsicums*, 254. *Love apples*, 264. *Herbs* of all sorts, 252, &c. *Grass seeds* for plats. *Strawberries* in pots, particularly the alpine sorts, 78.

PLANT

Trees and *shrubs*, 30, 98, 111, 115. *Herbs* in rooted slips or cuttings, 252, &c. *Strawberries*, 39. *Asparagus* 210. *Artichokes* 208. *Jerusalem artichokes*, 228. *Lettuces*, 231. *Cauliflowers*, 220. *Other things* as directed last month.

PROPAGATE

Trees and *shrubs* by graffing, 84; by suckers, offsets, layers, and cuttings, 65. *Herbaceous plants*, by parting roots, &c. 17, vol. 2.

FLOWERS.

The *hardy* kinds of flowers in *pots* that have been housed, should be inured by degrees to the weather, and soon left out on nights: Let no flowers be housed, or under cover more than necessary.

Pot desirable hardy plants for moveable ornaments, when in flower; not too many, 9, 11, vol. 2.

Carnations, and *auriculas*, if not before, dress, 91, vol. 2.

Tulips, *hyacinths*, &c. of the best sorts, protect, 21, vol. 2.

Water potted plants as the weather is, 10, vol. 2. *auriculas* will want it most as pushing to flower.

Sow annuals, 6. vol. 2. *Biennials*, 15, vol. 2. *Perennials*, 17, vol. 2.

Take up, remove offsets, and divide fibrous rooted *perennial* flowers early in the month, 17, vol. 2.

Layers of carnations, pinks, and sweet williams, take up carefully, and plant with earth to the roots, 93, vol. 2,

Anemonies and *ranunculuses* may be put in *(east* border) the first week; but they will blow late, 19, vol. 2.

Bulbous

SECT. XX.   APRIL.   109

Bulbous roots may also yet be put in, first week, with prospect of a like success, 20, vol. 2.
Box, thrift, daises, pinks, &c. plant soon for edgings.

NURSERY.

Remove litter, weed, stir the ground, rake neatly.
Prune plants into form, taking off side shoots, shortening the leader, &c. to make a head, &c. 70.
Graffs of last year cut down to a few eyes; but at the end of the month is soon enough.
Transplant and *sow* as last month, and do it quickly.
Exotics, or tender plants, sow on a gentle hot bed.
Water give in a dry time, to seeds, seedlings, cuttings, and newly planted things; but not over much.

* * * * * *

APRIL.

IF by any means the proper early cropping of the ground has been prevented, make no *delay* to finish, and to get the garden into a complete state of cultivation. This month may be mild enough to invite us abroad, to traverse the walks, and view nature in her *spring* attire, " *all blooming and benevolent.*" Let nothing therefore be met with that appears slovingly, or disgusting. See page 54.

MISCELLANEOUS WORK.

Borders, &c. weed, stir, rake, and clean up neatly, 49.
Gravel walks and *grass plats,* put in order, roll, &c. 55.
Edgings of box, &c. make, repair, trim, or cut, 55.
Watering omit not where necessary in a dry time, 50.
Pruning finish soon, head down young trees, 133, 147.
Graffs, see to, that the claying remains safe on, 86.
Blossoms of wall fruit, protect in bad weather, 148.

Dung

Dung for hot beds, collect and take due care of, 176.
Hot beds, make in time for fruiting *cucumbers.*
Melons, tender *annuals,* &c. 188, 199, 6, vol. 2. 11, vol. 2.
Asparagus, strawberries, artichokes, see last month.
Cauliflowers, stir mould about, and earth up, 220.
Peas, earth up, and stick before they droop, 237.
Beans in blossoms, crop and earth up firmly.
Thin in time all seedling crops, by hand or hoe, 49.
Prick out plants of every kind as soon as fit, 50.
Potatoes, early sort, earth up, protect from frost, 241.
Lettuces, tie up, and stir the ground about, 233.
Cabbages, earth up, and also tie up forward ones, 217.

SOW

As *soon* as possible, what may have been omitted last month, or the preceding. *Then, Salsafy,* 246. *Scorzonera,* 247. *Pumpions* and *gourds,* 243. *Boorcole,* 215. *Broccoli,* 216. *Brussels sprouts,* 217. *Chou Milan,* 224. *Chardons,* 223. *Kidney beans,* the ground being dry, 229. *Cabbages,* chiefly the large *sugar loaf,* for autumn *coleworts,* 217, 224. *Herbs,* culinary and medicinal, 252, &c. *Nasturtiums,* cold ground, 259. *Basil,* on heat, 253.
Succession crops of *cucumbers* and *melons,* for bringing up under hand-glasses, &c. 193, 204. 224, 233. *Peas,* large and small. *Beans,* the broad sort. *Savoys, spinach, carrots, turnips, celery, radishes, lettuces, finochio, small sallading, onions* to draw young. Observe that *succession crops* should have cooler situations as the summer advances.

PLANT

Strawberries yet but *alpines* succeed best so late, 39.
Asparagus, 210. *Artichokes,* 208. *Lettuces,* 231.
Chives, garlick, rocombole and *shalots,* first week, see February. *Cabbages,* (if any remain) 217. *Cauliflowers,* 220. *Kidney beans* that have been raised on heat,

SECT. XX.   APRIL.   111

heat, 229. *Potatoes* for a full crop, 239. *Herbs* in rooted flips, 252, &c. *Trees* and *shrubs* immediately, and do it in the best manner, water, cover the roots, and stake the stems, 98, 102, &c.

PROPAGATE

Trees and *shrubs*, by graffing, layers, cuttings, and sowing, which may yet be performed, 65, 72, 84.
Herbs, by flips, or cuttings, in a good soil, and a shady situation, but not under trees, 252, &c.

FLOWERS.

Sow, in the first week, (if not done before) *annuals*, 6, 11, 13, vol. 2. *Biennials*, 15, vol. 2. *Perennials*, 17, vol. 2.
Plant, or prick out, *annuals* in fresh hot beds, pots, or borders, as the several sorts require, 7, vol. 2. *Biennials* and *perennials* of the late blowers, may yet be transplanted into borders or pots, giving an immediate watering, and shading a few days from sun, 12 vol. 2. *Carnation layers*, taking them up carefully with a scoop trowel, 9, vol. 2. *Pinks*, the same. *Tuberose*, as directed, page 99, vol. 2.
Tulips, ranunculuses, anemonies, &c. of choice sorts, protect in severe weather, as cutting wind, 21, vol. 2.
Auriculas in bloom, shelter from rain, wind, sun, and support the stems by neat forked sticks.
Pots of flowers, shift, and dress, tie up, water, &c.

NURSERY.

Weed, water, stir the soil, rake neatly, and *clean up*.
Transplant (yet) seedlings of trees and shrubs; the *evergreen* sorts it is now a good time for, 72.
Sow (if not done before) the seeds of forest trees, flowering shrubs and evergreens; but keep them *cool*, by watering, as every thing should be, that is sown or transplanted late in the spring: Yet they must not be soaked with wet.

VOL. II.   K   MAY.

MAY.

Let this *charming* month be ushered in with due respect, by the gardens being in excellent order, to which end let no help be spared, when the *gardener* is not competent to perform the work himself: It is often too much for the most industrious man.

We now gather vegetables that have stood the *winter*, and been the care of many months, with some of the products of *spring* also; and it is the hope and fruition of reward that sweetens labour: All the senses are gratified,

—— The softening air is balm;
And every sense and every heart is joy!

Thomson.

MISCELLANEOUS WORK.

Neatness must be pursued, stir the ground, rake, &c. 49.
Gravel walks and *grass plats*, keep in good order, 55.
Weeds, destroy every where, by the hand or hoe, 49, 54.
Water, if dry weather, new planted trees, shrubs and flowers, strawberries, cauliflowers, &c. 40, 51.
Thin all sorts of seedling crops enough, and in time, 49.
Prick out lettuces, celery, broccoli, boorcole, cauliflowers, savoys, cabbages, leeks, &c. 51.
Earth up potatoes, peas, broad beans, kidney beans, cabbages, savoys, forward celery, &c.
Tie up forward lettuces, and early cabbages, 217 233.
Cucumber plants, air, water, shade, train, 190, &c.
Hot beds, make for cucumbers & melons, 178, 194, 205.
Prune figs, first week, regulate wall-trees, 135, 154, 156.
Graffs, see to, and repair the claying, if they have not taken, and made some shoot, 86.
Thin fruit that is superabundant on wall trees, 150.
Beans, top, when in blossom, as it helps to forward the crop, and prevents their being top heavy.

SOW

Nasturtiums, herbs, and tall *kidney beans,* first week, 259. *Endive,* 226, and *purslain,* 261, second week, *Cauliflowers* about the middle for a late autumn crop, 221. *Pumpions* and *gourds,* 243.

Succession crops of cucumbers for picklers, 195. *Melons* for mangoes, 206. *Dwarf kidney beans, celery, radishes, turnips, cabbages, savoys, broccoli, peas, beans, finochio, salsafy, scorzonera, chardons, spinach, lettuces, radishes,* and *small sallading;* chiefly in the first week.

PLANT

Kidney beans that have been forwarded on heat, 229. *Cucumbers* and *melons,* second crop, 194, 205. Forward *gourds,* 243. *Lettuces,* 232. *Cauliflowers, savoys, cabbages, coleworts,* 217, 224. *Celery,* if forward, in trenches, 222. *Artichokes,* 208. *Potatoes,* 239. *Nasturtiums,* 259. *Capsicums,* 254. *Love-apples,* 264, and basil, 253, towards the end of the month. *Herbs,* by parted roots, 252, &c. *Trees* and *shrubs* may yet succeed under good management, 103.

PROPAGATE

Herbs, culinary and medicinal, by slips and cuttings, but rather the latter. For *sage* it is now the best time, 252, &c.

FLOWERS.

Sow annuals of all sorts for a late blow. *Scarlet bean,* sow as a flower to run up pales, &c. 6, vol. 2. &c.
Thin seedlings soon, that they may not be weak, 6, vol. 2.
Prick out, or *plant,* the *tender annuals* in new hot beds, pots, &c. as directed, 7, 9, 11, vol. 2.

Hot beds

Hot beds of flowers, manage, as to air, water, &c. 6. vol. 2.

Biennials and *perennials*, thin in time, and water them; also prick out any that are forward enough; they may yet be sown, 15, 16, vol. 2.

Auriculas out of flower, remove out of the sun.

Tuberoses, pot on heat, or under a south wall, 99, vol. 2.

Tulips, *anemonies*, &c. in beds and in flower, protect, 21, vol. 2.

Bulbs and *tubers* of dying spring flowers, take up, 18, vol. 2.

Slips and *cuttings* of *pinks*, double *wall flowers*, double *sweet williams*, double *scarlet lychnis*, double *rockets*, and *lychnidea*, plant as soon as the young shoots are forward enough.

Geraniums plant cuttings of last year's shoots, 94, vol. 2.

Water seed beds lightly and moderately in a dry time, 13, vol. 2: and pots of flowers, regularly, 10. vol. 2.

Air, give to housed plants freely, as the season is.

Dress, *shift*, and *tie up*, flowers and shrubs in pots.

Pot some ten week stocks, mignonette, &c. 9, 11, vol. 2.

Support spindling flowers and weak shrubs, 56.

NURSERY.

Weed, *water*, and occasionally *shade* tender seedlings.

Seed beds, keep cool, for without moisture, germination cannot be expected; but give water lightly, so as not to cake the ground, 51.

* * * * *

JUNE.

IN this month the gardener begins to find *some* pause to his labour. The ground is now fully cropped, as to principals, and the *chief* business is to see that the various plants, according to their different ages of growth, do not stand in need of the necessary assistance of *culture*, or good management.

MISCEL.

MISCELLANEOUS WORK.

Weed, &c. keeping the crops and ground neat, 54.
Gravel walks, grafs plats, and *edgings,* fee to, 55.
Water, let it be duly applied where neceſſary, 51.
Thin by hoe, or hand, all forts of crops, 49.
Prick out celery, endive, favoys, broccoli, &c. 50.
Cauliflowers ſhewing head, break leaves over, 221.
Earth up high peas, beans, &c. fee the laſt month.
Tie up the leaves of garlick and rocambole, 227.
Blanch lettuce, white beat, and finochio, 215, 233, 256.
Stick peas and *top beans,* when in full flower, 237.
Cucumbers, attend duly, to air, water, train, &c. 190.
Melons, ditto, prune and lay tile under the fruit, 201.
Prune wall trees, vines and eſpaliers, 135, 154, 164.
Blighted trees, pull off curled leaves, in time, and water them frequently with an engine, 52.
Graffs that have taken, unclay and unbind, 86.
Bud, or inoculate, at Midſummer, or foon after, 91.
Aſparagus, finiſh cutting by Midſummer, 212.
Herbs for drying, gather as directed, page 252.

SOW

Cucumbers, laſt crop, for picklers may do in cold ground, if a good foil and funny fituation, 195. *Pumpions* and *gourds* may fucceed as ditto, 243. *Turnip radiſhes* of all forts, but chiefly the large white and black Spaniſh for autumn uſe, in cool ground, 245. *Endive* for a principal crop, 226.
Succeſſion crops of *broccoli, peas, broad beans, kidney beans, ſpindle rooted radiſhes, lettuces, ſmall ſallading, purſlain, turnips, cabbages, carrots, finochio,* and *ſpinach,* which will however foon run.

PLANT

Cucumbers, 194. *Melons,* 205. *Pumpions* and *gourds,* 243. *Naſturtiums,* 259. *Capſicums,* 254. *Love apples,* 264. *Leeks,* 231. *Celery,* 222. *Cauliflowers, broccoli,*

broccoli, borecole, savoys, cabbages, and such like greens, at two and a half feet, or rather more for *cauliflowers;* less for *broccoli,* and *cabbages* if a small sort. Seedling *herbs,* 252, &c. *Moist weather* at this season is very advantageous for pricking out, or planting, and it must not be neglected if it occurs: Water at the time, and afterwards as the weather may require.

PROPAGATE

Herbs by slips, or cuttings, in a good soil, and as cool a situation as may be, not under trees, 252, &c.

Layer the young shoots of *roses, evergreens,* or any shrub, or tree, that does not readily strike root from older wood, or send forth suckers, 69.

Cuttings, or the young shoots of some woody plants, may be made to strike root, see page 43, vol. 2.

FLOWERS.

Annuals, tender sorts, pot and plant out into the borders; they will require a good soil, water, and a little shade at first, and chuse rainy or cloudy weather, 9, vol. 2.

Pots of flowers set where they have only the morning sun, but not under trees, or any roof, except for ornament, when in blow.

Trim, from dead parts, &c. perennials and biennials, 57.

Carnations, and other spindling flowers, support, 56.

Water pots of flowers duly, borders occasionally, 10, vol. 2.

Prick out seedlings of biennial and perennial flowers, particularly *carnations,* 93, vol. 2. *Pinks,* 98, vol. 2. *Auriculas,* 92, vol. 2, and *polyanthuses,* 98, vol. 2, into shady places.

Plant slips, or cuttings of walls, &c. see last month.

Layer carnations, pinks, and sweet williams.

Auriculas should be set in shade, except for seed.

Spring bulbs, the leaves being decayed, take up, 18, vol. 2.

Autumnal bulbs, plant at the end of the month, 18, vol. 2.

NURSERY.

NURSERY.

Weed, water, stir the soil, *rake* and clean up.
Shade tender seedlings, and late planted things.
Seed beds, spring sown, keep moist, and earthed up; in very hot weather, an awning of mats is advantageous.
Thin young plants from growing thick and weak.

* * * * * *

JULY.

THOUGH in this month there is a cessation from the great bustle, and more laborious works of gardening, yet "*its many cares*" still find employment for the willing hand; and most assuredly a good success in the *end* will not be attained without perseverance in the *means*. Let nothing therefore be omitted, that may tend to crown the gardener's credit with a continued production of *fine vegetables*, *fruits*, and *flowers*. The garden now abundantly gratifies the *sight*, the *taste*, the *smell;* and those who have the opportunity to enjoy it, should be grateful to GOD—and the *gardener*.

MISCELLANEOUS WORK.

Prepare vacant ground for cropping, and let as little of it as possible lay rude and unproductive.
Weed, stir the borders, hoe between crops, &c. 54.
Water cauliflowers, and whatever else may need it, 51.
Gravel walks, grass plats, and *edgings*, keep in order, 55.
Box, yew, &c. should be clipped after, or in rain.
Earth peas, broad and kid. beans, celery, cabbages, &c.
Blanch lettuce, white beet, and finochio, 215, 233, 256.
Stick peas, and running kidney beans in time, 237, 230.
Thin all small crops to their due distances, 49.
Prick out celery, broccoli, cabbages, savoys, &c. 50.

Seeds,

Seeds, gather as they ripen, left the beft are loft, 59.
Herbs for drying, gather as foon as in flower, 252.
Take up garlick, rocambole, fhalots, 227, 249, 261.
Cucumbers and *melons,* attend, water, train, &c. 190, 201.
Pumpions and *gourds,* train, and water plentifully, 243.
Artichokes, take off fmall fide heads in time, 208.
Wall trees, &c. regulate and occafionally prune ; alfo ftop *vines,* and take off fide fhoots, 135, 154, 159,&c.
Thin wall trees, &c. of fuperabundant fruit, 150, 161.
Bud-graff, or inoculate, fruit trees, rofes, &c. 91.
Blighted wall trees, attend to, fee the laft month.

SOW.

Broccoli, firft week, cool ground a little, for late ufe.
Endive, principal winter crop, in open ground, 226.
Peas and *beans,* of any kind, may yet be fown, if ground to fpare, before the 15th, and chance to do tolerably ; prefer the *mazagan* bean and *Leadman's* dwarf peas, 238: Sow under fhelter, if convenient, from N. & E.
Kidney beans, dwarfs, firft week, fouth border, 230.
Carrots, a few, cool ground, to draw young late in autumn, water both feeds and roots occafionally in dry weather to forward them.
Radifhes of any kind, but chiefly the large black and white Spanifh turnip forts, 245.
Lettuces, the hardier, or winter forts, open ground, 231.
Spinach, beginning of the month the *round,* and towards the end the *prickly* feeded, 249.
Onions, a few Welch, and Strafburgh, fecond week, 234,
Coleworts, firft week for winter, laft week fpring, 224.
Turnips, any fort, both early and late in the month, 250.

PLANT

Celery and *leeks* at fix inches. *Endive, lettuces, coleworts* at a foot. *Cabbages, favoys, broccoli, boorcole,* and *cauliflowers,* at two feet, or a little more, in a rich foil, particularly the latter : Give *water* at planting;

SECT. XX.   JULY.   119

planting, and two or three times after, if not much rain should fall.

PROPAGATE

Herbs, particularly sage, propagate yet, by cuttings, or slips, occasionally watering, 252, &c.
Trees and *shrubs,* by laying shoots of the present year; i. e. of those that are not apt to strike from older wood. Slips and cuttings of some sorts, may strike, by the help of a *hand-glass,* 67. 122, 43, vol. 2.

FLOWERS.

Stir flower borders, and rake them neatly, 54.
Pots of flowers, set in shade, and regularly water, 10, vol. 2.
Carnations and double *sweet williams,* layers, 92, vol. 2.
Pinks, plant slips, cuttings, pipings, or layers, 97, vol. 2.
Geraniums, double, scarlet lychnis, lychnideas and *double wall flowers,* plant cuttings, or slips of, 94, vol. 2.
Annuals, the beginning of this month is a good time to plant out the tender sorts into borders; any that are in too small pots, shift into bigger, 12, vol. 2.
Biennials, thin seed beds of, prick out, water, &c. 15, vol. 2.
Perennials, ditto, particularly auriculas, 92, vol. 2. Carnations, 93. vol. 2. Pinks, 98, vol. 2, and polyanthus, 98, vol. 2.
Larkspurs and *stocks,* pull up single ones; i. e. all the former, and most of the latter, 58, vol. 2.
Seeds, gather very regularly as they ripen, 57, 66.
Bulbous and *tuberous* roots take up in due time, 19, vol. 2.
Trim off dead stems, or other parts of plants and shrubs, straggling branches, &c. 57.
Support weak flowers and shrubs by proper ties, 56.

NURSERY.

Weed, water, shade, young tender seedlings, &c. 70.
Prune away suckers, or shoots from stems, &c. particularly those that have been graffed, 96.   *Thin*

Thin seedlings that grow thick; if those drawn are planted out, afford occasional watering, and the shade of a single mat, which should only be over on days, for the night dews greatly refresh new planted things. A little *moss* laid round the roots of any curious sorts would preserve them from drought.

* * * * * *

AUGUST.

IN this month (as in some measure before) the gardener anticipates products of the *future* year, and sows various vegetables in *autumn* to stand the *winter*, for *spring* and *summer* use; so that, in this, and other respects, *August* is in truth an important season, as will be seen by the work directed to be done. The *times* for several *sowings* should be pretty exactly observed in order to success.

MISCELLANEOUS WORK.

Weed and *water, stir borders, clean up, be neat,* 50, 54.
Walks and *grass plats,* attend, roll, mow, sweep, 55.
Thin by hoe, or hand, young crops, in dry weather, 49.
Prick out celery, and other things that are ready, 50.
Earth up peas, beans, kidney beans, celery, cauliflowers, cabbages, savoys, winter greens, &c. 49.
Blanch endive, beet, chardon, finochio, 226, 215, 223.
Dig, or use a strong hoe, between rows of plants, and water to settle earth about the roots, 49.
Vacant ground, clean, and, considering how it will be best disposed of, prepare accordingly, 46, &c.
Stick peas, and take up the haulm of old crops, 237.
Stake tall plants which are standing for seed, 59.
Seeds, gather as they ripen, left the best shed, 60.
Herbs, gather for drying just when in flower, 252.
Onions, press down the leaves to the ground, 235.

Grape

SECT. XX.   AUGUST.   121

Grape vines, prune, and keep in due order, 155.
Wall trees, espaliers, climbing shrubs, &c. regulate, 136.
Insects about wall trees, see to, and hang up vials of sugar and water for wasps, &c. See blight, *June.*
Budding may yet be performed, first week, 91; *buds* that have taken of former work, unbind, 96.
Net fruit trees to keep off birds and also fingers.
Gather fruit before the sun has been long on it.
Mat currants and gooseberries for late fruit, 169.
Strawberries, clear from runners, weeds, leaves, 171.
Cucumbers, melons, pumpions, and *gourds,* train, water, &c. but melons like not much wet, 202, &c.
Pickling cucumbers should be gathered twice a week.

SOW

Coleworts in the first week, 224; *cabbages* in the second, 217; and *cauliflowers* in the third, 220. *Onions* for winter and spring, a full crop of *Welch,* and a few *Strasburgh* in a warm border, first week, 234. *Lettuces* at the beginning, middle, and end of the month, 231. *Small sallading,* in a shady place, and water it, 255. *American cress,* it is the best time for, second week, 256. *Radish,* both spindle and round rooted, but chiefly the large Spanish turnip sorts, cool ground, 245. *Peas,* early frame, and Leadman's dwarf, may be tried first week, for the chance of a *rarity,* close under a warm wall, 238. *Kidney beans,* dwarf, as ditto, 230. *Spinach,* round and prickly, first and third weeks, the former at broad cast, and the latter rather in drills, 249. *Turnips,* first or second week, 250. *Carrots,* ditto, but they will be sticky. *Herbs* may be sown, first week, 252, &c.

PLANT

Leeks, celery, lettuces, endive, cabbages, coleworts, late broccoli, and boorcole, distance as last month, though every thing planted late, may be so much the

the nigher. *Strawberries* and *herbs*, culinary and medicinal, towards the end of the month, that they may be well rooted before winter, 39, 252, &c.

PROPAGATE

Trees and *shrubs*, by laying *young* shoots in fine rich earth, and keep the ground cool about them, 69.

FLOWERS.

Decayed parts, take off, trim, and tie to sticks, 56, 57.
Shrubs, ditto, thin a little, and prune off suckers, 114.
Edgings, or *hedges* of box, yew, &c, may be cut now.
Water potted flowers regularly, others occasionally, and particularly new planted things, 10, vol. 2.
Annuals, hardy, sow towards end of the month, 13, vol. 2.
Biennials and *perennials*, plant, last week, 15, 17, vol. 2.
Saxifrage pyramidal, and double plant in pots, 81, vol. 2.
Geraniums, raised from cuttings, (or seed) pot soon.
Auriculas and *polyanthus*, transplant, part the roots, &c. any time this month, 91, 98, vol. 2.
Carnations may yet be layered; early layered ones will be rooted, which carefully take up, and plant in pots, or open ground, water and shade, 92, vol. 2.
Pinks from cuttings, &c. and *sweet william* layers may be fit to move; but, if late and weak, leave some of them till spring, 97, vol. 2.
Bulbous roots, as lilies, &c. take up for planting, 18, vol. 2.
Bulbous offsets, replant without delay, 19, vol. 2.
Bulbs of autumn flowers, plant in first or second week: see *atamasco*, *Guernsey*, *belladonna*, and *pancratium* lilies.

NURSERY.

Prune suckers, side stem shoots, straggling and luxuriant ones from the head; *stir* the ground, *weed*, *water*, *thin seedlings*, &c. See last month.

SEPTEMBER.

SEPTEMBER.

Gardens begin now to fail of their wonted *beauty*, and therefore dying flowers, all litter, and every thing unsightly, admonish the gardener to trim his plants, and clean the ground frequently, that all may be neat, if not gay. An attention of this sort, stirring the ground, and raking it, will give an air of *freshness* and *culture* highly pleasing and creditable.

MISCELLANEOUS WORK.

See beginning of last month, *twelve* first articles.
Prepare ground for planting trees and shrubs, 108.
Turf, lay as a good time, beat, roll, and, if dry, water.
Gather fruits as they ripen, and store them well, 269.
Grapes, tie fine ripe bunches up in gauze or crape.
Figs, keep in close training to ripen the fruit.
Cucumbers and *melons*, cover the frames, &c. on nights; melons *must* be protected from cold and wet, 206.
Pickling cucumbers, gather before they spot.
Cauliflowers, prick out, and some on a slight hot bed to strengthen them, at three inches, to grow three weeks; these must then be put under the protection of frames, or hand-glasses, as choice plants; every other may be drawn, and the rest remain to be covered. The *Michaelmas* crop, if dry weather, water to bring forward.
Herb beds should be cleaned and dressed this month, 252.
Onions, being dry and hard, take in and sort, to rope, &c. 235.
Garlick, *shalots*, and *rocambole*, tie up, and store, 227.
Seeds, such as are well dried, dress and put up, 57, 60.

SOW

Spinach, turnips, Welch onions, and *endive,* first week, for late spring use. Radishes of all sorts, but chiefly the large black turnip, 245. *Small sallading,* every ten days, warm borders, 215. *Corn sallad,* 255. *Chervil,* 254, and *sorrel,* 263.

PLANT

At distances as before, *coleworts, endive, lettuces,* and yet winter *cabbages, savoys, broccoli, boorcole, Brussels, sprouts, chou-milan,* and *celery.* The *lettuces* should be on dry warm ground, 232. *Herbs,* pot and medicinal, from parted roots, or offsets, 252, &c. *Strawberries,* any time this month, but the sooner the better; dress old beds and plants, 39, 171. *Shrubs,* begin to plant towards the end, especially if moist weather, but let not the roots be long out of ground, 110, &c.

PROPAGATE

Trees and *shrubs,* by laying young shoots, and at the end of the month, cuttings may be planted, as of *gooseberries, currants, laurels, honeysuckles, jasmines,* &c. 65, &c.

FLOWERS.

Remove dead ones, *trim* the decaying, tie up, &c. 56, 57.
Annuals, sow some of the hardy sorts, first week, 13, vol. 2.
Biennials, plant out, reserving a few for spring, 15. vol. 2.
Perennials, ditto, also take up, and part old roots 17, vol. 2.
Pinks, from cuttings, &c. (if well rooted) plant out; also *carnations, sweet williams,* &c. from layers, 97, vol. 2.
Geraniums, from cuttings, or seed, plant without delay, in small pots, shortening the roots, &c.

Auriculas,

SECT. XX.   OCTOBER.

Auriculas, dress pots, shift plants, or sow, 91, vol. 2.
Polyanthus, plant, part roots, or sow the seed, 272.
Bulbs of autumn flowers, plant yet in first week, see last month; and those of spring in last week, as *crocuses,* early *tulips,* common *anemonies,* &c. 18, vol. 2.
Lilies and other scaly bulbous roots, plant soon, 19, vol. 2.   [vol. 2.
Offsets from bulbs must be planted immediately, 19,
Beds for choice bulbous and tuberous roots, prepare for planting next month, 19, vol. 2.
Edgings of box, or thrift, plant, cut, or repair.
Pots of flowers bring from shady situations to more sunny ones; the *exotics,* or tender plants, begin (second week) to put under some degree of shelter, according to their nature.
Succulent plants are impatient of wet, and more so of frost, but still do not well endure housing, therefore they require a peculiar attention at this season, so as to have the open air as long as may be exposed without danger.

NURSERY.

Weed, stir the soil, clean up, and water, if dry weather.
Dig about young trees, at the end of this, or the beginning of next month, as directed, 80.
Prepare ground for planting next month. Stocks and seedlings, and sowing seeds of trees and shrubs, 72, 73. *Evergreen* seedlings should be planted out by the end of this month, and be watered regularly, if a dry time.

* * * * * *

OCTOBER.

THIS is the *chief* month of the year for planting trees, shrubs, &c. No part of it should be lost, in either working the ground *well* for the purpose, or putting

putting in the plants as soon as possible : Early planting, if the ground is fit, is of more consequence than many of those who do, or ought to know better, will admit of.

Now the virtues of *industry* and *perseverance* will be tried, to keep the grounds clean from falling leaves, &c. The *garden*, however, ought yet to be a source of pleasure, and the weather is often still inviting abroad : All impediments should be surmounted.

MISCELLANEOUS WORK.

Dig, dung, trench, and *drain,* ground thoroughly, 46.
Prepare for planting, lay open the holes for trees, 99.
Rake leaves off borders and quarters, sweep, &c.
Gravel walks and *grass plats,* cleanse, roll, mow, &c.
Turf will be well laid now, and do the work soon.
Caterpillars, destroy, for they do mischief rapidly.
Thin by hoe, spinach, &c. small crops, by hand, 49.
Prick out cabbages for winter or spring planting, 217.
Hoe between roes of cabbages, &c. and earth up, 49.
Blanch celery, finochio by earthing up ; endive, beet,
 chardons, by tying up, 223, 226, 256, 215, 223.
Cauliflowers that are heading, break leaves over, 221.
Asparagus beds and seedlings, dress, second week, 212.
Strawberries, if not before, dress out of hand, 171.
Raspberries, dress, and plant coleworts between, 169.
Seeds, gather duly, and lay up thoroughly dry, 60.
Fruits, gather carefully, and house well, 269, 274.
Dig up, and store clean and dry, carrots, 219; potatoes,
 242 ; parsneps, 235 ; Jerusalem artichokes, 228.
Dress (for fine fruit) about currant and gooseberry
 bushes, by digging in a little manure.
Herb beds should always be dressed at this time, 252.
Vines, wall-trees, &c. regulate, if not prune, 146.

SOW

SOW

Beans, mazagan, 213. *Peas*, early sorts, 236. *Lettuces*, hardy sorts, first week, warm border, 231. *Small sallading*, warm border, under glass, 255. *Radishes*, early purple short top, may succeed, south aspect, 245. *Carrots*, a few early horn, warm border, but they will prove sticky.

PLANT

Broccoli, a few, first week, for latest spring use, at eighteen inches, but the heads will be small. *Coleworts*, first week, at about a foot, 224. *Cabbages*, any time, chusing strong plants, 217. *Endive*, first week, warm border, 226. *Celery*, first week, open ground, for late spring use, 222. *Cauliflowers*, settle soon in their winter quarters, and manage well, 220. *Lettuces* treat as cauliflowers, 232. *Shalots*, *garlick*, *rocambole*, dry ground, 249, 227, 261. *Strawberries*, first week, 39. *Wall trees*, and other *shrubs*, but evergreens in the first week. *Herbs*, rooted sorts, 252, &c. *Mint* on a little heat, protecting it, 259. *Layers* of trees and shrubs made last year; being rooted, take them up well, and plant immediately, 99, &c.

PROPAGATE

Trees and *shrubs*, by *suckers*, 65. By *layers* of the young wood, roses, jasmines, bay, laurel, laurustinus, vines, figs, filberts, codlins, mulberries, &c. See lists of trees and shrubs. By *cuttings* or *slips*, gooseberries, currants, berberry, jasmines honeysuckles, laurels, box, &c. See lists.

FLOWERS.

Look over, trim, tie up, gather ripe seeds, &c, 56, 57, 60. *Geraniums*, and other tender plants, dress, house, 97, vol. 2.

Auriculas

Auriculas and *carnations* in pots, preserve from much wet, and set in sunny situations.

Seeds, or *seedlings*, in pots, or boxes, ditto, and shelter from the cutting N. E. winds.

Annuals, self sown, &c. may be taken up with a little earth, and planted where wanted.

Biennials, plant out, but leave a few for spring, 15, vol. 2.

Perennials, ditto, also slip or divide old roots, 17, vol. 2.

Bulbous, *tuberous* and *fleshy* roots of spring and summer flowers, plant, but the earliest first, 18, vol. 2.

Saxifrage, pyramidal and double, plant in pots, 81, vol. 2.

Edging of dwarf flowers, box, &c. plant, or repair.

NURSERY.

Stir, and fork in neatly a little well rotted manure, 71.

Dig ground to be planted, a week before wanted.

Sow seeds of trees, &c. and guard against mice, &c. 72, 80.

Transplant seedlings to wider distances, as those designed for stocks, &c. at about two feet, 73, 74.

Suckers of plums, &c. plant for stocks, and *cuttings* of codlin, quince, and mulberry, for trees, 75.

Prune, or dress up, young trees and shrubs from suckers, straggling shoots, and form the heads.

* * * * * *

NOVEMBER.

Though the *last* be the better month for planting, yet this is more commonly the time adopted : It cannot be now proper to delay it. The leaves not being all off should be no obstacle.

The object of *pleasure* should not yet be given up ; and let the gardener do all in his power to be cleanly and neat, giving his grounds that proof of good culture, which is so essential to his credit.

MISCEL.

SECT. XX. NOVEMBER. 129

MISCELLANEOUS WORK.

Wet, if water stands any where, let it be well drained.
Vacant ground, dig, manure, trench, or at least hoe, 49.
Clear away dead plants, leaves, and all litter, 54.
Weed borders and crops, as spinach, winter onions, &c.
Grass plats, cleanse, roll, mow, and lay *turf* soon.
Gravel walks, weed, clean and roll hard after rain.
Composts, collect, and mix well the materials for.
Cucumber and *melon* earth, store in dry time, 183, 200.
Earth up peas and beans as soon as above ground ;
 celery, cauliflowers, broccoli, and winter greens.
Blanch endive, 226, chardons, 223, and finochio, 256.
Dig up carrots, potatoes, Jerusalem artichokes, and pars-
 neps, but not all the latter, 235. Also when in
 prospect of *frost*, some red beet, scorzonera, salsify,
 skirrets, Hamburgh parsley, leeks, turnip radishes,
 and horseradish, all of them to be preserved a while
 in a cellar, or longer in *dry* sand. See cauliflowers
 farther on.
Cauliflowers and *lettuces* in frames, &c. attend, 220, 232.
Artichokes, see to, when in prospect of frost, 209.
Asparagus, dress beds of, and also seedlings soon, 212.
Raspberries, dress in the first week ; see last month.
Hot beds may be used for small sallading, 255, mint,
 259, lettuces, 233, or for radishes at Christmas, 245.
Frost, consider what should be protected from it.
Fruit, latest sorts, gather in the first week ; and man-
 age that already housed, 269, 273.
Onions, store of, look over to remove decayed ones, 235.
Seeds, dress, and put up clean and dry, and keep so.
Caterpillars on winter greens, pick off in time.
Grubs about the roots of lettuces, search for.
Shrubs, prune and dig about ; fasten trained ones, 114.
Prune all trees, except figs, but cherries first, 146.
Figs, pull off green fruit, and fasten the shoots as close
 as may be without force, 156.
Cover the roots, and *stake* new planted trees, or tall
 shrubs ; fasten those of the wall, 102.

Cauliflowers

Cauliflowers in head, break leaves over. This vegetable, and *broccoli*, may be taken up when in profpect of froft, and planted with balls of earth, and only laid in a cellar, where they will keep (perhaps) a month; but tie the leaves together at the tops with a hay band before taken up.

SOW

Small fallading and *lap lettuce*, under glafs, warm border, or on a little heat, 233, 255. *Radifhes*, purple fhort top, warm border, 244. *Carrots*, early horn, may chance to fucceed. *Beans* and *peas* for firft principal crop, 213, 235.

PLANT

Celery yet, 222. *Lettuces*, 232; and *cauliflowers* yet, in frames, under hand-glaffes, or clofe under a fouth wall, 220. *Coleworts*, 224. *Cabbages*, 217; and all in the firft week, though the latter may be later. *Mint* on heat, 259. *Wall trees*, and others foon, 30, &c. 98, &c. *Shrubs*, deciduous, but not evergreens, 110, &c. *Strawberries*, if defired, but foon, 39.

PROPAGATE

See laft month, by cuttings, flips, layers, and fuckers; or divided roots, as rofes, &c. 66, &c.

FLOWERS.

Take up dead ones, *trim* and *tie* thofe in blow.
Froft, beware of, as to the care of tender ones.
Auriculas and *carnations* in pots, (tho' hardy) protect.
Seedlings in boxes, &c. place in the fun, and protect.
Pots

Pots of hardy flowers are themselves preserved, as well as the plants, by plunging (rather above their rims) in the ground; place a bit of tile under them to keep out worms. If the soil is moist, lay drift sand, or ashes, about the pots.

Bulbous and *tuberous* roots, plant early; and valuable sorts protect from much wet and frost, 21, vol. 2.

Biennials and *perennials* of hardy sorts, plant early, in dry soils, and water in the morning, 15, 16, vol. 2.

Thrift, or *box*, plant or repair, as soon as may be.

NURSERY.

See last month; and do soon what was omitted.

Transplant hardy seedlings, in fine broke earth, 73.

Cover the roots of newly planted things, 73.

Traps, set for mice, &c. about seed beds, 73.

* * * * *

DECEMBER.

THE garden is no longer decorated with flowers, or verdure; but it contains many things of *promise*, which demand attention, and which the industrious gardener will duly afford, agreeable to the culture that each requires.

There are still some works of *labour;* and where there is plenty of dung and frames, *hot beds* may be made use of, and *spring* anticipated.

If this month be called *dreary*, yet still the face of nature has its charms, and invites us sometimes abroad, even when covered with snow. Frost is cleanly and beneficial, it dries the path, it strings our nerves, exhilarates our spirits, purifies the air, and prepares the ground for future produce.

All

> All *nature* feels the renovating force
> Of *winter*, only to the thoughtless eye
> In ruin seen. The frost-concocted glebe
> Draws in abundant vegetable soul,
> And gathers vigour for the coming year.
>
> THOMSON.

MISCELLANEOUS WORK.

Weed crops, &c. *clean up* litter, and still be neat.
Gravel walks, roll hard, if dry, against wet and frost.
Grass plats, cleanse from worm casts, sweep and roll.
Mice traps, set about peas, beans, cauliflowers, &c. 239.
Caterpillars, snails and *slugs*, see after duly.
Tools, make, repair, grind, and keep bright, 9, vol. 2.
Seeds, look over the stock to keep clean, dry, &c.
Fruit and *onions*, examine, to remove decaying, 235.
Straw, damp or musty, remove from store rooms.
Frost, guard against ill effects of every where.
Wheat straw, useful to protect things, see radish, 244.
Vegetables, before hard frost, take up, see last month.
Artichokes, asparagus and *raspberries*, (if not before) give their winter dressing soon, 209, 212, 169.
Endive, tie up when perfectly dry, and ridge some, 226.
Earth up high celery, cauliflowers, chardons, broccoli, savoys, cabbages, &c. pressing the mould to.
Cauliflowers and *lettuces* in frames, &c. manage, 220, 232.
Planting, prepare for, and open the holes ready, 29, 98.
Vacant ground, clean, dung, rough dig, or trench, 46.
Barrow, make use of in frost to wheel in dung, &c.
Hot beds, see and manage the materials well for, 174.
Cucumbers may be sown in the last week, 178, 181.
Composts, make, and incorporate well by turning over.
Orchards, prune trees, dress, dig, or plough the soil, 43.
Prune wall pear trees, espaliers and shrubs, 146, 157.
Hedges and *ditches*, manage as the case requires.
Drain wet from standing in gardens, or plantations.
Spring, have a constant eye to, and prepare for.

SOW

SECT. XX.   DECEMBER.   133

SOW

Beans, 213. *Peas*, 237. *Radishes*, 244. *Carrots* may be tried as radishes, 218. *Lettuces* under glafs in a warm border. *Small fallad* and *lap lettuce* on a flight heat, 255, 233.

PLANT

Mint on heat, 259. *Trees* and *fhrubs* of the deciduous kind, covering the roots and ftaking; if againft a wall, faften them to it, 99, &c.

PROPAGATE

By *fuckers, cuttings, layers*, &c. fee *October*, 65, &c.

FLOWERS,

Take care of, but neither fow nor plant; yet fome chufe to fow *auriculas* in this month.
Covering of every kind is to be no clofer, or longer kept on than *neceffary*, for great dangers arife from much nurfing, when plants come to be expofed, fee laft month.

NURSERY.

Protect feed beds, as the froft may require.
New planted things, cover the roots of well.
Seedlings of tender things may be covered lightly all over, but uncover in time.
Froft-cracks in beds, fill up with fifted mould.
Wet (much of) gives froft fo great hold, that it fhould be particularly guarded againft.
Vermin muft be attended to, particularly mice, which are even apt to bark young trees, 73.

CLOSE.

CLOSE.

As it has been one of the objects of this book to afford some entertainment and moral instruction, the following lines from *Thomson* may properly follow the calendar, and will serve for a finish.

ON THE SEASONS.

THESE, as they change, ALMIGHTY FATHER, these
Are but the *varied* GOD. The rolling year
Is full of THEE.———

Nature attend! join every living soul,
Beneath the spacious temple of the sky,
In adoration join; and, ardent raise
One general song.———

Soft roll your incense, herbs, and fruits, and flowers—
In mingled clouds to HIM, whose sun exalts,
Whose breath perfumes you, and whose pencil paints.

Great source of Day! best image here below
Of thy CREATOR, ever pouring wide,
From world to world, the vital ocean round,
On nature write with every beam his praise.

For *me*, when I forget the darling theme,
Whether the blossom blows, the summer ray,
Russets the plain, *inspiring* autumn gleams;
Or winter rises in the blackening east;
Be my tongue mute, my fancy paint no more,
And, dead to joy, forget my heart to beat!

THOMSON.

THE END.

AN ESSAY ON QUICK-LIME,

AS A CEMENT

AND AS A MANURE.

BY

JAMES ANDERSON, L.L.D.

F.R.S. F.A.S. S.

Author of " Essays relating to Agriculture and Rural Affairs," 3 Vols. 8vo, and of several other Performances.

Honorary Member of the Society of Arts, Agriculture, &c. at *Bath*; of the Philosophical, and of the Agricultural Societies in *Manchester*; of the Society for Promoting Natural History, *London*; of the Academy of Arts, Sciences, and Belles Lettres, *Dijon*; of the Philosophical Society, *Philadelphia*; of the Royal Economical Society, *Berlin*; and correspondent Member of the Royal Society of Agriculture, *Paris*.

And he gave it for his opinion, that whoever could make two ears of corn, or two blades of grass, to grow upon a spot of ground where only one grew before, would deserve better of mankind, and do more essential service to his country, than the whole race of Politicians put together.

SWIFT.

Boston :

PRINTED BY *SAMUEL ETHERIDGE*,

For JOSEPH NANCREDE, NO. 49, *Marlboro'-Street*.

1799.

AN ESSAY ON QUICK-LIME,

AS A

CEMENT

AND AS A

MANURE.

ADVERTISEMENT.

THE nature of the subject discussed in the following Essay, necessarily required that it should be treated in a scientific manner. The Author has endeavoured to render it as perspicuous as possible; but is afraid, that, to those who may never have been versant in studies of this sort, it may still in some places appear a little abstruse. On this occasion, he hopes to meet with the indulgence of those who think no exertion

of

of mind improperly beftowed, when it is in the purfuit of ufeful knowledge.— Others who do not care to engage in intricate difcuffions of any fort, he would advife to pafs over this Effay entirely; or at leaft the *firſt part* of it. The *reaſons* for what is advanced in the fecond part, will not indeed be in that cafe fo clearly feen; but the practical farmer, if not thoroughly *inſtructed* by that, may at leaft be *directed* to what he ought to do.

AN ESSAY ON QUICK-LIME.

QUICK-LIME is a *calx*, or a very fine powder, obtained by burning marble, chalk, or lime-ftone, and afterwards throwing water upon it.

This powder, when newly burnt, is foluble* in water;—is capable of being formed into a firm cement, if properly mixed up with water,—and is poffeffed of many other peculiar qualities that it is unneceffary here to enumerate.

But if this powder has been expofed to the influence of the air for fome time, it is found to be no longer capable of being diffolved in water;—it has become incapable of being formed into a cement, and has loft many of the other peculiar qualities for which it was at firft remarkable.

In common language, this powder is ufually diftinguifhed by the name of LIME fimply. But, in the language of philofophic precifion, it is called QUICK-LIME, fo long as it remains foluble in water, and capable of being ufed as a cement. After it lofes thefe properties, it is diftinguifhed by the name of EFFETE-LIME.

In either of thefe ftates, it is employed by the farmer as a manure: And as it is a manure of the moft univerfal utility that has yet been difcovered, its nature and qualities deferve to be very particularly invefligated.

The defign of this Effay, is to point out fome of the peculiarities that conftitute the excellence of this fubftance, as a manure, and as a cement: And as what may be faid of it as a manure, will be better underftood after its nature as a cement has been explained, it will be neceffary to confider it firft in that point of view.

PART

---

* Capable of being diffolved.

To avoid difagreeable circumlocution, I fhall be obliged, in this Effay, to employ fome technical terms not commonly underftood; but fhall explain their meaning as I go along.

PART FIRST.

Of *QUICK-LIME* as a Cement.

§ 1.

IF lime-ftone or marble be expofed to the action of a pretty intenfe fire for a fufficient length of time, its colour is altered, and its weight confiderably diminifhed: but it retains its former figure and dimenfions.

In this ftate of burnt ftone, it is in many places diftinguifhed by the name of *lime-fhells,* or *fhell-lime,* or fimply *fhells.*

§ 2.

If water be thrown upon thefe *lime-fhells,* a confiderable heat is in a fhort time generated; the burnt ftones begin to crack and fall afunder, and the mafs increafes in bulk as it gradually crumbles down, or *falls,* as it is more commonly faid, into a fine powder; which is always of a white colour, whatever was the colour of the ftone before calcination.*

This powder is called *flacked lime,* or fimply *lime;* and the operation that reduces it from *fhells* to this ftate, is called *flacking.*

§ 3.

If this powder is intimately mixed with as much water as reduces it to the confiftence of a thin pafte, and afterwards dried, it concretes into one coherent mafs,

---

* *Calcination* is the operation by which any folid compact body is, by means of fire, reduced from its former coherent ftate, to that of a dry incoherent powder, which is called a *calx.*

mafs, which adheres to ftones, or other unpolifhed bodies, very firmly; and thus it becomes a proper cement for building walls of any fort.

After this pafte has been once fully dried, it becomes indiffoluble in water, fo as never to be foftened by the moifture of the air; on which account, it greatly excels clay, or any other cement that can be eafily obtained.

This cement, when compofed for building walls, is called *mortar*. When intended to be applied only as a fmooth coating upon the furface of any place, without being mixed with ftones, it is called in this country fimply *plafter*.

§ 4.

It has been found by experience, that the cement made of lime that had been obtained from a lime-ftone which confifted of pure *calcerous** earth alone, without any proportion of fand, never attained any great degree of hardnefs but remained a foft crumbly mafs, that might be eafily broken down by any fmall force applied to it.

And, on the contrary, if the original lime-ftone contained a very large proportion of fand, the cement made of it alone was a much harder, firmer, and more durable fubftance.

And as it was difcovered, that the pureft lime might be rendered a very firm cement by the addition of a due proportion of clean hard fand, the practice of mixing fand with lime, when intended for mortar, came to prevail very univerfally.—The oldeft lime built walls that are now to be found, clearly fhow that this practice has been adopted before thefe were built.

But

* *Calcerous* is a general term denoting all thofe fubftances that confift of the matter of which lime may be made, in whatever ftate it may be found—whether alone—or mixed with other fubftances, that prevent it from being reduced to powder after calcination.

But it still remains a *desideratum* to ascertain the due proportion of sand; as authors, as well as practical masons, differ very much from one another as to this particular.

They likewise differ very much in their directions about the mode of mixing the materials, and of applying the cement;—some modern authors especially, attributing amazing effects to a small variation in these particulars, while others deny that these circumstances have any sensible effect on the durability or firmness of the cement.

These different and contradictory opinions seem to arise from an imperfect knowledge of the nature of quick-lime, and the variations it may admit of: For, these variations are so very great, as to render it impossible to give any general rules that can possibly apply in all cases. It therefore behoves those who wish to attain any consistency of knowledge on this subject, to endeavour, first, to ascertain the circumstances that render calcareous substances capable of becoming a cement *at all*, and then to trace the several changes that may be produced upon it by other extraneous causes.

This I shall endeavour briefly to do.

§ 5.

Lime-stone and marble are nothing else than a calcareous matter *chrystallized*,* and assume different appearances, according to accidental circumstances that have occurred at the time of their original formation.

1st. The

---

* Saline substances, when dissolved in water, and put into proper circumstances for that purpose, separate from the water, and *shoot* into regular figures, which assume different forms, and are more or less transparent according to the different nature of the salt, as nitre, alum, &c. These regular transparent bodies are properly called *chrystals*.—Hence every body in nature that assumes a form and appearance similar to these, and is produced in the same manner, is said to be *chrystallized*.

1*st*. The more perfect these chrystals are, the *harder*, and more compact, will the stone be that consists of them.

2*d*. The smaller the proportion of extraneous matter that is entangled among these chrystals, the *purer* and finer will the lime be that is made from the stone which consisted of them.

From a variation in one or other of these two particulars, arise all the varieties of calcareous matter that can be converted into lime; which varieties may be distinguished from one another by the following particulars.

1*st*. When the calcareous matter is *pure*, and perfectly chrystallized; when it assumes a clear and somewhat transparent appearance, and is found in regular *strata*, without many fissures, it is then called *marble*.

2*d*. When the calcareous matter, is *pure*, but the chrystallization less perfect, though in regular strata, it still obtains the name of marble; but as it is more opaque, and less compact than the former, it is reckoned less valuable, and coarser.

3*d*. When the calcareous matter is still pretty pure, but hastily concreted into an uniform mass, without having been in a state that permitted it to chrystallize, or to subside into regular strata, it is called *chalk*; which, when reduced to a powder without calcination, is called *whiting*.

4*th*. When the chrystals are tolerably perfect, but have had a considerable proportion of sand entangled among them, it is no longer called marble, but *limestone*. And this is more or less *pure*, or affords a richer or poorer lime, as it contains a greater or smaller proportion of calcareous matter; and is more or less *hard*, according to the degree of perfection of the chrystals.

Even the purest calcareous matter, perfectly chrystallized, is called lime-stone, and not marble, when it consists of small pieces that have not been concreted into regular strata.

5*th*. When

5*th.* When the calcareous matter is perfectly pure, and shot into smaller chrystals, of a transparent whiteness, it is called *sparr*—and, in other circumstances, *stalactites.*

6*th.* When the calcareous matter has been formed by nature as a covering for animals, it is called *shell;* in which class may be included *corals* and *corallines.*

These are all the substances that have hitherto been employed for making lime. The other varieties of calcareous matter, (that I may bring them all under one view, and point out their essential distinctions) are as follow:

7*th.* When the calcareous matter, while in its fluid state, has been absorbed into a bed of clayey matter, and with it concreted into an uniform, compact, unchrystallized mass, it has been denominated *marle;* which is more or less *pure,* according to the proportion of calcareous matter it contains; and more or less *hard,* according to the nature of the clay, and the proportion of sand that may have been mixed with it. And,

8*th.* When *shells,* by the lapse of time, and by long macerating in water, have lost the animal gluten that cemented them, and are crumbled down to a fine whitish powder, they are denominated *shell-marle.*

9*th.* When shells are broken into down small fragments, that are still hard and gritty, it is called *shell-sand.*

It would be a curious disquisition to inquire how these masses of calcareous matter were originally formed?—How they were reduced to a state that rendered them soluble in water, which must have been the case before they could admit of being chrystallized?—What were the circumstances which contributed to render some of these chrystals so much more perfect than others? &c. &c.—But these disquisitions, however curious they might be, are here omitted, as not absolutely necessary for the elucidation of our subject. The explanation of the nature of the different calcareous matters

matters above given, was neceſſary; as, without a knowledge of theſe, it would have been impoſſible to have explained, in a ſatisfactory manner, the way in which theſe ſubſtances are more or leſs fitted to be employed as a cement, or a manure.

To avoid unneceſſary repetitions, the Reader is deſired to obſerve, that for the future, I ſhall mention all matters that can be converted into quick-lime, under the name of *lime-ſtone*, whether they be in the form of marble, chalk, or common lime-ſtone, diſtinguiſhing either of theſe when it may become neceſſary.

§ 6.

Lime-ſtone, in the ſtate we find it, is always a compound ſubſtance.—In its pureſt ſtate, it conſiſts of a calcareous earth, united with a conſiderable proportion of water; for ſaline matters, when chryſtallized, always contain water.

Lime-ſtone likewiſe contains another ſubſtance, the nature of which will be afterwards explained.

When lime-ſtone has been expoſed for a ſufficient length of time to the action of a ſufficiently intenſe fire, the whole of the water it contained is evaporated: So that lime-ſhells are always lighter than the ſtone of which they are made, by the whole weight, at leaſt, of the water the chryſtals contained.

And as perfect chryſtals always contain a much larger proportion of water than thoſe that are leſs perfect, it follows, that of two kinds of lime-ſtone of equal *purity*, that which is hardeſt, and moſt tranſparent, will loſe a greater proportion of its weight in calcination, than that which is ſofter and more opaque.—Hence *marble* loſes more weight by burning than *chalk*.[*]

Again,—

---

[*] Such readers as are totally unacquainted with the circumſtances that are neceſſary to the formation of chryſtals in general, will probably be at a loſs eaſily to comprehend the chain of argumentation followed here, and in ſome other parts of this Eſſay. The following explanation will make it more intelligible: As

Again,—As fand lofes nothing of its weight by calcination, it likewife follows, that in two kinds of limeftone equally firm and well chryftallized, the *pureft,* or that which contains the greateft proportion of calcareous

As faline matters, properly fo called, are more eafily chryftallized by art than any others, it will be beft to take our illuftrations from that clafs of bodies.

It is a property of faline bodies, that they may all be diffolved in water.

They may alfo be feparated from that water, and obtained in a dry form; but they affume very different appearances, according to the nature of the procefs that is followed for feparating them from that water.

If a watery folution of any falt be fuddenly evaporated by means of fire, there remains behind a white fubftance, fometimes flightly coherent, as in pearl-afhes, &c. and fometimes it falls into a powdery calx, as in evaporating a folution of Glauber's falts, alum, &c.

But if the water be gently evaporated by a moderate heat—before it becomes a dry powder, the falt quits the water, and fhoots out into regular figures of a tranfparent glaffy-like appearance, which have obtained the name of chryftals.

Thefe chryftals vary in figure, hardnefs, &c. according to the nature of the falts of which they are compofed.

But they all agree in one refpect, that they contain a confiderable proportion of water united with the faline matter.—Some kinds of falt abforb a very large proportion of water in this way.—Chryftallized Glauber's falts contain two thirds of their weight of water.—Common falt does not contain near fuch a large proportion.

Hence it happens, that no chryftals of any kind of falt can poffibly be formed, unlefs thefe falts have been perfectly diffolved in water.

And the perfection and tranfparency of thefe chryftals depend entirely on their being allowed to fhoot leifurely, in that degree of heat which is beft adapted to the nature of each particular kind of falt.

For it often happens, that water can be made to diffolve a much larger proportion of falt, when it is hot, than when it is cold; fo that if a folution of thefe kinds of falts is continued in a confiderable heat, it will ftill remain fluid, even after it has lefs water than would be neceffary for forming the chryftals.—In which cafe, if it is taken from the fire, and allowed to cool, it fuddenly *concretes* into a folid opaque kind of mafs

between

careous matter, will lose in calcination, the greatest proportion of weight.

From thefe facts it appears, that no rule can be given for afcertaining the proportion of weight *that* lime-ftone lofes by calcination. It muft vary in all poffible degrees, according to circumftances.

§ 7.

Lime-ftone, befides the ingredients abovementioned, contains a confiderable proportion of another fluid, that enters into its compofition, and greatly alters its chemical qualities, to which philofophers have given the name of *fixed air*.* This is alfo difentangled from the ftone, and difperfed, in the act of calcination; as has been demonftrated by the very ingenious Dr. Black, of Edinburgh, to whofe moft fatisfactory Effay on this fubject,

between a chryftal and a calx—as may eafily be experienced, by melting chryftallized Glauber's falt in a fire-fhovel, and allowing it to cool before it is entirely evaporated to drynefs.

The fame circumftances contribute to the formation of calcareous matters into chryftals, and may be eafily applied by the Reader.——Lime is the *calx* produced by evaporating the chryftals to drynefs;—and it only differs from other *faline calces* in this refpect, that *they* always retain the quality of being foluble in water, and may be converted into a liquid mafs, and again chryftallized whenever that is adminiftered to them:—whereas lime lofes that quality in a fhort time; and if it has not been diffolved, and again chryftallized, in that fhort fpace, it muft ever remain unalterably in the ftate it chanced to be in when it loft its faline quality.—Hence it appears in all the different ftages of more or lefs perfect chryftallization, from the moft tranfparent fpar, or marble, to the moft opaque chalk,—from the hardnefs nearly of a flint, to the loofenefs of an almoft incoherent powder.

* Since this Effay was written, a total change has taken place in regard to the names of chemical fubftances—but I do not think it neceffary here to make any change in that refpect, the terms being here all explained as they occur, fo as to prevent ambiguity.

subject, in the Physical and Literary Essays, I refer the curious Reader.

When lime-stone is thus deprived of its *fixed air*, it acquires many of the properties of saline bodies. It is in consequence of this that it then becomes capable of being dissolved in water,—is extremely acrid,—and acts most powerfully on many bodies upon which it has no sensible effect while in the state of lime-stone.

On these accounts, chemists have given it the appellation of *caustic*, when in this state, in contradistinction to its ordinary state before calcination, or after it is again united with its fixed air, when it is said to be in its *mild* state.

Hence, then, the phrase *mild* when applied to calcareous earth, denotes that it is *then* united with its fixed air ; which may be said equally of it before calcination, when it is called lime-stone ; or after calcination, when it is denominated *effete* lime : And *caustic* calcareous earth is a phrase exactly synonymous with *quick-lime*, in its strict and philosophical acceptation ;—that is, calcareous earth perfectly detached, in a chemical sense, from every other substance.

§ 8.

But although it is possible by art to free lime-stone from its water and air, and reduce it to the state of an unmixed acrid saline *calx* ;—yet no art can keep it long in that state, as it has an irresistible propensity to unite itself again to these substances.

If water is poured upon the stone immediately after calcination, which in that state is usually called *lime-shells*, it has been already said, that it pervades every part of the stone ; each particle of the lime seems greedily to seize some portion of the water, with which it instantly and intimately unites. In the act of union, a considerable heat is generated, and in a short time its whole particles are perfectly detached from one another,

other, so as to fall down in the form of a fine, white, and seemingly dry powder, notwithstanding the large quantity of water that is thus united with it.*

If lime-shells be exposed to the influence of the air, without throwing water upon them, they quickly attract moisture from thence, which slowly, and without any sensible heat, flakes the lime-shells, and reduces them to powder.

Still, however, the lime retains its *caustic* quality, even after its partial union with the water: But it as irresistibly, though more slowly, continues to absorb the *air*, as the *water* of which it had been deprived by this calcination, and without intermission, perpetually tends towards that *mild* state which seems to be natural to it.

§ 9.

If water is poured upon flaked lime in large quantities, that water dissolves a certain portion of the saline *calx*, which forms the solution called *lime-water*, that has been much praised as a medicine by physicians.

But the lime has hardly had time to be dissolved by the water, before the calcareous earth absorbs a proportion of its fixed air from the water itself, and the surrounding atmosphere; with which it forcibly unites, and immediately again becomes *mild* calcareous earth, or, if you will, lime-stone. And as it is not *in this state* soluble in water, it immediately separates from it, and forms a thin film of chrystallized lime-stone on the surface of the water.　　　　　　　　　　　　　In

---

* The quantity of water contained in dry flaked lime, is much greater than any one could possibly imagine.—By experiment, I find that *pure* lime *perfectly calcined*, requires *at least* its own weight of water, before it can be reduced to a powder. By the heat generated in the operation, about one tenth of that water is evaporated,—so that the *driest* flaked lime, if pure, consists of about equal parts of calcareous earth and water.—Such as is flaked to the *ordinary degree*, contains a great deal more water than is here mentioned.

In this way, all the lime is in a short time separated from the lime water; and it quickly loses all those qualities for which it was remarkable, becoming pure and simple water again, unless some caustic lime be allowed to remain at the bottom of the vessel, upon which the water may again act, after what it had formerly dissolved had left it.

§ 10.

It is by a process somewhat similar to the former, that calcareous *stalactites* are formed in caverns under the earth, depending from the roof in the form of very large icicles, and other grotesque figures, that afford matter of admiration and astonishment to the curious who visit these subterraneous caverns. It is but seldom that we are able to give such a distinct account of the operations of nature, as in the present case.

These *stalactites* are always formed by water dropping from the roof. This water, in these cases, is always slightly impregnated with caustic calcareous matter, which it meets with in the bowels of the earth, and dissolves.—By what process that calcareous matter is there rendered *caustic*, remains as yet to be explained, and affords a subject well worthy the investigation of the curious.*

This natural lime-water, when it comes to the roof of the cavern, hangs for some time in the form of a drop, till at length so much water is accumulated there, as, by its natural gravity, overcomes the power of cohesion, and makes it fall to the ground. But it is no sooner fallen, than it is again succeeded by another,—and another,—and so on *ad infinitum*.

While

---

* Chemical philosophers have now been enabled to account for this phenomenon by the solvent power of certain *gases*—but it is unnecessary here to enter more at large into that discussion, as it does not affect the explanation in the text.

While these drops remain suspended from the roof, the calcareous matter contained in them greedily attracts the air all around the surface of the drop; and before it falls, a small part of it is reduced to a *mild* state, leaves the water with which it was formerly united, and adheres firmly to the roof; which in time accumulates so much solid matter as to form a sort of nipple depending directly downwards.

After this nipple is formed, each drop, as it descends, flows from its root towards its point, so as to be diffused in a thin stream over its whole surface. In this situation, the water is so much exposed to the action of the air in its descent, that a part of the calcareous matter is rendered *mild*, and is left adhering to the former, so as to increase its diameter towards the root; while a part flows forward to the point, and adds to its strength, in the same manner as it first began to be formed.

In this manner these tangles* continue to increase in size so long as they are suffered to remain,—and as ought to be expected from the above induction, there is always a small hole through the heart of each of them.

The tangles under bridges, and other artificial arches through which water is permitted to percolate, are found exactly in the same manner, though usually they are less perfectly chrystallized.

All sorts of calcareous *spars* owe their origin to a similar cause.

While

---

* It is doubtful, if *tangles*, in the sense here used, is a proper English word; but as it is common in Scotland, and as I know no single English word that is equivalent to it, I have ventured to adopt it. It denotes any kind of pendent concretion, resembling the shape of an icicle, of whatever kind it is formed. Any person who reflects on this subject, will feel what a want it would be in the language, if the word icicle were abolished: the want would hardly be less perceptible, if I were debarred the use of this term.

While these natural *stalactites* are of a small size, they will continue to be regularly formed, and retain the figure of icicles; because the water, as it oozes out, will be sufficient to surround the whole of the nipple, and augment it equally on every side. But, in time, these will become so large, as to cause the water to flow down only on one side, after which the figure will become distorted and irregular. Two or more will sometimes unite into one; and, in the course of ages, an infinite diversity of fantastic forms will gradually be produced which may exhibit, on many occasions, figures of stupendous magnificence.

§ 11.

The operations of nature are so simple, that when we once get a glimpse of the manner in which they are effected in one instance, it is easy to extend our observations, in a satisfactory manner, to others of a similar nature. When we once perceive the manner in which calcareous *stalactites* are formed, it is easy to comprehend the way in which more regular strata of calcareous substances have been produced. The same cavern that produces the one, will always afford examples of the other.

The drop of lime-water that falls from the roof of the cavern, although it has lost some of the calcareous matter with which it was impregnated, still retains a part. When it reaches the ground, it either remains stagnant, so as to form a poole, or flows over a smooth surface. In either of these cases, it will be allowed time to absorb some more of its air; and a part, or the whole, of the calcareous earth will be rendered *mild*, and remain in a firm chrystallized solid cake of marble.

If the stream is considerable, the sheet of calcareous matter may be extended to a great distance, thinly spread over a large declivity, as the water flows in its course, till at last the whole cavity may be filled with a regular stratum of lime-stone or marble. In

In this manner, within the memory of man, have huge rocks of marble been formed near Matlock, in Derbyshire, which furnish matter of astonishment to those numerous travellers who flock to see this uncommon phenomenon. It is seldom that nature's operations are so rapid as in this instance. But there is no room to doubt, that all the strata of calcareous matter in the world, have been formed by a process exactly similar to this.

When the drops are smaller, so as not to be sufficient to form a large stream, but still to flow over a small part of the surface, irregular swelling cakes of lime stone are produced.—When smaller still, they rise up into high prominences, with roundish heads,—sometimes resembling collyflower, and sometimes broccoli-heads.

If a current of air hastily promotes the evaporation of the water, the chrystallization will be less perfect. But enough has already been said to illustrate the subject I have undertaken.

I now return from the operations of Nature, to those of Art.

§ 12.

If flaked lime be exposed to the air for any length of time, in the form of a dry powder, it absorbs the fixed air also in this state, in a short time loses all its qualities as a quick-lime, and, chemically considered, differs in no respect from the stone of which it was composed.

If no more water has been added at flaking than was barely sufficient to make it *fall*, and if it be kept dry ever afterwards, or mixed with any dry powder, it does not harden as it absorbs its air, but remains in a powdery state, to all appearance in no respect differing from *quick-lime*.

But if a larger proportion of water has been added than was necessary for flaking the lime,—in proportion

tion as it abforbs its air, and becomes *mild*, it concretes into a coherent mafs; firft, upon the furface, which quickly becomes covered with a hard cruft, greatly refembling the thin cruft that is formed on the furface of moift earth by a moderate froft. Mafons, ignorant of the real caufe of this phenomenon, call it *frofted* lime; although, their own experience ought to fatisfy them, that this cruft is formed as readily in fummer as in winter.

As lime that has abforbed its air in any of thefe ways, is altogether unfit for becoming a cement, it is evident, that a great change may be produced upon the quality of any lime, by having allowed lefs or more of it to be in this ftate, before it is worked up into mortar.

§ 13.

If a large quantity of water be added to frefh flaked quick-lime, and beat up with it into a thin pafte, the water diffolves a fmall proportion of the lime, which, as it gradually abforbs its air, is converted into chryftals; between the particles of which chryftals, that part of the lime which was not diffolved, and the other extraneous matters that may have been mixed with it, are entangled, fo as to form a firm coherent mafs of the whole.

The pafte formed in this manner, is called *mortar*; and this heterogenous, imperfectly femi-chryftallized mafs, conftitutes the common cement ufed for building ordinary walls.

Thefe circumftances being premifed, it will not be difficult to comprehend what are the particulars that are neceffary to form the moft perfect cement of this fort.

§ 14.

Since lime becomes a cement only in confequence of a certain degree of chryftallization taking place in the whole mafs, it is fufficiently obvious, that the firmnefs
and

and perfection of that cement, must depend upon the perfection of the chrystals, and the hardness of the matters that are entangled among them. For, if the chrystals are ever so perfect and hard of themselves, if they be separated from one another by any brittle incoherent medium, it is evident, that the whole mass must remain in some degree brittle and incoherent.

§ 15.

Water can only dissolve a very small proportion of lime, even when in its most perfect saline state*; and, as happens with all other saline matters, no more of the lime can be reduced to a chrystalline mass, than has been actually dissolved in the water.—Hence it happens, that if mortar be made of pure lime and water alone, a very small proportion of the lime only can be dissolved by that small quantity of water that is added to it: And as this small proportion alone, can be afterwards chrystallized, all the remaining undissolved particles of the lime will be entangled among the few chrystals that are formed.

And as the undissolved lime in this mass will in time absorb its air, and be converted into *mild* calcareous earth without having had a sufficiency of water to allow it to chrystallize, it must concrete into a friable mass, exactly resembling chalk: It follows, that this kind of mortar, when as dry as it can be made, and in its highest degree of perfection, will be always soft, and easily crumbled into powder.

§ 16.

But if, instead of forming the mortar of pure lime alone, a large proportion of sand be added to it, the water

---

* The reader will observe, that I often speak of lime in its *saline* state. I presume, he will easily understand, that, by that phrase, is meant lime while it remains capable of being dissolved in water:—that is, as long as it remains deprived of its fixed air;—or, in other words, while in its *caustic* state.

water will, in this case, dissolve as much of the lime as in the former, and the particles of hard sand, like sticks or threads, when making sugar-candy or other chrystals, while surrounded by the watery solution, will help to forward the chrystallization, and render it more perfect than it otherwise would have been, so as firmly to cement the particles of sand to one another.

And as the granules of sand are perfectly hard of themselves, so as not to admit of being broken down like the particles of chalk, it necessarily follows, that the cement made of these materials must be much more perfect, in every respect, than the former.

§ 17.

That the reader may see the full force of the above reasoning, it is necessary he should be informed, that when calcareous matter is reduced to a caustic calx, it becomes, in every sense of the word, a perfect saline substance, and is in this state as entirely soluble in water as common salt or sugar; although with this difference, that lime can be suspended by water only in a much smaller proportion. Water can dissolve one third of its weight of common salt, and keep it suspended in a fluid state; but it can hardly dissolve one thousandth part of quick-lime before it is saturated*.

But

---

* The term *saturation* is employed to denote that state of a fluid, when it has dissolved as much of a solid body as it can possibly suspend in it at one time.

When any saline substance is put into water, it is dissolved by the water, and suspended in it till it attains what is called the point of saturation;—after which, if ever so much salt be added, not one particle more will be dissolved,—but it will remain at the bottom in its original solid state.

Water dissolves very different proportions of different salts before it is saturated. It will dissolve its own weight of Glauber's salt, one-third of its weight of common salt, and not one-thousandth of its weight of lime.

Hence it may very readily happen, that although any particular salt could be wholly dissolved in water, a part of the

salt

But although lime be as entirely soluble in water *when in its caustic state*, as any other purely saline substance, it so quickly absorbs its air, as to have some part of it rendered *mild*, before it can be wholly dissolved on any occasion, in which state water cannot act upon it; so that to obtain a total solution, that proportion of it that becomes mild, requires to be again and again calcined, after fresh solutions have been drawn from it.

As such a large proportion of water is necessary to dissolve any quantity of lime, it seldom happens, even in making lime water, but that more lime is added than is sufficient to saturate the whole of the water: In which case, some of it still remains at the bottom; in a condition capable of being dissolved, if more water be added to it.

But lime, it has been already said, differs from purely saline substances, in this respect: that it cannot possibly be long suspended in water; for it soon absorbs its air even from that element, and is thus reduced to a mild state, when it immediately chrystallizes, and separates from the water.* In

salt may remain untouched, if too much has been added. Thus, if one ounce of lime is put into ten ounces of water, that water will become saturated before it shall have dissolved one-third of the quick-lime, and the remainder will remain in a solid state, untouched.

* Although purely saline substances, *in every state*, continue to be soluble in water, yet many of them become more or less so, in proportion to the quantity of air that is united with them at the time; and *in so far* resemble lime in this particular, that they are more easily dissolved when deprived of their air, than when united with it.

Alkaline† salts, strictly so called, like lime, may be either in a *caustic* or *mild* state; which appellations they in like manner obtain when they are deprived of their air, or united with it. When

† The term *alkali* is employed to denote a certain class of saline bodies, whose certain distinguishing characteristic is, that they may be united with acids, and with them form *neutral* salts, as nitre, common salt, &c..

In consequence of this peculiarity, it necessarily happens, that in proportion as these chrystals separate from lime-water, a part of it becomes pure water again, and is instantly capable of dissolving as much caustic

When these salts are in a *caustic* state, they are soluble in water *in any proportion*. They have even such a tendency to unite with it when in this state, that it is extremely difficult, if not altogether impossible, to free them from the water till they are reduced to a mild state. No art has ever yet been discovered, by which a caustic volatile alkali could be exhibited in a solid form; and although dry concretions of the fixed alkali are sometimes obtained while it is possessed of a certain degree of *causticity*, yet these concretions are only obtained in consequence of some part of it becoming mild in the operation: nor can they be kept in that state without the utmost care.

Ordinary pot-ash is an alkaline salt, obtained from the ashes of burnt vegetables. This is, in some measure deprived of its air in burning the plant; but during the process, before the watery solution is thoroughly evaporated to dryness, the alkali has absorbed some part of its air, and is in some measure rendered mild, so as to admit of being reduced to a dry state by the force of fire. But as the salt is not in this state *perfectly* mild, the caustic part of the alkali attracts the moisture from the air with so much power as soon to obtain enough to reduce the whole to a watery solution, if it is not preserved from damp air with the utmost care.

This, and every other saline substance, which attracts moisture from the air, and dissolves in it, is called a *deliquescent* salt.

But if this alkali be exposed to the air for a sufficient length of time, till it has slowly absorbed its whole proportion of fixed air, and with it has become one chemical mixt, forming a *perfectly* mild alkali, it is then capable of being dissolved in water, *only in one certain proportion*, like other salts; and may be made to shoot into regular chrystals, which may be kept in a solid dry state, when the atmosphere is in a due temperature of heat, in the same manner as any other salt.

In this case, the alkali, it is plain, leaves the water as soon as it has united with its air, in the same manner as lime separates from water, and assumes a dry chrystalline form. The alkali may, indeed, be again dissolved, by adding a larger proportion of water, which the other cannot; but, in the first particular, the parallel is alike.

Common

caustic lime as it had lost by the former chrystallization; so that it immediately acts upon, and dissolves another portion of the quick-lime that remained below after the water was saturated. This portion of lime is also chrystallized in its turn, and a fresh solution takes place; and so on, it continues constantly chrystallizing

Common salt is, in like manner, in part decomposed* by the violent heat that takes place in our ordinary way of boiling it. A part of its acid is dissipated; the alkali that remains, is left in its *caustic* state. Hence it has a perpetual tendency to absorb water; in consequence of which, the whole becomes a deliquescent salt. If the evaporation is made slowly enough, the chrystals are more perfect; and it may be easily kept dry in the ordinary state of our atmosphere.— This is the reason why great salt may be more easily kept dry than small salt.

If, however, the alkali that is mixed with the salt had not been in a caustic state, it is well known it would not have *deliquesced*; for the *natrum* of the Ancients, or the *fossil alkali* of the Moderns, in its native *mild* state, is a firm chrystalline salt, much resembling nitre, from whence it originally derives its name.

Exactly similar to these are the changes produced upon common sugar, by the different processes it may be made to undergo. Sugar is a solid concrete, obtained by evaporating to dryness the juice of the sugar cane. In the ordinary process for obtaining that substance, it is deprived of some part of its fixed air,—and is hastily concreted into an imperfect sort of chrystalline mass. In this state, it is possessed of a certain degree of acrid causticity, and can be dissolved in water in any proportion from the slightest degree of impregnation to perfect dryness.—But when it is placed in proper circumstances, and is allowed time to absorb its air,—like the other substances above mentioned, it can only be dissolved in certain proportions; and therefore quits the water as it gradually unites with its air, and assumes a regular chrystalline form.

These chrystals are distinguished by the name of *sugar-candy*, and are well known to be more difficultly soluble in water,— to be a milder and less acrid sweet,—and to possess many other qualities different from the sugar of which they were originally formed.

* Common salt is a compound substance, formed by the union of a particular acid with the *fossil alkali*.

chryftallizing and diffolving anew, as long as any cauftic lime remains in the water to be diffolved.

It is in confequence of this conftant action of the water and air, that lime-water always continues of an equal degree of ftrength, fo long as any cauftic lime remains in the veffel for the water to act upon, notwithftanding the large proportions of calcareous chryftals that are continually feparating from it.

§ 18.

From the foregoing induction, it appears, that when a large quantity of fand is mixed in the mortar, that fand will bear a great proportion to the whole mafs; fo that the water that may be mixed with the mortar will be much greater in proportion to the quantity of lime contained in this mortar, than if the whole had confifted of pure calcareous matter.—And as the fand abforbs none of that water, after a part of the lime is chryftallized, and feparated from the water, that water, now pure, is left at liberty to act once more upon thofe few particles of cauftic lime that may ftill remain in the mortar, which will be diffolved and converted into chryftals in their turn.

In this manner, it may happen, in fome circumftances, that a very large proportion of the lime may become chryftallized; fo that the mortar fhall confift almoft entirely of fand enveloped in chryftalline matter, and become, in due time, as hard as ftone itfelf; whereas mortar, confifting of pure lime, without fand, can hardly ever be much harder than chalk.

§ 19.

It is not, however, to be expected, that in any cafe, this dried mortar will affume that tranfparent chryftalline form, or the compact firmnefs of marble, or limeftone.—In mortar, in fpite of the utmoft care that can ever be taken, a very confiderable quantity of the lime muft must remain undissolved ; which undissolved lime, although it may be so much separated by the sand and chrystallized lime-stone, as not much to affect the hardness of the mortar, yet it must still retain its white chalky-like appearance.

But, as marble and lime-stone, are always formed by those particles of lime that have been wholly dissolved in water, and from which, they have been gradually separated by a more slow and more perfect mode of chrystallization, they have nothing of that opaque *calx*-like appearance, but assume other colours, and appear more firm, uniform, and compact ; the sand, and other matters that may be enveloped in them, being entirely surrounded with a pure chrystallized matter.

§ 20.

To obtain the most perfect kind of mortar, however, it is not enough that a large proportion of sand should be employed, and that the sand should be intimately mixed with the lime. It is also of the utmost importance, that a large proportion of water be added: For, without this, it is impossible that a large proportion of the lime can be chrystallized ; and the mortar, in that case, would consist only of a mixture of chalky matter and sand, which could hardly be made to unite all—would be little more coherent than sand by itself, and less so than pure chalk. In that case, pure lime alone would afford rather a firmer cement than lime with sand.

§ 21.

It is also of very great importance, that the water be retained as long in the mortar as possible : For, if it be suddenly evaporated, it will not only be prevented from acting a second time upon the lime, after a part of what was first dissolved has been chrystallized, but even the few chrystals that would be formed when the water was suddenly evaporating, would be of themselves,

selves, much more imperfect than they otherwife moft certainly would have been.

Common falt, which confifts of chryftals haftily formed by a fudden evaporation of fea-water by means of fire, has the appearance of a dry whitifh calx, that may be eafily broken to pieces:—The fame falt, when flowly chryftallized by a gentle evaporation in the fhade, confifts of large cubical chryftals, as tranfparent, and little fofter, than crown-glafs.

Ordinary lump fugar, it has been faid, likewife confifts of another fubftance haftily concreted by a fudden evaporation of the fluid in which it was diffolved:— Sugar-candy, is the fame fubftance, flowly chryftallized by a more moderate evaporation. Every one knows, what a difference there is between the firmnefs of thefe two fubftances. As great muft be the difference between the firmnefs of that cement which has been flowly dried, and that which has been haftily hardened by the powerful action of a warm air.

It is owing to this circumftance, that the lime which remains all winter in a mortar-tub filled with water, is always found to be much firmer, and more coherent than the mortar that was taken from the fame tub, and ufed in any work of mafonry; although, in this cafe, the materials were exactly the fame. From the fame caufe, any work cemented with lime under water, if it has been allowed to remain unhurt till it has once become hard, is always much firmer than that which is above the furface of the water.

§ 22.

To make the reader comprehend the full force of the foregoing reafoning, I would compare lime-cement, or mortar, to a mafs of matter confifting of a congeries of ftones clofely compacted together, and united by a ftrong cementing matter, that had, while in a fluid ftate, pervaded all the interftices between the ftones, and had afterwards become a folid indiffoluble fubftance. If

If the cementing matter be exceedingly hard and coherent, and if the stones bedded among it are also very hard and firm, the whole mass will become like a solid rock, without fissures, that can hardly be broken to pieces by the power of man.

But although the cement should be equally firm, if the stone of which it consists be of a soft and friable nature, suppose chalk or sand-stone, the whole mass will never be capable of attaining such a degree of firmness as in the former case; for, when any force is applied to break it in pieces, although the cement should keep its hold, the solid matter cemented by it would give way, and the whole would be easily broke to pieces.

Now—in mortar, the sand that is added to it represents the stones of a solid matter in the composition, the particles of which are united together by the lime that had been formerly dissolved, and now chrystallized, which becomes an exceedingly solid and indissoluble concretion.

And as the particles of sand are of themselves exceedingly hard, and the cement by which they are united equally so, it is plain, that the whole concretion must become extremely firm, so as to require a very great force to disunite any particle of it from the whole mass.

But if, instead of employing sand, the only solid body that is entangled among the cementing matter should be chalk (which, as has been said, must always be the case when the mortar consists of pure lime alone) or any other slightly coherent substance, let the cementing particles of that composition be ever so perfect, it is impossible that the whole can ever attain a great degree of firmness; as these chalky matters will be easily broken asunder.

§ 23.

Many conjectures have been made about the nature of the lime-cement employed by the Ancients. It has been

been thought they poffeffed an art of making mortar, that has been long fince entirely loft ; as the cement in the walls that have been built by them, appears to be, in many cafes, much firmer than that which has been made in modern times.—Yet, when the mortar of thefe old buildings is analized, it is found to confift of the fame materials, and nearly in the fame proportions, which we now employ.

It is probable, however, that their only fecret confifted in mixing the materials more perfectly than the rapidity or avarice of modern builders will permit ; in employing their mortar in a much more fluid ftate than we do now ; and in allowing it to dry more flowly, which the immoderate thicknefs of many of their walls would naturally produce, without any preconcerted defign on their part.

Tradition has even handed down to our times the memory of the moft effential of thefe particulars ; as the lower clafs of people, in every part of the country, at this moment, invariably believe that thefe old walls were compofed of a mortar fo very thin, as to admit of its being poured, like a fluid, between the ftones, after they were laid in the wall. And the appearance of thefe old walls, when taken down, feems to favour this popular tradition.

Nor have I any doubt but this may have been actually the cafe. The ftones in the outer part of the wall were probably bedded in mortar, nearly as we practife at prefent ; and the heart, after being packed well with irregular ftones, might have the interftices between them entirely filled up with fluid mortar, which would infinuate itfelf into every cranny, and in time adhere as firmly as the ftones themfelves, or even more fo, if the ftones were of a fandy friable nature.

As thefe walls were ufually of very great thicknefs, it might often happen that the water in this mortar, by acting fucceffively upon different particles of caufticlime, would at length be entirely abforbed by fucceffive

five chryſtallizations, ſo as to become perfectly dry, without any evaporation at all; in which caſe, a very large proportion of the original lime muſt have been regularly chryſtallized in a ſlow and tolerably perfect manner, ſo as to attain a firmneſs little inferior to lime-ſtone or marble itſelf.

Upon theſe principles, it is eaſy to account for the ſuperior hardneſs of ſome old cement, when compared with that of modern times, in which a practice very different is uſually followed, without having recourſe to any wonderful *arcana* whatever.

§ 24.

A modern French author, *Monſieur Loriot*, after meditating much upon this ſubject, imagines, he has made a perfect diſcovery of the way in which the Ancients employed their quick-lime, ſo as to obtain ſuch an extraordinary firm cement; from which diſcovery, he thinks very important benefits may be derived to ſociety.

According to his opinion, the ancient cement conſiſted of lime and ſand, nearly in the ſame proportions as are commonly employed, for that purpoſe at preſent. But inſtead of making it of flaked lime entirely, as we do now, he ſays they employed a certain proportion of their lime *unflaked*, which they mixed with their mortar immediately before it was uſed.

This compoſition, he ſays, forms a firm and durable cement, poſſeſſing ſo many valuable properties, that I chooſe to give them in words of his own panegyriſt:

"In the courſe of the 1770,*" ſays he,† "Monſieur Loriot

* It deſerves to be noted, that about the ſame period, Mr. Doſſie, ſecretary to the Society of Agriculture and Arts, in the Strand, London, publiſhed a receipt for making mortar, in imitation of that of the Ancients, which was in every reſpect the ſame with this of Monſieur Loriot.—Which of theſe was the original diſcoverer, let the parties themſelves determine.

† Theſe extracts are taken from a Treatiſe, entitled, *A Practical*

Loriot had the happiness to discover a kind of mystery in Nature, which for several ages past, had not, it is most probable, manifested itself to any body but himself;—a mystery on which all the merit of his discovery is founded.

" Taking some lime which had been a long time slaked, out of a pit covered with boards, and a considerable quantity of earth over them again, by which means the lime had preserved all its original freshness, he made two parts of it, and plashed and beat them both perfectly well.

" He then put one of these parts, without any addition, into a glazed earthen pot, and in that condition set it to dry of itself in the shade. Here, in proportion as it lost its moisture by evaporation, it cracked and split in every direction; parted from the sides of the pot, and crumbled into a thousand pieces, all of them equally friable with the bits of lime dried up with the sun, which we usually meet on the banks of our lime-pits.* " With

Practical Essay on Cement and Artificial Stone, justly supposed to be that of the Greeks and Romans, lately rediscovered by Monsieur Loriot, Master of Mechanics to his Most Christian Majesty, &c. Translated from the French Original, lately published by the express order of the above Monarch. London, Cadel, 1775.—It appears to have been written not by M. Loriot himself, but some of his friends, as he is always mentioned in the third person.

* It is impossible, in reading this Essay, not to remark the extreme ignorance or inaccuracy of the compiler of it, on many occasions. The present paragraph affords a proof of it. There can be no doubt, but that lime, if it has been *very long flaked*, will lose all its qualities as a *quick-lime*, and become perfectly *effette*, let it be ever so carefully covered.—He gives no other test of the lime being still possessed of its caustic quality, but that it was covered.—For ought that appears, it might have been entirely *effette*-lime; in which case, it is not at all surprising if it should not be capable of being converted into a cement of any kind.—Indeed the effects he describes, could only arise from its having been actually in this state: For, there is no man, who does not know, that lime which has been some time flaked, may, on many occasions, be employed,

"With regard to the other part, Monſieur Loriot, juſt added to it one-third of its quantity of powdered quick-lime, and then had the whole well kneaded, in order to make the two kinds of lime perfectly incorporate with each other. This done, he put this mixture likewiſe into a glazed earthen pot, as he had done the firſt; when, behold, it ſoon began to heat, and, in the ſpace of a few minutes, acquired a degree of conſiſtence equal to the beſt plaſter, when prepared in the beſt manner. In ſhort, it ſet and conſolidated as readily as metals in fuſion when taken from the fire, and turned out a kind of inſtantaneous lapidification, having dried completely within a very ſmall ſpace of time, and that too without the leaſt crack or flaw; nay, it adhered ſo ſtrongly to the ſides of the pot, as not to be parted from them without breaking it."

As to this paſſage, I ſhall only ſay, that I repeated the above experiment ſeveral times, with all the accuracy I was capable of; with this only difference, that I employed lime that had lain a conſidrable time beat up with water, as is uſual, to allow it to *ſour*, in the common language of maſons, inſtead of lime that had been long covered up in a pit, like that which he employed.

The reſult was, what any man who beſtows a moderate degree of attention to the ſubject, and the experience of maſons, might have expected,—but extremely different from that of Monſieur Loriot.

The paſte made of the old ſlaked lime alone, dried ſlowly,—became in time a maſs ſlightly coherent, ſomewhat harder than chalk, it having been very pure lime I employed, without ſand or any other addition.

That which was made with the ſame ſlaked lime, with one-third of its quantity of unſlaked lime reduced to powder, kneaded through it, did indeed heat, as is uſual

ployed as a cement, which, at leaſt, is capable of adhering together, and not falling down at once into a looſe powder as it dries.

ufual in all cafes when the lime is flaked,—fwelled up, as is alfo ufual;—but acquired no degree of hardnefs greater than the other, nor differed in any refpect from it, excepting that it abforbed the water more quickly; and in a day or fo after it was kneaded up, when it became pretty dry, fome particles of lime-ftone, which had not been burnt fo perfectly as the reft, and were therefore longer of flaking, began to heave up afrefh, having lain till this time unflaked.

On this account, although it muft only be confidered as an accidental misfortune that will not always happen, it was evidently a much worfe cement than the other.

Such is the fact. Nor is it eafy to fee a reafon why any beneficial confequences fhould refult from the practice recommended.—It is well known, that if water be added to burnt lime-ftone *in any way*, the firft effect is, that it heats, fwells, and falls down to a powder.—Even under the water, the effect is the fame. After that powder is formed, it may, by remaining under water, concrete into a folid mafs; but with whatever fubftances it is mixed, it muft firft feparate before it unites. In the name of common fenfe, then, where can be the difference in firft reducing it to that powdery ftate, and then beating it up with the water; or in pouring the water that is neceffary to reduce it to powder upon it, and allowing that powder to remain as it may fall, without being beat up with the materials?—Some of the watery particles will at firft be abforbed, which is evidently a lofs to the mortar; and the lime will be far lefs intimately mixed with the other ingredients, than if it had been properly blended and beat up with them after it was in its fmalleft powdery ftate; which muft tend to render the mortar ftill lefs perfect.

Monfieur Loriot's panegyrift, however, is at no lofs to produce reafons for thefe wonderful effects, that feem to him to be entirely fatisfactory. He thus proceeds: " The

" The result of this addition of the quick-lime, surprising as at first sight it might seem, is, notwithstanding, so easily explained and accounted for, that it seems somewhat strange that Monsieur Loriot should be the first to suspect and discover it. In fact, what can be plainer than that the sudden setting and consolidating of these two substances must necessarily arise from the quick-lime's being carried, by a perfect amalgamation, or admixture, into the inmost recesses of the slaked lime, saturating itself with the moisture it there meets with, and thereby effecting that instantaneous and absolute desiccation*, which, because we are so well accustomed to it, we so little mind in the use of gypses or plaster?"

If I understand this paragraph, it means neither more nor less than that these two substances unite, because they necessarily do unite most perfectly. If it has any other meaning, I am dull enough not to perceive it.

It

---

* Any one who has bestowed a moderate degree of attention to the operation of slaking lime, as it is usually performed, must have observed many instances of that sort of sudden desiccation,—but without perceiving any of the other effects her mentioned.

In slaking lime-stones, especially when of the purest sort, so much water is necessary, and it is imbibed so slowly, that the operators, knowing it will be all drunk up in due time, often to throw so much on one place at once, as to reduce it to almost a fluid state.—This water soon sinks through it to the unslaked lime below.—But if the lime on the top was regularly slaked before the last effusion of water, it retains a smooth uniform surface, like plaster, is dried almost entirely in a few minutes,—and, if not broke by the swelling of the lime below, continues ever afterwards to retain that form without crumbling away at all. If this is allowed to dry perfectly, and no more water is poured on it, till it has absorbed all its air, it is perfect chalk. It has the same hardness, consistency, &c. and cannot be distinguished from it, either in appearance or by any other property.

This, however, will never be the case, unless the lime has been perfectly pure, so as to dissolve in acids as entirely as sugar does in water.

It would be tiresome to quote more passages from this Treatise. Let it suffice to observe, that the author proceeds to tell, that this newly discovered cement dries and hardens almost under the hand of the operator, without cracks or flaws of any sort;* that it neither expands nor contracts with the air;†—that it is impervious to moisture,‡—and may not only be employed for making roofs to houses that are subjected to the continual dropping of water,§ basons, acqueducts, canals,‖ &c. that will instantly contain water in any quantities, but even finer works of the pottery kind:¶ that it perfectly resists frosts; with a long *et cœtera* of other qualities which it would be tiresome to enumerate; for an account of which I must refer to the pamphlet itself.

That Monsieur Loriot has not discovered a cement possessing these peculiar qualities, it would be unbecoming in me to say; seeing *it is affirmed*, that works have been erected with it that prove the facts in the clearest manner. But that such effects will be invariably produced, merely by adding a certain proportion of unslaked lime in powder to mortar, as he asserts, or even by making the mortar entirely with powdered quick-lime, I may without hesitation venture to deny, not only from the reasoning above given, but from actual experiment again and again repeated by myself; which is likewise in some measure corroborated by the experience of Mr. Dossie.*

For

---

*P. 31. †P. 32. ‡Ibid. §P. 44. ‖P. 44, 45, 46. ¶P. 52.

* Although Mr. Dossie recommends his new discovered cement for many qualities, yet he differs extremely from M. Loriot in his account of the manner in which the union is effected: For, instead of saying that 'it consolidates as readily as metals in fusion when newly taken from the fire,' he says, 'it continues soft for some time, and only gradually hardens in the air.' See Dossie's Mem. of Agriculture, vol. II. p. 20.

Mr. Dossie

For thefe reafons, I am induced to think, that if Monfieur Loriot has really experienced thefe uncommon effects from the mortar he has tried, it muft have been occafioned by fome other unobferved peculiarity, and not merely by the circumftance to which he feems to afcribe it. Poffibly it may have been impregnated with *gypfum*,* a faline fubftance, naturally abounding in France; and as one of its principal ingredients is lime-ftone, there is nothing extraordinary in its being found in the fame quarry chryftallized along with the lime-ftone, nor any impoffibility of its efcaping undecompofed, on fome occafions, during the calcination of the lime. Or it may perhaps have been otherwife accidentally mixed with the lime in thefe experiments.

But in whatever way the *gypfum* may come there, if it be prefent, it is not to be doubted but effects fimilar in kind (though not in degree) to what M. Loriot defcribes, would, in fome meafure, refult from the practice he recommends: For, if *gypfum* be deprived of its moifture by calcination, it becomes a fine powder, greatly refembling the pureft lime, which coagulates, if I may ufe that phrafe, immediately upon the addition of water, and acquires at once all the firmnefs that it ever can be made to attain.

Thefe properties of *gypfum* have been long well enough known; but it never acquires the ftony hardnefs that lime-cement is fometimes endowed with, although

Mr. Doffie does indeed afcribe to his cement fome of the fame qualities that M. Loriot attributes to his.—Some of thefe, however, are common to every fort of lime-mortar, when carefully made; and were it not a little foreign from our fubject, it would be no difficult matter to fhow in what manner an inexperienced perfon might have his judgment mifled with regard to fome of the other qualities that may be called more equivocal.—The imagination is a more powerful magician than all the wife men of Egypt!

* *Gypfum* is an earthly falt, confifting of the vitriolic acid and calcareous earth.—It is beft known among artizans in this country, by the name of *Plafter of Paris*.

though it takes the smoothest polish of any cement we know : on which account, it has long been employed as a plaster where fine ornaments are required.

I have bestowed more attention on this performance of M. Loriot than my own opinion of its importance would have exacted from me ; and it is purely in deference to the opinion of others that I have endeavoured to account for some of those *phænomena* he describes, supposing they have really happened. The inaccurate and unscientific manner in which that pamphlet is written, makes it afford the philosophic reader but very little satisfaction ; and that affectation of the marvellous which runs through the whole, and the many hyperbolic compliments paid to M. Loriot with which it abounds, are but ill calculated for giving the reader a favourable opinion of the intention of the compiler. Future experiments will bring to light those circumstances which seem to be at present doubtful and mysterious.—I now proceed to point out some other circumstances, that may influence the quality of lime-mortar.

§ 25.

If lime-stone be sufficiently calcined, it is deprived of all its moisture, and of *all* its fixed air. But experience shows, that lime-stone will fall to a powder on the effusion of water upon it, when it is much less perfectly calcined, and while it still retains almost the whole of its fixed air. And as masons have hardly any other rule for judging whether lime-stone be sufficiently calcined, except this single circumstance of its falling to a powder when water is poured upon it, we may thus easily perceive, that the same lime may be more or less fitted for making good mortar, according to a circumstance that, in a great measure, eludes the observation of operative masons : For, if it should happen that all the lime-shells drawn from a kiln at one time, were just sufficiently calcined to make it fall to

a powder

a powder with water, and no more, that powder would be altogether unfit for making mortar of any kind.

This is a case that can seldom happen.—But as there are a great many intermediate degrees between that state and perfect calcination, it must often happen that the stone will approach nearer to one of these extremes at one time, than at another, so that mortar may be much more perfect at one time than at another; owing to a variation as to this particular.

§ 26.

Every author who has written on the subject of lime as a cement, has endeavoured to ascertain what is the due proportion of sand for making the most perfect cement. But a litle attention to the subject will show, that all rules that could be prescribed as to this particular, must be so vague and uncertain, as to be of little use to the practical mason. For,

Besides the variation that may arise from a more or less perfect degree of calcination, and which has just now been taken notice of, it is a certain fact, that some kinds of lime-stone are much more pure and contain a much smaller proportion of sand, than others do.

I have examined lime-stone that was so perfectly free from any mixture of sand whatever, as to dissolve in acids as entirely as sugar does among water: I have also tried another kind that contained eleven-twelfths of its whole weight of sand, and only one-twelfth part of lime; and have met with other sorts in all the intermediate proportions between these two extremes.

Now it would surely be absurd to say, that the pure lime would require as small a proportion of sand when made into mortar, as that which originally contained in itself a much larger proportion of sand than any writer on the subject has ever ventured to prescribe for being put into mortar.

What adds to this uncertainty is, the variation that may arise from the circumstance last mentioned, *viz.* the greater or less perfect degree of calcination that the stone may have undergone. For it ought to be remarked, that although lime-stone, when pure, requires a very intense degree of heat to convert it into a *vitrified** mass; yet when sand is mixed with the lime-stone in certain proportions, a very moderate heat is sufficient to convert the whole mass into vitrified *scoriæ*, or in the common language of the country, make it *run into danders*.

From this circumstance, it happens, that those who are possessed of a very impure lime-stone, are obliged to be extremely cautious not to give it an over proportion of fuel, lest it should vitrify the stone; and they are very happy if they can get their stone calcined just enough to make it fall with water, and no more; so that, in general, it may be presumed, that a very large proportion of *such* lime is *never* so sufficiently burnt as to be reduced to a perfectly caustic state, or to be capable of forming a cement.

But as there is no danger at any time of giving *pure* lime-stone too much fire, those who possess such a lime-stone are not under the necessity of being afraid of erring on that side: And as it is a loss to them if the whole does not fall after it is drawn from the kiln, it is natural to think they will in general give it a full proportion of fuel. From hence it may be reasonably concluded, that, in general, a much larger proportion of this kind of stone will be perfectly calcined, than of the other sort.

At a venture, we may with some show of probability, conclude, that about one-tenth of *pure* lime-stone is not enough calcined to admit of being made into mortar; and that, of the most impure sorts of lime-stone,

---

* A *vitrified* substance is one that has been melted by heat, and assumes somewhat of a glass-like appearance.

ſtone, not above one-fourth part of the lime contained in it is ſo much calcined as to be in a cauſtic ſtate.

Let us ſee what variation this ought to produce as to the proportion of ſand that might be added to the lime in the one or the other caſe : and, that the calculation may be more eaſily made, we ſhall ſuppoſe that the pooreſt lime-ſtone that is ever burnt, contains one-tenth of its whole weight of lime.

Ten parts of pure lime, before it could be reduced to the ſame degree of ſandineſs with the other, without conſidering the variation that ariſes from the burning, would require each of them nine parts of ſand to be added : Therefore, ninety parts of ſand ſhould be added to the ten, to reduce them to an equality with the other lime in its native ſtate.

But if we are likewiſe to take into the account the variation above ſuppoſed, that ariſes from their different degrees of calcination, the account will ſtand thus:

Of the ten parts of pure lime, one is ſuppoſed to be not enough burnt to be capable of acting as a cement ; ſo that there remains nine only in a perfectly cauſtic ſtate.

Of the ten parts of impure lime, nine are ſand, and only one is lime ;—and from this one is to be deduced three-fourths as not enough calcined. Hence there remains juſt one-fourth of one tenth-part (one-fortieth) of pure cauſtic lime.

But this fortieth part of the whole is united to thirty-nine other equal parts of ſand and uncalcined lime-ſtone.

There remained nine whole tenth parts of the pure lime in a cauſtic ſtate ; to each of which muſt be added thirty-nine tenths, including the one-tenth of uncalcined lime ;—ſo that to reduce it to the ſame ſtate with the former, there would need to be three hundred and fifty parts of ſand added.

It ſeems to be altogether inconceivable, that ſuch a ſmall proportion of calcareous matter could ever become

come sufficient to cement firmly together such a prodigious mass of other matters: Nor do I pretend to say, that this could actually be the case, as there may be some error in the *data*. The following, however, I know to be a fact:

The best modern mortar I ever saw, was made of lime, that I myself had analyfed, and found it contained eleven parts of sand to one of lime. To this there was added between twice and thrice its whole bulk of sand *by measure;* which may be allowed to have been at least three times its quantity *by weight*.

Now, supposing that every particle of that lime had been so perfectly calcined as to be in a caustic state, there could not be less than forty-seven parts of sand to one of lime. The reader may allow what he pleases for the uncaustic part of the lime, and make his calculation accordingly. But it is hardly possible to suppose, that above one-hundredth part of this mass, independent of the water, consisted of pure caustic calcareous earth.

But, whatever was the exact proportion of caustic lime, the mortar was made of these materials in the proportions expressed, and was employed for pinning the outside joints of the stone-walls of a house situated in a tempestuous climate, and exposed to every blast. It is now about fourteen years since it was finished; and I do not believe there has fallen to the ground, in all that time, one pound weight of the mortar.*

Had this mortar been employed in building a thick wall, where it would have been suffered to dry slow enough, there seems to be little reason to doubt but it would in time have become as firm as the stones of the wall itself.

From these considerations we may clearly see, that it is impossible to prescribe any determinate proportion of

---

* After seven years longer trial, the mortar still proves good and firm, and exhibits no appearance of ever falling.

of sand to lime, as that must vary according to the nature of the lime, and other incidental circumstances, which it would be tiresome to enumerate, and which would form an infinity of exceptions to any general rule.

But it would seem we might safely infer, that the moderns in general, rather err in giving too little sand, than in giving too much.

It deserves, however, to be remarked, that the sand, when naturally in the lime-stone, is more intimately blended with the lime, than can possibly be ever effected by any mechanical operation;—so that it would be in vain to hope to make good mortar artificially from pure lime, with such a small proportion of caustic calcareous matter as may sometimes be effected when the lime naturally contains a very large proportion of sand. But, there seems to be no doubt, that if a much larger proportion of sand were employed, and if that were more carefully blended and expeditiously worked than is common, the mortar would be much more perfect than usual in modern times.

This I have tried experimentally, with the desired success.

§ 27.

Another circumstance that tends greatly to vary the quality of the cement, and to make a greater or smaller proportion of sand necessary, is the mode of preparing lime before it is beaten up into mortar.

When lime is to be employed for making plaster, it is of great importance that every particle of the lime-stone be slaked before it is worked up: For, as the smoothness of the surface is the circumstance most wished for in plaster, if any particles of lime should be beaten up in it, and employed in work before they had had sufficient time to *fall*, the water still continuing to act upon them after it was worked up, would infallibly *slake* these particles, which would then expand them-

selves

selves with great force; and produce those excrescences upon the surface of the plaster, that are commonly known by the name of *blisters*.

Hence, therefore, if we hope to obtain a perfect kind of plaster, that shall remain smooth on the surface, and free of blisters, there is an absolute necessity to allow the lime to lie for a considerable time macerating in water before it is worked up.

This operation is called in this country, *souring*.

If the lime-stone be pure, and has been very perfectly calcined, there will be little danger but that the whole of the lime will fall at first: But if it has been less perfectly burnt, there will be many particles that will require to lie a long time before they will be reduced to powder. This operation is therefore more necessary with impure than pure lime; but it ought on no occasion to be omitted, as there is not the smallest probability but *some* blisters would appear on plaster made even of the *purest* lime, if worked up and used immediately after it has been flaked.

It is also a common practice to *sour* the lime when it is intended to be used in *mortar*. And although it is not so indispensably necessary in this case as when it is intended for plaster, yet, if properly performed, it is evident, that it must, even here, be of use; as any dry knots that may fall after the mortar is used, must tend to disunite the parts of it that had been already united, and render the cement much less perfect than if the whole had been properly mixed up with the materials before using.

But more circumspection is requisite in souring lime for mortar, than for plaster. For,

As it is not necessary that plaster should be endowed with a stony degree of hardness, there is no loss sustained by allowing a great proportion of the lime that is intended for that purpose, to absorb its air before it be used; for a very small quantity of *quick-lime* will be sufficient to unite the whole into one slightly coherent mass. Therefore,

Therefore, the only circumftance neceffary to be attended to in fouring lime for plafter, is, that it be allowed to macerate long enough, as there is no danger of ever erring on the oppofite extreme. It is indeed neceffary that it fhould lie a very long time on fome occafions, before we can be certain that all the particles are thoroughly flaked. I have known pieces of lime-fhells lie upwards of fix months expofed to all the viciffitudes of winter-weather, and *fall* after that time. Such flightly burnt ftones are indeed ufually feparated in fifting the lime for plafter ; but as fome fmall chips may efcape, it is always fafeft to allow it to lie *in the four* a very long time.

This practice is alfo attended with another advantage of fome confequence.—For, if by this means a great proportion of the lime be allowed to abforb its air, and become *effette*, when it is beaten up for ufe, the water can have no fenfible effect upon that *effette*-lime—it will only feparate the particles of cauftic lime more perfectly from one another, fo as to fuffer it to dry without cracks of any fort, and render the furface of the plafter much more fmooth and entire than it could have been if the whole had been employed while in its perfectly cauftic ftate. By this means alfo, thofe chryftalline exudations, fo common on newly plaftered walls, will be moft effectually obviated. On all which accounts, the practice of allowing lime intended for plafter to macerate *very long* with water, ought never to be omitted but in cafes of neceffity.

But as lime is no fooner flaked than it begins to abforb its air, and as it continues to abforb more and more every minute from that period, till it becomes entirely *effette*, fo as to be rendered gradually lefs and lefs fit for forming a cement of any fort :—it follows, that if lime intended for *mortar* is allowed to lie long *in the four*, much of it will be converted into chalk, or unchryftallized *effette-lime* ; in which condition it will neither admit of fo much fand in ufing, nor ever become such a firm cement, as if a larger proportion of sand had been employed at first, and worked up as quickly as possible into mortar, and used.

This malady will be increased, if the lime-stone has not been very well burnt; therefore care ought to be taken to choose the very best burnt lime for *mortar*; in which case, a very short time, if it has been carefully sifted after flaking, will be sufficient to make it *fall* as much as is necessary. For the object of principal importance here, is to have the cement as *firm* as possible; and the bursting of a very small particle of unslaked lime amongst it afterwards, will not produce such a sensible inconvenience as it would have done in plaster.

Those, therefore, who wish to obtain the hardest and firmest *mortar*, will be careful to get *well-burnt* lime, and allow it to macerate with the water only a *very short time* before it is used. But the best burnt lime I ever saw, would require to macerate some days in the water, before there can be a certainty that the whole will be sufficiently flaked.*

§ 28.

---

* It is no unsatisfactory proof of the justness of the foregoing reasoning, to observe, that the practice which would necessarily follow from it, is exactly what was followed by the ancients, if we can rely on the account given of this matter by *Vitruvius* and *Pliny*.

Vitruvius, so far from recommending unflaked lime for making plaster, as Monsieur Loriot would suggest, recommends expressly that it should be *soured* or macerated in water—for the very same reasons as are given above; as it is only by that means, he says, that the plaster can be prevented from blistering—His words are (lib. vii. cap. 2) . . . "Tunc de albariis operibus est explicandum. Id autem erit recte, si glebae calcis optimae, ante multo tempore quam opus fuerit, macerabuntur. Namque cum non penitus macerata, sed recens sumitur - - - habens latentes crudos calculos, pustulas emittit - - - Qui calculi dissolvent, et dissipant tectorii politiones."

Pliny points out, still more clearly, the difference between the quality of the lime necessary for making *mortar* and *plaster*
—a certain

§ 28.

The reader, if he has followed me thus far, will easily perceive, that although it be in vain to expect those wonderful effects from the practice recommended by Monsieur Loriot, that he so pompously describes, yet it may happen, that if circumstances accidentally concur

—a certain proof that the ancients had been very accurate in observing *facts*, as they could have no idea of the reasoning by which these facts might have been explained or corroborated.

'Ruinarum urbis,' says he, ' ea maxime causa, quod furto, calcis *sine ferrumine suo cæmenta* componuntur. *Intrita* quoque *quo vetustior, eo melior*. In antiquarum (antiquis) ædiuin legibus invenitur, ne recentiore trima uteretur redemptor ; idio nulla (nullæ) tectoria eorum rimæ fœdavere.' Plin. Hist. lib. xxxvi. cap. 23.

In this passage, Pliny strongly contrasts *mortar (cæmenta)* with *plaster (intria.)* The first, he says (by implication) ought always to be composed of lime *cum ferrumine suo*, that is, lime that still retains its *gluten*,—lime that still retains that quality by which it is enabled to unite detached matters into a solid body, and *glue* them as it were together. In other places of his work, he describes it as *calcis quam vehementissimæ*, lime in its most acrid state, that is, perfectly *caustic* lime.

This quality, he plainly hints, it gradually loses by time, so as to come at length to be *sine ferrumine suo ;* in which state, as it is impossible to become a firm cement for building, he severely reprehends those who use it as such.

But although he condemns the practice of using that old and inert lime for mortar, he immediately adds, that for plaster it is better than new, because it is not so subject to crack in the work. " *Intrita* quoque quo vetustior, eo melior......... *ideo nulla tectoria corum rimæ fœdavere*."

Monsieur Loriot quotes this passage, and contends, that *calcis sine ferrumine suo*, means merely flaked lime, in opposition to his favourite powdered lime-shells.—What reason he has to think so, the reader is left to judge.—It is to be observed, however, that Monsieur Loriot does not confine the use of his cement to making mortar.—Like those medicines that cure all diseases, it is equally proper for plaster, and indeed it is as a plaster he chiefly recommends it. There can be no doubt, however, from the authorities above quoted, that the *Ancients* were as great strangers to the use of it in this sense, as the *Moderns*.

concur to that end, a very perfect mortar may be obtained, by following his directions. For, if the flaked lime that shall be employed has not had time to become, in a great measure, *effette* ;—if the unflaked shells that are to be pounded have been *perfectly* calcined ;—if the lime-stone has been of a sandy sort of itself ;—if the sand added to it has been of a proper kind, and in due proportion ; and if these materials be carefully mixed before they are applied, there can be no doubt but the mortar would be very good : So that it may *sometimes* happen, that those who follow the practice recommended by him, in making mortar for ordinary uses, may be lucky enough to succeed to their wish. But, as these favourable circumstances may not chance to occur in other cases, they may be at other times very far from succeeding.

That gentleman, with his usual want of accuracy, takes no notice of any of these circumstances.—He only recommends that powdered quick-lime, by which he means pounded lime-shells, be mixed up with common mortar, made of old flaked lime, in certain proportions. He does not give the smallest hint as to the state of *old flaked lime* to be used as common mortar ; but seems to think it a matter of no moment, whether it shall have been so long flaked, as to be perfectly *effette*, or the reverse ;—he does not, indeed, seem to know any thing about that peculiarity of lime distinguished by that term.

But, independent of that circumstance, the practice he recommends is much worse in other respects than that usually followed in modern times, either for making plaster or cement, especially the first. For, in the ordinary operation of flaking, those lime-shells that are not enough burnt, have some chance of being rejected when the lime is sifted ; whereas, in this method of pounding the whole promiscuously, these will be mixed with the others ; and therefore it may be expected that some of the particles will remain unflaked

for

§ 29.

for a very long time, which will be in danger of disuniting, and bliſtering the work long after it is put up.

Authors almoſt univerſally agree in aſſerting, that the hardeſt lime-ſtone affords a lime that will conſolidate into the firmeſt cement; and hence it has been, in general concluded, that lime made of chalk, affords a much weaker cement than what is made of marble or lime-ſtone.

It appears, however, from the foregoing obſervations, that if ever this be the caſe, it is only *incidentally*, and not *neceſſarily* ſo.

Lime made of pure chalk, differs not in the leaſt from lime made of the pureſt marble. Both conſiſt of a fine impalpable powder, without any mixture of extraneous matter; and if they have been equally calcined, are poſſeſſed of the ſame chemical qualities in every reſpect. Indeed, nothing is more eaſy, than to form artificial chalk from pure lime-ſtone, as I have more than once experienced, which the reader may alſo do, by following the directions in the margin,* if his curioſity prompts him to it.

And

---

* In flaking lime compoſed of *pure* lime-ſtone, it will be obſerved, that the pieces fall into powder much more ſlowly than when the lime-ſtone has contained any ſand in it.

If a great quantity of water be ſucceſſively poured upon a large heap of theſe pure lime-ſhells, without ſtirring them, and if it be allowed to lie ſome time afterwards, it will be found, on opening the heap, that ſome pieces of lime-ſhells have only expanded conſiderably in bulk by the operation of flaking, without being crumbled down to a powder. Theſe pieces, if allowed to remain in a cloſe place, where they are not expoſed to the viciſſitudes of the weather, will ſtill retain their form; and as they gradually abſorb their air, they acquire a ſort of firmneſs of conſiſtence, and in time become chalk in every ſenſe of the word,—having the ſame degree of firmneſs, of ſoftneſs, and every other quality of chalk.

This is the moſt perfect reſemblance of chalk that can be made: but, if any quantity of that pure lime be reduced to a

very

And the practice of the southern provinces of Britain, sufficiently confirms the justness of these observations. For, to the south of the Humber, on the east coast, almost all the lime they use is made of chalk; yet, there are many buildings in these counties, in which the cement is as firm as in any part of the island. Nor does the ordinary mode of building in these places, indicate any deficiency in the quality of their mortar; for many of their houses are coated on the outside with a crust of lime, stuck full of small pebbles, which remain in it very firmly for many years. We know well, that this is the most trying manner of employing mortar.

There is, however, greater danger that lime made of chalk, should form, on some occasions, a weak cement, than that from lime-stone.

For, as chalk never contains any sand, its lime will always form a very soft cement, unless care be taken to mix a large proportion of sand with it, in beating up the mortar; which is not so indispensably necessary in forming mortar from lime-stone, as it sometimes contains so much sand as to form a pretty firm cement, without any additional sand at all.

Even if the lime-stone should be equally *pure* calcareous matter as the chalk, the lime of the first has a chance of becoming a firmer cement than that of the last.

For, as it is impossible to reduce the pure *lime-stone* to

very thin paste, at the time of flaking, and be hastily dried to a certain degree, it acquires a sort of consistency so as to be capable of retaining its form. And if this be kept in a place not exposed to the vicissitudes of the weather, till it has attained its whole air, it will resemble chalk almost as much as the former, and might be employed for every purpose that the chalk is used for.

The reader will please to observe, that this can only be done with lime that is *perfectly* free of sand; for if it has the least particle of sand among it, no art can give it the softness of chalk.

to a powdery *calx*, without subjecting it to the action of a very strong fire, which, while it dissipates the water, and fully dries the chrystals, carries off the *whole* of its fixed air; so that the *calx* is almost entirely caustic.

But *chalk* may be reduced to *calx*, by such a moderate heat as is scarcely sufficient to dissipate any of its air;—so, that what assumes the appearance of lime made from it, may be nothing else than a powdered *effette* calcareous earth, which never can become a cement of any sort. But as there is no danger of vitrifying chalk by over-burning, this inconvenience may be entirely obviated by a careful and perfect calcination.

In those countries, therefore, where chalk-lime is common, care ought to be taken to choose only that kind of it for mortar, that has been calcined by a *very strong* fire, and to reject that which has been burnt by furze or brakes, as unfit for that purpose.

But it is obvious, that as this defect arises entirely from the unskilfulness of the operator, which may be easily avoided, it ought not to be considered as any objection to the quality of the lime, considered in itself.

§ 30.

It is unnecessary to extend our observations to all the other kinds of lime-stone that may be met with; as these general observations on the two extremes, marble and chalk, may be easily applied to all the intermediate kinds. It has been already said, that the different friability of different sorts of lime-stone arises entirely from a smaller or greater degree of perfection in the chrystallization, which must have been occasioned by accidental circumstances that have occurred at the time the concretion was effected, and can have no influence on the quality of the lime when it is once more reduced to the state of a *caustic calx*.

And

And as it does not yet appear that there is the smallest difference between the chemical qualities of any one kind of fossile calcareous earth and another, *when perfectly pure*, there is no reason to suspect that there can be any difference between one kind of *lime* and another, *as a cement*, unless what may arise from the nature of the extraneous bodies that may be accidentally mixed with that calcareous matter in its native state, or from its being more or less perfectly calcined.

But the only extraneous matter that is ever found in lime-stone is *sand*,* in greater or smaller proportions. And as no lime-stone that *can be calcined*, contains such a large proportion of sand as is necessary for making a perfect cement, we may naturally conclude, that every kind of lime is equally fit for becoming a firm cement, if it be first reduced to a proper degree of causticity, and has afterwards a due proportion of sand *properly* mixed with it, before it be employed in work.

Different sorts of lime, no doubt, vary very much from one another in the proportion of sand they naturally contain, and therefore must require very different proportions of sand to be added to them before they can be made equally perfect as a cement. This is an economical consideration, of no small moment in some cases, as it may make one sort of lime vastly *cheaper* than another on some occasions, and therefore deserves to be attended to by every builder. Directions shall be given in the Second Part of this Essay, by the help of which he may be enabled to discover the exact proportion of sand contained in any sort of lime he may wish to examine.

§ 31.

In the preceding parts of this Essay, I have spoken of *sand* as the only substance that is ever added to lime in

---

* This expression requires some limitation. See the Postscript to this Essay.

in forming cement; but as others have, on some occasions, been employed for this purpose, it will be proper here to point out their several excellencies and defects.

Almost the only substances that I have known used as an addition to mortar, besides sand of various denominations, are *powdered sand-stone, brick-dust,* and *sea-shells,* that have been broken into small fragments.

And for forming plaster, where closeness rather than hardness is required, the useful additions are, lime that has been flaked, and kept long in a dry place, till it has become nearly *effette;* powdered chalk or whiting, and *gypsum* in various proportions; besides hair, and other substances of that sort.

Others that have been lately recommended by Monf. Loriot, are, balls of any sort of earth slightly burnt and pounded;—the rubbish of old buildings (by which I understand the old mortar after it has been separated from the stones) reduced to powder, and sifted; or almost any other thing that can be reduced to a moderately fine powder.

From what has incidentally occurred relating to this head, the reader will be able to judge, in some measure, of the comparative value of these several additions. But, to render the subject still more clear, the following observations may be of use:

It is sufficiently certain, that none of these additions enter into the composition, so as to affect its qualities as a *chemical mixt;* they only operate in a manner purely *mechanical:* For, whatever the nature of the addition may be, it possesses the same qualities, when so united, as if by itself, and may be separated by mechanical means from the compound, unaltered. Therefore, we need give ourselves no trouble about ascertaining their chemical qualities, but consider them merely as masses of matter that may be more or less fitted for this purpose by their peculiar form, degrees of hardness, &c.

It

It has been already shown, that *sand* ought to be preferred to chalky matters, chiefly on account of the hardness and firmness of the particles of which it consists. And as the purest sand consists of detached chrystals, which are so hard as scarcely to admit of being broken into smaller parts, this kind of pure chrystalline transparent sand is, perhaps, on this account, the most proper addition that can possibly be made to lime in forming *mortar*.

Sand-stone consists of an almost innumerable congeries of small particles of sand united to one another, in a slight manner, by some kind of natural cement. But as it is troublesome to reduce this kind of stone to its smallest component parts, and as the particles of it, when not reduced to that ultimate degree of fineness, may be easily broken into smaller parts, it can never be looked upon as such a proper addition for a lime-cement as the purest sand.

There are also many substances that are called *sand*, which are nothing else than fragments of decomposed granite, moor-stone, sand-stone, &c. all of which may be easily reduced into smaller particles by moderate triture, and are liable to the same objections as pounded sand-stone.

But almost any of these is preferable to *brick-dust*. Fine clay, when *perfectly* burnt in the fire, may be made to assume almost a stony hardness. But common brick is so imperfectly burnt, as to admit of being reduced, without much trouble, to a fine impalpable powder; insomuch, that it is often used, when in this state, for scouring polished iron or brass, especially if the brick has had no fine sharp sand in its composition.

As the rough particles of brick-dust may be so easily reduced to a fine powder, the mortar formed with it can in no case be of the most perfect sort.

But brick-dust is still liable to a greater objection, when considered as a component part of mortar.

Clay

Clay only loofes its quality of abforbing water, and in fome meafure of diffolving in it, by a very perfect degree of burning; fo that if any part of it has efcaped the violent action of the fire, that part, when mixed in mortar, will ftill be apt to abforb water whenever it may reach it, and lofe its firmnefs, and make the mafs of which it is a part, crumble to duft.

It is exactly in this manner that all forts of *marle* are liable to fall into powder when drenched in water, and expofed to the air; even although they fometimes appear, when dry, to be endowed with a ftony hardnefs.

On this account, brick-duft, which ufually confifts of the imperfect burnt bricks, ought to be confidered as a very dangerous mixture for mortar, and fhould never be employed but in cafes of abfolute neceffity.

But the balls of other forts of earth, flightly burned, as recommended by Monfieur Loriot, muft be, on many accounts, far lefs proper; as many of thefe forts of earth cannot, by the action of fire, be deprived of their quality of abforbing water, and of becoming foft with it. So that he who fhould be foolifh enough to employ thefe fubftances, may be certain that his cement will not only be incapable of attaining any confiderable degree of hardnefs at any time, but will alfo be liable to turn moift in a damp air, nor will be capable of retaining its firmnefs or cohefive quality in an expofed fituation.

Powdered *lime-rubbifh* is liable to the fame objections with the fofteft fand-ftone or brick-duft; as the particles of which it confifts, never can be endowed with the adhefive firmnefs that is neceffary for forming a perfect cement.

Fine fhells are perhaps firmer than any other fubftance, next to pure fand, and may be employed where the other cannot be got, if this abounds. I have feen a cement that was as little affected by the weather as any other, and had ftood firm in the work a great many years,

years, that had been originally formed with a sand consisting almost entirely of the fragments of shells. But it had not the rocky hardness of some old mortar that we frequently meet with.

Roughly *powdered glass*, if such a thing could be got, at a moderate expense, would form a most perfect sort of mortar; as it would not be liable to be affected with the weather, would be sufficiently hard, and consist of very irregular fragments.

Thus it appears, that of all the substances that can be easily met with, *sand* forms the most proper addition to lime in making mortar; on which account, it has been justly preferred to all others for that purpose.

Pure firm chrystallized sand is better than any other sort:—But all pure sands are not equally proper for this use.

§ 32.

It has been already shown, that the principal advantages which resulted from the addition of sand in making lime-mortar, were, that it augmented the quantity of hard indissoluble matter,—and put it in our power to employ a larger quantity of water in proportion to the lime, and thus forwarded the chrystallization of the calcareous matter, augmented the *quantity* of these chrystals, and rendered their quality more perfect. Those kinds of sand, therefore, which promote these purposes in the highest degree, will be best adapted for mixing with mortar.

But if sand consists of irregular angular particles, a greater quantity of water will be retained in the vacuities formed between these angular pieces, than could have been if the whole had consisted of round smooth globules; and therefore it is natural to think, that rough angular sand, will be more proper for this use than that which is smoother.

Hence, if equally pure, sea-sand, which consists of round globules, that have been worn perfectly smooth

by

by the continued attrition upon one another on the shore, (like the larger pebbles in the same situation) will be worse than any other sort.—River-sand will be better than it;—and pit-sand, when quite free of earth, the best of all.

§ 33.

If the sand be hard, and the particles angular, it is perhaps of very little importance whether these be very small, or of a larger size.—The sand in the lime that formed the extraordinary firm cement mentioned § 26, was as small as could well be imagined.

Because sea-sand is usually smaller than any other sort, and is acknowledged to be less proper for making mortar than many other kinds of sand, a prejudice has been in general adopted against *fine* sand for this purpose. But this, there is reason to imagine, is only a vulgar prejudice, arising from the peculiar figure of that sort of sand.

§ 34.

There is another and better reason for not employing sea-sand in mortar, *viz.* that there is always a chance that some particles of salt may be formed among it, by the evaporation of the sea-water upon the shore. And as common salt continues always to be a deliquescent substance, it will have a perpetual tendency to attract moisture from a humid air, and thus render the wall in which this mortar has been employed extremely damp and unwholesome.

It is from the same cause that any porous sort of stone, that has been taken from the sea shore, continues at all times to be wet in damp weather: For, while the stone remained on the shore, its pores would be, from time to time, filled with salt water; upon the evaporation of which, the salt it contained would remain behind, within the pores of the stone, which would thus become endowed with the quality of attracting moisture from a damp air, sufficient to dissolve the salt, and make the watery solution ooze out through all its pores.

This is a phenomenon for which it is more easy to account, than to prescribe an effectual cure.—Perhaps, no art can render the stone sufficiently dry, after it is once put into the wall.—To let it lie for a considerable time in a stream of running fresh water before it was employed, might mitigate, at least, if not entirely obviate, the disease.

§ 35.

For the same reason, lime that has been slaked with sea-water, is always unfit for being used as a mortar. For, as it is impossible ever to extract that salt from the mortar, it continually attracts moisture from the air in damp weather, and oozes through the pores of the wall in form of drops of sweat, which again disappear when the weather becomes dry.

This is an inconvenience often felt :—But as the real cause of it is seldom known, few persons are at proper pains to guard against it. Those who obtain their lime by water-carriage, are in a peculiar manner liable to be hurt by this circumstance, as the lime is, for the most part, slaked at the ship's side, by the sea-water, which is more easily got than any other.

When lime that has been slaked in this manner is employed as a plaster, it is rather worse than when used as a mortar, as it has less sand added to it, and has fewer pores in the inside, in which the drops of water might be allowed to lodge ; so that the wall becomes alternately covered with a crust of dry powdery salt, and with damp tears running down its surface.

Too much care, therefore, cannot be taken to avoid using lime that has been slaked with sea-water,—as it will be impossible, or extremely difficult, ever to render these walls perfectly dry.

I have thus enumerated at much greater length than I originally intended, the several circumstances that
contribute

contribute to render lime-cement more or less perfect. In doing this, I have had occasion to explain the nature of many of those calcareous matters which have been generally used as a manure, which will considerably shorten our labour in what remains of this Essay.

If I have reprehended, with some degree of asperity, those who, either through ignorance, or a wilful intention to deceive, have endeavoured, by specious pretexts, to mislead the ignorant, I hope the candid will be rather ready to ascribe this to a desire of rectifying those abuses that might have been introduced by their means, than to any other motive. I have never found fault, but where it was necessary to correct.*

I now

* Before I quit this branch of our subject, I may be allowed to remark, that although the discoveries of Modern Philosophers have enabled us to account for some of the *phænomena* relating to quick-lime as a cement, that were altogether inexplicable to the Ancients, yet here, as in almost every branch of natural knowledge, we are still far from having attained that summit of perfection which some may, perhaps too hastily, be disposed to imagine.—In many respects, we have as yet been just able to penetrate the mysterious veil of nature, so far, as to let us know that much remains to be discovered, of which we have now only a very faint idea.—The following hints will illustrate my meaning, and deserve the consideration of Chemical Philosophers;

There is little reason to doubt, that *flint* is nothing else than calcareous matter combined with some substance that has hitherto eluded the knowledge of Chymists.

It is likewise highly probable, that the native chrystalline concretion called *quartz*, by Naturalists, is only another modification of the same calcareous matter, combined with some other substances that prevents the action of acids upon it, and gives it other sensible qualities very different from calcareous substances in their ordinary state.

There is even some reason to suspect, that all the other varieties of *chrystalline* earths, including sand of every denomination, are other modifications of the same calcareous matter.

Even *argillaceous* earths (clays) however different in appearance and natural qualities, in their ordinary state, afford evident marks of the same original. But

I now go on to confider calcareous matters as a manure.

But in what manner it comes to be fo differently difguifed in thefe feveral bodies,—what are their feveral component parts,—how they may be analyfed and recompounded, are fecrets of Nature, referved for the difcovery of future ages: And, till thefe are difcovered, it is probable, we will never be able to account for the manner in which the moft perfect cement may be fometimes produced.

PART

PART SECOND.

Of QUICK-LIME and other Calcareous Substances, as a Manure.

IN the First Part of this Essay, I have been able to give, as I hope, a tolerably satisfactory account of the *rationale* of the operation of lime *as a cement;* and it is much to be wished, that I could pursue the same method in the investigation of this substance *as a manure*. But in this respect, I have as yet been able to discover no clue that could, with safety, be trusted for leading through the intricate labyrinth that lies before us; on which account, I willingly shun the arduous undertaking.

It would be easy for me here to amuse the reader with a critical analysis of the several theories that have been invented by ingenious men, to account for the *manner* in which lime operates as a manure. It would be no difficult matter to demonstrate the defects of their several systems; and I might, with great facility, make an idle display of *apparent* superiority by ridiculing their several hypotheses. But as I could not substitute any thing in their stead, that would be more satisfactory to the sensible Reader, I choose to wave this ungracious discussion; and shall content myself with enumerating a few *facts* concerning the use of calcareous substances as a manure, that it much imports the practical farmer fully to understand.

§ 1.

The first idea that occurs in reflecting on this subject, is, that all substances in which calcareous matter is contained, have been successfully employed as a manure, at different times, and in different places.

Thus—*lime,*—*marle* of all sorts,—*chalk,*—*lime-stone-gravel,*—

gravel,—*shelly* sand, or pure *shells* of every denomination, have all been employed as manures, with the greatest success.

§ 2.

And as all these, excepting lime, always contain the calcareous matter in its *mild* state, we are led to conclude, that *they* operate on the soil merely as *calcareous*, and not as *saline* substances.

Lime, indeed, is sometimes applied to the soil in its *caustic* state, as it comes fresh from being slaked, but more commonly at some considerable distance of time after it has been burnt. However, as burning is the only mode usually employed for reducing lime-stone to powder, and thus preparing it for a manure, the opinion in general prevails, that calcination is as necessary for rendering lime capable of becoming a manure, as for making it fit to be employed as a cement.

It is, however, of importance to the practical farmer, to be informed that this is not the case.—Mr. Du-Hamel, was the first, who, from an accidental experiment, was led to believe that *powdered lime-stone* was a manure equally efficacious with *lime* itself. He recorded the experiment as a great discovery.

Having had occasion to dress a marble chimney-piece, for repairing one of his country-houses, the mason chose a lawn near the house, as the most convenient place for hewing the stone. After the operation was finished, all the large chips were picked up and carried away, that they might not disfigure the lawn; but the fine powder that had been grinded off by the action of the chissel, mixed so intimately with the grass, that it could not be gathered up.—In consequence of this very full dressing of powdered lime-stone, the grass afterwards grew upon that spot with much greater luxuriance than on any other part of the lawn, and always continued to have a much livelier verdure. From

From hence, he, with good reason, concluded, that powdered lime-stone might be employed as a manure with success. To try if this would always be the case, he repeated the experiment several times, by causing some lime-stone to be pounded on purpose; and found that it never failed to promote the fertility of the spot on which he applied it, in a very high degree.

§ 3.

I chose to relate this experiment at large, for the satisfaction of those who may be unacquainted with the *physical* cause of the difference between lime and lime-stone. To such as are fully apprised of this, a little reasoning might have been sufficient to afford a certain conviction, that the result of the experiment must have been what Mr. Du-Hamel found it.

Lime is no sooner slaked, than it immediately begins to absorb its air, and return to its former *mild* state; or, in other words, it becomes *effette*; in which state it possesses the same chemical qualities, in every respect, as lime-stone.

If this be spread out thinly upon the surface of the earth, it absorbs its air in a very short time.—A few hours, in this situation, restores a large proportion of its air; and, in a day or two, at most, it becomes perfectly *effette*, as masons experience when they sweep together the scattered particles that have lain round their heaps of lime, and attempt to use it in mortar by itself, for it is then no more coherent than sand, or moistened earth.

Hence, then, it must follow, that in every case, *lime* is converted into the same state with *lime-stone*, in a few days after it is mixed with the soil; so that if it produces any effect at all as *lime*, as a *saline* substance, —it must only be at the *very first*, when it is applied; and it must act ever afterwards merely as *powdered lime-stone*.

But it is well known, that lime produces scarcely any

any sensible effect as a manure at the beginning. Even the first year after it is applied to the soil, its effects are inconsiderable, in comparison of what it produces in the second and succeeding years. From whence we must conclude, that it operates upon the soil, merely as a *mild* calcareous earth ; and that its calcination is of no farther utility in preparing it for manure, than as a cheap and efficacious method of reducing the lime-stone to a fine powder.

§ 4.

It is of importance, that these facts should be generally known ; because it may sometimes happen, that good lime-stone shall be found in places where fuel could not be obtained for burning it ; in which case, such lime-stone could be of no use to the farmer, if calcination were absolutely necessary. But, seeing this is not the case, lime-stone, even in these situations, may be converted into a most beneficial manure, if a stream of water can be commanded, sufficient for driving a mill, for reducing the stone to powder.

I have seen the model of a mill that had been invented for that purpose, which was constructed on the same principles with an ordinary gun-powder mill. It had several large massy stampers, composed of huge blocks of cast-iron, that were successively lifted up and let fall by a wheel that catched their handles, and, after a proper time, slipped them again as it revolved round its axis. These stampers fell with great force upon the lime-stone, that had been previously broken into pieces of a moderate size, and placed in a strong trough, formed for that purpose. Through this trough, a small stream of water was conveyed, which washed away with it, the small pieces of lime-stone, as they were successively reduced to powder by the stampers. This stream of water was received into a large reservoir, in which it was allowed to stagnate, and deposit,

posit, as a sediment, the lime-stone powder it brought along with it ; the pure water flowing gently over a part of the brim, which was made lower for that purpose.

When the reservoir was nearly full of this fine powder, the work was stopped ; the water was drawn off from the reservoir; by taking out some plugs left for that purpose, at different heights, till all that was clear had run off: the powdered stone was afterwards thrown out to the bank, and allowed to dry sufficiently for use.

I have heard that a mill, upon these principles, was erected by the Honourable the Trustees for managing the forfeited estates in Scotland, and that a good deal of lime-stone was pounded with it. But, as it was erected in the Highlands of Scotland, where roads were bad, and where there was but little, spirit for improvements in agriculture ; as there was no public demand for the manure, after the experiment was sufficiently tried to show that it might be practised with advantage in other places, the mill was suffered to lie unemployed.

§ 5.

But although this may be considered as a most valuable discovery for those who may have a good lime-quarry so situated as not to be within the reach of any kind of fuel for burning lime-stone ; yet, to such as can obtain fuel at a moderate expense, there can be no doubt but that burning is the easiest and most efficacious mode of reducing lime-stone to powder that ever was invented, and therefore ought always to be adopted where necessity does not prevent it.

Reducing lime-stone to powder by calcination, is attended with this farther advantage to the farmer, that it considerably diminishes his expense of carriage. *Pure* lime-stone loses about two-thirds of its weight by being

being thoroughly burned; so that the man who is obliged to drive this manure from a great distance, will find a very considerable saving by driving it in the state of *shells*. But if it were reduced to a powder by mechanical triture, he could not be benefitted by this circumstance.

Many persons choose to drive lime-stone from a considerable distance, and burn it at home: But it is obvious they then subject themselves to a very heavy charge in carriage, which would be avoided by an opposite conduct. This, therefore, ought never to be practised but where other circumstances may counterbalance this unfavourable one.

§ 6.

But as lime-stone is often, in its native state, mixed with sand in various proportions; and as sand loses nothing of its weight by calcination, it must happen, that those kinds of lime-stone which contain the largest proportion of sand, will lose least in calcination, and of course afford the weightiest lime-shells.

Hence it is obvious, that those who are under the necessity of driving lime from a great distance, ought to be particularly careful to make choice of a kind of lime-stone as free from sand as possible, and to drive it in the state of *shells*; as they will thus obtain an equal quantity of manure, at the least expense of carriage that is possible; and the lightest shells ought, of course, to be always preferred.

§ 7.

When lime is flaked, that which contains most sand *falls* most quickly, and absorbs the smallest proportion of water. What is pure, requires a very large proportion of water, and is much longer before it begins to fall.

Hence it happens, that those who drive sandy lime-shells in open carriages, must be very careful to guard
against

against rain; because a heavy shower would make the whole fall, and generate such a heat as to be in danger of setting the carts on fire; whereas *pure* lime-shells are in no danger of being damaged by that circumstance. I have seen a cart loaded with such shells, which had been exposed to a continued shower of rain, as violent as is ever known in this country, for more than three hours, and seemed hardly to be affected by it in the smallest degree. I ought to observe, however, that my experiments were confined to only one kind of pure lime, so that it is not from hence demonstrated, that *all* kinds of pure lime will be possessed of the same qualities.

§ 8.

Lime shells formed from the purest lime-stone, require more than their own weight of water to slake them properly;* whereas some kinds of lime-shells that contain much sand, do not require above one-fourth part of that quantity.

Hence it is much worse economy in those who have pure lime-shells, to slake and carry them home in the state of powdered lime, than it is in those who have only a sandy kind of lime-shells.

§ 9.

It is even, on some occasions, more advisable for those who have very sandy lime, to drive it in the state of powdered lime, than in that of *shells*: For, as it is dangerous to give that kind of lime-stone too much heat, lest it should be vetrified, those who burn it can never be *certain* that the whole of the stone will fall to powder when water is added, till they have actually tried

---

* I have found, by experiment, that pure lime-shells cannot be flaked with less than about one-fourth more than their own weight of water. When flaked in the ordinary way, the same lime-shells took more than double their weight of water.

tried it; nor do they think it a great loss if some part of it should be imperfectly burned, as it requires much less fuel on a future occasion than fresh lime-stone; and therefore they much rather choose to err on this, than on the opposite extreme.

But, should any one attempt to drive this *poor* sort of lime in the state of *shells*, he would be in danger of carrying home many stones that would never *fall*, which would more than counterbalance the benefit he would derive from the want of the small quantity of water that is required to slake it.

On these accounts, it may be admitted, as a general rule, that those who can have access to lime-stone which is free of sand, will save a *great deal* in the carriage of it, by driving it in the state of *shells*;—and that, on the contrary, it will be most economical in those who can only get lime of a very sandy quality, to drive it in the state of powdered lime.

From hence it follows, that the practice which now prevails, of carrying shell-lime by water from one part of the country to another, is only an imaginary saving, obtained at a very high risque, to those who drive shells of a sandy quality;—but a real and unequivocal advantage, of very high importance to the community at large, if these *shells* are obtained from a pure lime-stone.

These observations relate only to the saving of carriage to the farmer; an article of capital importance to him. It is proper now to take notice of some other particulars that may equally affect him in this way, as well as in the application of the lime to his ground.

§ 10.

A vague opinion, in general, prevails in every part of the country, that one sort of lime may be more valuable than another: but it does not appear that farmers have hitherto had almost any rule to direct them

them in the choice of different forts of lime ; fome efteeming one fort *ftrongeft,* as they term it, and fome valuing another fort more highly, without being able to affign any fatisfactory reafon for the preference they give, in either cafe.

It is of importance, that this matter fhould be elucidated.

Although it does not always happen, yet, in many parts of the country, the real nature of lime is fo little underftood, that the weightieft lime is preferred, as a manure, to that which is lighter ; becaufe it is imagined the firft has more *fubftance,* and will therefore produce a more powerful effect upon ground, than the fineft and lighteft lime.

But, there feems to be no reafon to think, there is any difference in the fpecific gravity of different parcels of *pure* calcareous matter, when fully calcined ; therefore, if there is any difference in the weight of various forts of lime, it muft arife entirely from a variation in the quantity or *gravity* of fome extraneous matter that is mixed with the lime.

And as *fand* is almoft the only extraneous body that is ever found in lime-ftone, and is always of much greater fpecific gravity than pure quick-lime,—it follows, that the weighty lime only owes its fuperior gravity to a larger proportion of fand that is mixed with it.

But *fand* is of no value as a manure ; fo that he who voluntarily purchafes this kind of lime, in preference to the other, is guilty of a great degree of folly ; which will be the greater, if he has likewife to drive it from a confiderable diftance. It would be better for him, if he is determined to ufe nothing but weighty lime, to buy fuch as is pure, if it can be obtained, and mix it with fand after he has got it home, fo as to give it the gravity required. Some might laugh at this, as a proof of his folly, and juftly : but, it is, furely, lefs foolifh in him to do this, than to pay money for the fand which he would thus obtain for nothing, and drive it from a distance, when he might have it at his door. This practice would also be attended with the farther advantage of enabling him to know exactly, what quantity of *real* lime he applied to his ground, as he would not be in danger of considering the sand as a part of it.

§ II.

Those who have access to only one sort of lime-stone, must be contented with it, whatever may be its quality. But such as have an opportunity of choosing, may be benefitted by the following observations:

Pure lime-stone, when fully calcined and slaked, is reduced to a fine impalpable powder, that feels soft between the fingers, without the smallest tendency to grittiness. Such lime as contains sand, is never so fine nor so soft, but feels gritty between the fingers, and is more or less so as the sand is coarser or finer, or in greater or smaller proportions.

The lime from pure lime-stone, is always of a bright white, when perfectly calcined, without a tendency to any colour. When it has any colour, it proceeds from the sand, or other uncalcareous matters in its composition. There are, however, some sorts of sand, that are of such a pure whiteness, as not to debase the colour of the lime in the smallest degree; but these are rare:—And there are some matters that alter the colour of the lime a good deal, without debasing its quality in any considerable degree; but these are still more rare than the former.

Hence it follows, that the best lime for the purpose of the farmer, is that which is lightest, softest to the touch,* and whitest. The more they deviate from either of these tests of purity, the worse they are for him.   That

---

* Softness to the touch is not an unequivocal proof of the purity of lime. I have seen *one* kind of lime, that contained a large proportion of an uncalcareous impalpable powder, that was as soft to the touch as the purest lime; but this was a singular exception to a rule that is very general.

§ 12.

That the farmer may have under his eye, at one time, the several criteria of the purity of lime, that have been enumerated in different places of this Essay, I choose to mention them here all at once. If he is attentive to mark these peculiarities, he needs be very little solicitous about examining the qualities of his lime, by any more minute or troublesome trials. They are as under:

If the lime-stone loses much of its weight in calcination, and the lime-shells are extremely light; if the shells require a very large proportion of water to slake them fully; if it is long before they begin to fall; if the lime-stone is not apt to *run* (or be vitrified) in the operation of burning; if it falls entirely when it gets a sufficient quantity of water, after it has been properly calcined; if it swells very much in flaking, and if the lime is light, fine to the touch, and of a pure white; he may be satisfied, that it is extremely good, and may use it in preference to any other lime that is inferior to it in any of these respects.

These rules are perfectly sufficient to decide as to the comparative value of any two kinds of lime that may be opposed to one another and may be relied upon as sufficiently accurate for the ordinary purposes of the farmers.

§ 13.

But such as may discover a new quarry of lime stone, and who wish to ascertain with certainty its real value, before they put themselves to any expense about it, will do well to employ the following more accurate, and in that case, more easy analysis.

As all calcareous matters are capable of being dissolved in acids—and as no other earthy matter can be dissolved in them—it follows, that if a sufficient quantity of acid is poured upon any body that contains cal-
carcous

carcous matter, this matter will be quickly diſſolved, while the others are left behind ; and the proportions of each may be accurately aſcertained.

To try the exact value of any kind of lime-ſtone, or other calcareous matter,—take a quantity of aquafortis,* or ſpirit of ſalt ;† and having prepared them as in the margin,‡ put them into a glaſs or earthen veſſel ; —add to that, by little and little, a known quantity of the matter you mean to examine, which had been previouſly dried, and reduced to powder. After each addition, ſuffer the violent efferveſcence or ebullition that will enſue to abate before more is added. When the whole of the powder is put to the acid, and the efferveſcence

---

* Nitrous acid. † Muriatic acid.

‡ All the mineral acids efferveſce and unite with calcareous earths. But as the vitriolic acid (ſpirit or oil of vitriol) does not *diſſolve* the calcareous matter, but forms a new concrete, that ſtill retains its ſolid ſtate, it is not fit for this experiment.

And as it ſometimes happens, that a little vitriolic acid is mixed with either the nitrous or muriatic acids, it becomes neceſſary to be certain that this is not the caſe, before they are employed in this experiment.

The eaſieſt way of trying if theſe acids are free from the vitriolic, is to put a little chalk into them before you employ them. If the acid is pure, the chalk will diſſolve very readily ; but if not, ſome part of the chalk will fall to the bottom, in the form of a pure white ſediment. When this is the caſe, add ſmall bits of chalk, by little and little, till no more of that white ſediment appears ; after which, the acid may be kept for uſe, as ſufficiently pure.

If the nitrous acid is ſo ſtrong as to have a ſlight brown, or reddiſh appearance, it ought to be diluted with water, till it aſſumes a greeniſh look. As it is bought in the ſhops, for the uſe of dyers, &c. it is uſually weak enough.

If the muriatic acid is ſo ſtrong as to have a bright yellow colour, or emits fumes when the bottle is opened, it ought to be diluted, by adding water, till it aſſumes almoſt a colourleſs tranſparency, with a very faint tinge of yellow.

When they are thus prepared, either of theſe acids may be uſed indiſcriminately for this experiment, as they are equally proper.

vefcence entirely fubfided, ftir it about feveral times with a piece of tobacco-pipe, and allow it to remain for fome time, that the acid may act upon every particle of the matter, and thoroughly diffolve it. And to be certain that there has not been too little acid, put a few drops of frefh acid to the folution, which will excite a frefh effervefcence if the whole is not fully diffolved. When no change is produced by this addition, it is a certain proof that the whole of the calcareous matter is already diffolved.

Take then a piece of filtering paper, thoroughly dry, the weight of which is alfo known, fold it properly, and put it in a glafs funnel; pour the whole of the folution, with the matter that may have fubfided, into the funnel, and allow it to filtre through the paper flowly. When the fluid part has thus drained off, fill up the filtre again with pure water, to wafh off the whole of the faline parts from the *refiduum*.* Add water, in this manner, till it comes off without any faline tafte; fuffer it then to drop off entirely, dry it thoroughly, and weigh the paper, with its contents. The difference between which, and what the powder and paper were at the beginning, is the whole weight of the calcareous matter; fo that its proportion to the whole mafs is perfectly afcertained.

In this manner I have examined a great many different kinds of lime-ftone, and have found them vary in all degrees of purity, from fuch as were entirely foluble in acids, as fugar or falt is in water, to others that contained only one-twelfth of their weight of foluble matter, and eleven-twelfths of fand. The ordinary kinds of lime-ftone contain from one-third to two-thirds of their weight of fand. Hard chalk is ufually a pure calcareous earth, foluble in acids; and fome forts of lime-ftone may be met with that are equally pure, but thefe are rare. The only extenfive lime quarries

---

* The matter that remains undiffolved.

quarries of such pure lime-stone, that I have met with, are at Sunderland, in the county of Durham, where there are several quarries of exceedingly fine lime-stone, the best of which belonged, in the year 1777, to Mr. James Galley of that place. There are some quarries farther up the river WEAR, the stone of which is of a much inferior quality.

Were all the stones in the same quarry equally pure, the above would be a perfect and unexceptionable method of ascertaining the purity of any lime-stone: But it often happens, that in a quarry of the very worst quality, there are some pieces found that consist of pure spar, that are entirely free of any mixture of sand; and in other quarries of a better sort, there are often small veins of an impure sort of stone, mixed through the rock; so that if either of these should chance to be picked out as a specimen for trial, the result would not be just.

To avoid falling into this mistake, any one who wishes to make an accurate analysis of any newly discovered lime-stone, will do well to take eight or ten stones from different parts of the quarry, that are somewhat different in appearance from one another; and, having taken a chip from each, pound the whole together, to afford a proper subject for the experiment.

The same experiment might be tried with *lime*; but it is evident the proportions would be different in the same stone, from what they would be if tried before calcination—as lime wants its fixed air, &c. which it had when in the state of lime-stone. But as the lime is more liable to be varied by accidental circumstances, it is best to try the experiment with lime-stone.

§ 14.

It is in general believed, that the lime made of the hardest lime-stone is *stronger*, as it is called, by which is meant more powerfully efficacious as a manure, than that

that which is made from materials of a softer nature. Hence it is in general asserted, that lime made from chalk, is much weaker, as a manure, than that which is made from harder lime-stone.

Nothing, however, can be more erroneous than this hypothesis. In the former part of this Essay, I have had occasion to explain pretty fully what is the real difference between chalk and lime-stone; and nothing can be more certain, than that the lime made of chalk is purer than that made from almost any lime-stone, and contains a much larger proportion of calcareous matter; on which account, it must be more efficacious as a manure, than any of these more impure kinds of lime.

The hardest lime-stone that I know, is that belonging to Mr. Galley, at Sunderland. Its external appearance rather resembles flint than lime-stone; yet the lime made of this exceedingly hard stone, is as light, as white, and as soft to the touch, as the purest chalk-lime. It differs not from that in any respect, insomuch that I defy the greatest connoisseur in these matters to distinguish between it and the purest chalk-lime, when perfectly calcined, by any other means than by the pieces of flint that are so often met with among chalk-lime.

And from this lime, obtained from these very hard stones, as perfect chalk may be artificially made by the simple process described § 24, as was ever obtained from any quarry in England.

From these considerations, therefore, I am obliged to conclude, contrary to the common opinion, that chalk-lime is, almost in all cases, more efficacious as a manure, than any lime obtained from lime-stone, in equal quantities; as it is extremely rare to meet with a lime-stone that contains near such a large proportion of calcareous matter; on which account it ought always to be preferred by the farmer, where both can be had at the same price.

§ 15.

§ 15.

We know little certain about the mode in which lime operates, excepting that it acts merely in consequence of its being mixed with the soil in substance. If a heap of lime, of a considerable thickness, shall have lain ever so long upon one spot, and be afterwards carried clean away from it, so that none of the particles of the lime remain to be mixed with the soil,—that spot will not be richer, or carry more luxuriant crops, than the places around it; which, every one knows, is not the case with regard to dung.

Again—If lime be spread upon the surface of the soil, and allowed to remain there, without being ploughed in, its effects will scarcely be perceived for several years, till it has had time gradually to sink through the sward, and mix with the soil; after which, its effects begin to be perceived, although much less sensibly than if the same quantity of lime had been intimately mixed with the soil by means of the plough and harrow.

I am not a stranger to the improvements that have been made in Derbyshire, by means of lime, without the plough; but this is no exception to what I have said. The effects are slow though certain. Those who inhabit countries that admit of the plough, are often advised to lay lime upon the grass, and are made to believe that their pasture will be instantly mended by it, nearly in the same perceptible manner as if it had been dunged. This, I myself have tried, and have seen it tried by others, but always found that the grass for the first year was rather hurt than benefitted by it; nor was it so much improved in succeeding years, as if the same quantity of lime had been applied, and intimately mixed with the soil. In this mode of applying lime, therefore, it is long before it yields a proper return; and is not to be recommended to a poor man, unless where necessity obliges him to practise it.

§ 16.

§ 16.

If, then, lime acts upon the soil more efficaciously in consequence of being intimately mixed with it, we may naturally conclude, that it will produce a more sensible effect, when it is reduced to exceedingly small particles, than when it is applied to the soil in larger lumps; as these do not admit of being so intimately mixed with the particles of the soil.

But no method has ever yet been discovered for reducing calcareous matter to such small component parts, or of spreading it so evenly over a field, or of mixing it so intimately with the soil, as by calcination. Accordingly, it is found, that *lime* will produce a very sensible effect upon the soil, when applied in much smaller quantities, than any other calcareous matter whatever.

Considered in this view, it can never be expected that lime-stone, reduced to powder by any kind of mechanical triture, will produce, such a sensible effect upon the soil, as the same quantity of calcareous matter in the state of *lime, if properly applied;* because it is impossible, by mechanical means, ever to reduce it to such a fine powder as it naturally falls into after calcination.

§ 17.

Much, however, depends upon the mode of applying the lime to the soil, after calcination. If it is spread as soon as it is flaked, while yet in a powdery state, a very small quantity may be made to cover the whole surface of the ground, and to touch an exceedingly great number of particles of earth. But if it is suffered to lie for some time after flaking, and to get so much moisture as to make it run into clods, or cake into large lumps, it can never be again divided into such small parts; and, therefore, a much greater quantity is necessary to produce the same effect, than if it had been applied in its powdery state.

But if the soil is afterwards to be continued long in tillage—as these clods are annually broken smaller by the action of the plough and harrows, the lime must continue to exert its influence anew upon the soil for a great course of years:—it will produce an effect nearly similar to that which would be experienced by annually strewing a small quantity of powdered lime over the surface of the soil. But as the price of the lime must, in the first case, be paid by the farmer altogether, at the beginning, which only comes to be successively demanded in the other case, this deserves to be attended to, as it may become a consideration of some importance where lime is dear, and money not very plentiful.

§ 18.

In few particulars are practical farmers more divided in opinion, than about the quantity of lime that may be laid upon an acre of ground with profit, or even with safety. Some require that it should be applied in such small quantities, as thirty or forty bushels to the acre; and aver, that if more is used, the ground will be absolutely ruined: while others maintain, that ten times that quantity may be applied with safety.

A great variation may, no doubt, be produced in this respect, by a difference in the nature of the soil,—in the state of culture it is under at the time,—in the quantity of calcareous matter with which it may have been formerly impregnated;—and perhaps a variation may sometimes arise from other circumstances that have never yet been attended to.

A difference will likewise arise from the quality of the lime that is applied, and from the manner in which it is employed. Some kinds of lime contain, perhaps, ten times more calcareous matter than other kinds:—And it has been shown above, that a very great difference may arise from the mode of applying the lime.

Considering

Confidering all thefe circumftances, it would appear a little prefumptuous in any one to prefcribe pofitive rules that fhould be generally adopted in this refpect. This I fhall not attempt—but fhall relate, with candour, fuch obfervations as have occurred to myfelf, in the courfe of a pretty extenfive experience of this manure.

§ 19.

It is common to hear thofe, who have had little experience of lime as a manure, recommend very great caution, left too great a quantity be employed, for fear of *burning the foil*, as they exprefs it. This idea of *burning* has been evidently adopted, from what is experienced by applying cauftic lime to animals or vegetables, in large quantities, as it often corrodes and fhrivels them up, and produces other effects which greatly refemble thofe of fire : But it cannot produce any fuch effects, unlefs there are vegetables growing upon the foil at the time. In that cafe, the vegetables might, indeed, be corroded by the lime, if rain fhould fall immediately after it was fpread, when newly flaked ;—but as it lofes this fiery corrofive power in a few days after it is fpread, nothing of that kind can be expected to happen to the *foil*. Accordingly, we never hear of crops being burnt up with too great a quantity of lime, in thofe countries where it has long been ufed as a common manure—although it is there often employed in much larger quantities than in any other places where it is more rare.

I myfelf have had the experience of lime in all proportions, from one hundred to above feven hundred bufhels to the acre, upon a great variety of foils ; and have always found, that its effect in promoting the fertility of the foil, has been in proportion to the quantity employed, other circumftances being alike.

The expenfe in moft cafes prevents farmers from employing this manure in greater quantities than thofe
above

above mentioned; but accidental circumstances clearly show, that if it were applied in much larger quantities, the effect would only be to promote the luxuriance of the crop in a higher degree.

§ 20.

A gentleman of my acquaintance, in whose veracity I perfectly confide, happening to be from home when a large field was limed; and having no occasion for the whole quantity of lime that had been brought for that purpose, and laid down in one corner of the field, his servants, without driving it away, mixed what remained with the soil, although the lime lay there about four inches thick over the whole surface. The effect was, that for many years afterwards, the grain in that place was so immoderately luxuriant, that it fell over, and rotted before it came to the ear. After many years, this luxuriance abated a little, so as to allow the grain to ripen;—but it was there always much more luxuriant than in any other part of the field.

An accidental experiment, nearly similar to this, fell under my own observation. It happened that the servants of another farmer laid, by mistake, a few heaps of lime upon a grass field that he did not intend should be broken up at the time. The mistake was soon discovered, and no more lime was laid down at that place, and the few heaps (about a bushel in each) were allowed to lie, neglected, without being spread. The field was pastured upon for seven or eight years after that, before it was converted into tillage; and the heaps were by that time become so flat, and so far sunk into the ground, that they could hardly be discovered.

Before it was ploughed up, the whole of the field was limed, and this part of it equally so with the rest; nor were the old heaps touched till the plough went through them in tilling the field, when the lime was there turned up, with only a very small mixture of soil. The consequence was, that at every one of these heaps, a tuft of corn sprung up with such luxuriance as to be entirely rotted before harvest;—and for many years afterwards, these tufts could be distinguished from the other parts of the field, at a very great distance, like so many buttons on a coat;—and, perhaps, continue so to this day.

From these experiments, as well as other considerations that will afterwards occur,—there seems to be reason to conclude, that on soils which do not naturally abound with chalk, or other calcareous matter, there is less danger in giving too much lime, than in applying too little; except in those cases where an over-luxuriance is dreaded.

§ 21.

I have often heard it urged, as an objection to the use of lime as a manure, that although it does indeed promote the fertility of a soil, in a higher degree at first, yet, in the end, it renders it much more steril than formerly; on which account, they say, it ought not to be at all employed.

This, like many other objections to useful practices, takes its rise entirely from the avarice and unskilfulness of those who complain. It is chiefly heard of in those parts of the country where it is not uncommon for a farmer, after once liming a poor soil, to take fifteen or sixteen crops of oats successively, without any other dressing or alternation of crops. It must be a good manure that enables these soils to produce such a number of successive scourging crops of any sort: But it would be a marvellous one, indeed, if it should prevent those fields from being exhausted by them.

But, is it not well known, that in all the richest and best improved parts of the country, lime has been long employed as a manure? Yet, so far are these soils from being rendered steril by it, that it is doubtful if any art, without the affiftance of lime, or fome calcareous matter, could ever have brought thefe fields to their prefent degree of fertility. Thofe, therefore, who complain of the hurtful effects of lime as a manure, proclaim what they ought to conceal,—that they have had in their poffeffion a treafure, which might have enriched their pofterity, but which they have idly fquandered away in their own life-time.

§ 22.

We are not only unacquainted with the mode in which lime operates upon the foil, but we are even, in a great meafure, ignorant of the actual changes that are produced upon the earth, after this manure is applied. So much time is neceffary to difcover thefe, —and fuch accuracy of obfervation is required, that it will, perhaps, be long before the whole fhall be fully afcertained. I fhall mention a few that have occurred to myfelf.

It is often afked, how long the effects of lime may be perceived on the foil? and, if by this queftion it be meant to afcertain the length of time that the effects of lime will be perceptible in promoting the luxuriance of the crop after one manuring, it is no wonder that very different anfwers fhould be given, as the effects muft vary with the quantity or quality of the lime employed; the nature of the crops that follow, and many other circumftances, that it would be impoffible here to enumerate.

But if it be viewed in another light; if lime be fuppofed to alter the foil, fo as to render it fufceptible of being affected by other manures in a more fenfible degree, fo as to make it capable of producing crops, that no art could otherwife have effected, and to admit of being improved by modes of culture that would not otherwife have produced any fenfible benefit; the anfwer to the queftion would be more eafy, as, in this light, it is pretty plain, that its effects will be felt, perhaps, as long as the foil exifts. I believe,

I believe, farmers are seldom accustomed to consider lime, or other calcareous manures, in this last point of view; although, when it comes to be inquired into, I doubt not but this will be found to be by far the most valuable effect of these manures. A few facts will best illustrate my meaning:

In Derbyshire, the farmers have found, that by spreading lime in considerable quantities upon the surface of their heathy moors, after a few years, the heath disappears, and the whole surface becomes covered with a fine pile of grass, consisting of white clover, and the other valuable sorts of pasture-grasses. This shows, that lime renders the soil unfriendly to the growth of heath, and friendly to that of clover.

It is found by experience, that in all porous soils, which are not exposed to too much dampness, in every part of Scotland, where lime has not been employed, heath has a natural, and almost irresistible propensity to establish itself. In those parts of the country where lime has been much used as a manure, we find, that the fields may be allowed to remain long in grass, without being covered with that noxious plant.

Again:—It is well known by those who have been attentive, and have had opportunities of observing the fact, that peas, of any sort, can never be successfully cultivated in any part of the country, where the soil is not of a very strong clayey nature, or where lime or other calcareous manures have never been employed. If the ground be made as rich as possible with common dung, although the peas, in that case, will vegetate, and grow for some time with vigour; yet, before they begin to ripen, they become blighted; usually die away entirely before the pod is formed, and but rarely produce a few half-formed peas.

But if the ground has ever been limed, although, perhaps, at the distance of thousands of years before that period, it never loses its power of producing good crops of peas, if it is put in a proper tilth for carrying them at that time.   Again:—

Again:—In countries that have never been limed, the kinds of grafs that fpontaneoufly appear, if left to themfelves, are the fmall bent-grafs and feather-grafs. In places where lime has ever been ufed, the ground, if exhaufted, produces fewer plants of thefe graffes; but in their ftead, white clover, the poa and fefcue graffes, chiefly abound.

The foil, in either of thefe cafes, may become equally *poor*;—that is, may produce equally fcanty crops: But, the means of recovering them will be fomewhat different. In the laft cafe, a fallow feldom fails to prove beneficial. In the firft, it is often of no effect, fometimes, even hurtful. In the laft, a moderate dreffing of dung, produces a much more fenfible and lafting effect, than in the other. In the laft, the quality of the grafs, as well as its quantity, rather improves by age. In the firft, thefe circumftances are reverfed.

I might mention feveral other obfervations, tending to fhow that ground, which has been once impregnated with calcareous matter, acquires qualities from that moment which it did not poffefs before, which it ever afterwards retains, and never returns exactly to its former ftate. But, I have faid enough to fuggeft this idea:—future obfervations will fhow how juftly it is founded.

§ 23.

Although lime has fuch powerful effects on the foil, it does not feem ever to incorporate with the mould, fo as to form one homegeneous mafs; but the lime remains always in detached particles, which are larger or fmaller, in proportion as it has been more or lefs perfectly divided when it was fpread, or broken down by the fubfequent mechanical operations the foil may have been made to undergo.

Hence it happens, that in ploughing, if there chance to be any lumps of calcareous matter in a dry ftate,

upon

upon the furface, they naturally tumble into the bottom of the open furrow, as foon as the earth is edged up upon the mould-board, fo as to fall into the loweſt place that has been made by the plough before the furrow is fairly turned over.

In confequence of this circumſtance, it muſt happen, that, in the courfe of many repeated ploughings, more of the lime will be accumulated at the bottom of the foil, than in any other part of it. And as the plough fometimes goes a little deeper than ordinary, the lime, that on thefe occafions chances to be depofited in the bottom of thefe furrows will be *below* the ordinary ſtaple of the foil, it will be ufelefs for the purpofes of the farmer. It is commonly thought, that the lime has *funk* through the foil by its own gravity;—although it is certain, that lime is fpecifically lighter than any foil, and can only be accumulated at the bottom of the mould by the means above defcribed; others think, that the lime is chemically diffolved, and afterwards depofited there; but this idea is not corroborated by the facts that have fallen under my obfervation. The directions that follow are equally applicable in either cafe.

To obviate this inconvenience, it behoves the farmer, in the firſt place, to be extremely attentive to have his lime divided into as fmall particles as poſſible at the time of fpreading: For, if thefe are fufficiently fmall, they incorporate fo intimately with the mould, as to be incapable of being eafily detached from it. On this account, as well as others, it is always moſt advifable to fpread the lime when in its dry powdery ſtate, immediately after flaking, before it has had time to run into lumps.

It is alfo of importance to plough the foil with a more fhallow furrow than ufual, when lime is put upon it; efpecially the firſt time it is ploughed after the lime has been fpread upon its furface: Becaufe, at that ploughing, the lime being all on the furface, a

larger

larger proportion of it is turned into the bottom of the last-made furrow, than at any succeeding ploughing; and therefore more of it will be buried beneath the staple than at any other time, if the furrow shall have been very deep.

This circumstance becomes more essentially necessary in ploughing grass-ground that has been newly limed; because, in this case, the lime is less capable of being mixed with any part of the soil than in any other.

It also becomes extremely necessary, in all succeeding times, to guard as much as possible, against ploughing to unequal depths.

I have hitherto spoken only of *lime* as a manure; but most of these observations, it will appear, may be equally applied to other calcareous matters. That the comparative value of these, and the real difference between them, when compared separately with lime, as well as with one another, may be fully understood, it will be necessary to consider each class of these substances separately, and point out with precision its peculiar distinctive qualities.

§ 24.

OF CHALK.

All the writers on agriculture whom I have ever yet met with, have considered the several classes of calcareous substances as distinct kinds of manures, and as possessing qualities extremely different from one another on many occasions. And hence it happens, that sometimes one of these, which chances to have become the favourite of the author, and sometimes another, is highly recommended, while the others are despised as useless, or reprobated as pernicious.

In this manner, a very late Writer,* with whom chalk is a peculiar favourite, says, 'I will lay it down

---

* The Author of the Complete English Farmer.

down as a certain and incontrovertible maxim, that *chalk* fresh from the pit, laid on and managed as before directed, in the proper season, will enrich every sort of earth it is laid upon ; and that *lime*, on the contrary, laid on at whatever time, or managed in whatever manner, will, after the first or second year, impoverish every soil it mixes with.

It would be no difficult matter to produce other authors, who, in a like decisive manner, reprobate the use of *chalk*, while they enlarge, without bounds, on the qualities of *lime ;* and others who prefer *marle* of different sorts, or some of the other classes of calcareous earths, as the most valuable of all manures, while they condemn the others beyond all bounds of moderation.

The truth, however, is, that although these authors may be right in recommending their own favourite manures, the beneficial effects of which they may have often experienced ; as they usually condemn the others merely from early prejudices, or imperfect trials of them, which have not succeeded, their decisions ought only to be considered as a proof of their being unacquainted with the *real* qualities of the matters they condemn, and of that presumptuous weakness which is ever the attendant of ignorance.

Nothing can afford a stronger proof, that the author above mentioned was totally unacquainted, either in theory or practice, with the *real* difference between chalk and lime, than the positive distinction he has made between these two substances as a manure.*

§ 25.

It has been demonstrated in the preceding part of this Essay, that lime differs not in any of its qualities from chalk, except that it is deprived of its fixed air ; which can have no effect on it as a manure, because it again absorbs that fixed air before it has been a few days

* The Reader ought to be informed, that the *lime* he condemns, is lime made from the very *chalk* he so much approves of.

days applied to the foil. After this period, therefore, what was originally *lime*, is now chalk, and muſt have the ſame effects upon the ſoil *in every reſpect*, as an equal quantity of chalk, *equally ſpread upon it*, would have had.

It is eaſy, however, for thoſe who attend to the *practice* of this Gentleman, to account for his partiality to *chalk*. The quantity of chalk he recommends, is twenty-five loads *per* acre ; which, I ſuppoſe, may be about twelve hundred buſhels.* He adviſes only ten or fifteen buſhels of lime. Is it ſurpriſing that the effects of theſe two dreſſings ſhould be extremely different?

He ventured once to give a field of clay a dreſſing of ſixty buſhels of lime ; after which he took,

1. wheat,	produce	16 buſhels,
2. oats, . . .		4 quarters,
3. barley, . . .		5 buſhels,
4. clover, . . .		worth nothing.

Hence, ſays he, the lime has ruined my ſoil.

The ſoil was acknowledged to be poor—Inſtead of ſixty, it is doubtful if ſix hundred buſhels would have been ſufficient to make it produce good crops, under a management ſo execrable in other reſpects.

But—to leave off theſe ungracious ſtrictures, I now proceed—

§ 26.

CHALK, as has been often ſaid in the courſe of this Eſſay, is a pure calcareous earth, haſtily concreted. Sometimes it is mixed with a ſmall proportion of *argillaceous** matter, in which ſtate it approaches to the nature

---

* A *load*, I underſtand, to be a waggon-load---which, I ſuppoſe, may contain between five and ſix quarters.

* Clayey.

nature of *marle.* In either the one or the other of these states, it is employed as a manure in the countries where it abounds.

Chalk differs not from lime in any particular that can affect the farmer, unless it be that *lime*, by being in the state of a fine powder, admits of being more equally spread upon the ground, and more intimately mixed with the soil, than *chalk*;—from whence it follows, that a much smaller quantity of lime may be employed successfully as a dressing for ground, than could possibly be the case with chalk.

In order, therefore, to make chalk produce the greatest possible effect upon the soil, it becomes necessary to reduce it into as small pieces as can be done; so that it ought to be an object of great importance to those farmers who have an opportunity of employing this substance, to discover what is the easiest and least expensive method of reducing it, as soon as possible after it is spread upon the soil, into very small portions.

Chalk is such a porous substance, that when in its native bed, after long and continued rains, it is found to have imbibed a great deal of moisture, by which it assumes a softish feel to the touch.

But if chalk be dug out of the pit and dried slowly and perfectly by the heat of a summer's sun, its pores become in some degree contracted;—it resists, in a great measure, the fresh admission of water, and acquires a much greater degree of hardness, than when it was originally dug from the quarry.

On the contrary, if it be taken from the pit during the wet weather in winter, and exposed to the rains that usually fall at that season, it has never time to dry—its pores remain quite full of water; and when the frost comes on, that water in the act of freezing, being greatly expanded, bursts it forcibly asunder, and makes it crumble down into a slimy kind of powder. And as the pieces that may remain undecomposed, continue to absorb more as the rains fall from the heavens, the frosts that may succeed occasion a new dissolution ;—so that by these alternate rains and frosts, the whole is in time totally divided, so as to admit of being pretty evenly spread, and mixed with the soil.

For these reasons, it is always expedient to dig the chalk in the beginning of winter, and to spread it immediately upon the field as well as can be done, so as to expose it to the vicissitudes of the winter weather, before it has had time to harden after being taken from the pit.

§ 27.

As the chalk ought always to be carried to the field while yet wet, it, in a great measure, prevents those who may be at a distance from the place where it is found, from being benefitted by this manure; because the carriage of it would in these circumstances be extremely burdensome.

To obviate this inconvenience, it becomes a very economical practice, to reduce it to the state of lime before it is carried home: For, in this way, the weight is not only much diminished by the dissipation of all the moisture from the chalk, but it can also be carried home in summer, when the weather and roads are at the best; and a much smaller quantity will produce an equal effect, than when it is in the state of chalk.

Those, therefore, who have no other calcareous manure within reach of them but chalk, when that is at a considerable distance, ought always to drive it in the state of lime. But those who are close by the pit, will, in general, find it more economical to employ it in the state of chalk.

§ 28.

Chalk so much abounds in the southern parts of Britain, that ships sometimes bring it as a ballast to the north; on which occasions, it may be purchased at a moderate price by the farmer. But although it contains

contains perhaps nearly an equal quantity of calcareous matter as the same bulk of some very pure kinds of lime, yet it will not be good economy in him to purchase it at the same price with the lime, as at least three or four times more chalk than lime will need to be applied to his soil, before it produces an equal effect: For, as it is impossible to get that hard dry chalk reduced to small enough parts, a great quantity must be applied before it can produce any sensible effect; and although the effects of this manure may be lasting, yet it is never any thing near equal to lime, if applied in equal quantities.

Another calcareous matter, of great utility as a manure, is *marle*—The distinctive properties of which fall now to be considered.

§ 29.

OF MARLE.

Few substances appear under a greater diversity of forms, than marle. Hence it is usual for writers on agriculture, to enumerate, as distinct manures, the several varieties of this general class of bodies. But as all the different kinds of marle that have hitherto been discovered, may be reduced to two general classes, viz. *earthy* marles, which are always found in fossil strata under the earth, and *shell* marle, which always retains evident marks of its animal origin. I shall consider each of these separately, as distinct substances.

§ 30.

Of Earthy or Fossil Marle.

The varieties of this class of bodies are distinguished by names suggested by the appearance they assume when fresh dug from their native beds. When they are soft, and of an uniform texture, they are called clay marles; when firm and hard, stone marles; when these

these assume a thin foliacious appearance, they are denominated slate marles, and so on.

But whatever appearance they assume when fresh dug, or by whatever name they are known, they all agree in this, that if they be exposed for a sufficient time to the action of the air, they crumble into smaller parts, and fertilize the earth to which they have been properly applied.

The ingenious Dr. Ainslie has demonstrated, by an accurate set of experiments recorded in the Physical and Literary Essays, in the third vol. of my Agricultural Essays, That all the varieties of this class of bodies contain a considerable proportion of clay, united with calcareous matter; whereas lime-stone, if it does not consist of pure calcareous matter, is usually united with sand in various proportions.

The calcareous matter in marle, does not differ in any respect from that in lime-stone, and its proportions in many cases is the same in marle as in lime-stone;—so that the difference between the appearance and qualities of these two substances, arises entirely from the nature of the heterogeneous bodies mixed with the calcareous matters.

When *marle* is exposed to the air, the clay, in its composition, absorbs the moisture that falls from the clouds—swells with it—becomes soft—and, gradually losing its cohesion, crumbles to pieces. If lime-stone is exposed to the air, the sand in its composition is not in the least affected by moisture, and it retains its original figure and dimensions for a great length of time.

When sand is mixed with the clay that enters into the composition of marle, it assumes a stony-like appearance, and is more or less firm, according to the quantity of sand, or other circumstances. But where there is clay at all in the composition, it will be gradually softened by water acting upon it; and it is owing to this circumstance alone, that stone-marles fall in time to pieces when exposed to the air. But

But if marle be expofed to the action of a moderate fire, the clay in its compofition becomes hard—it is no longer capable of abforbing water, or of being affected by it in any degree ; fo that the marle, if not of a very pure fort, or fuch as contains only a very fmall proportion of clay mixed with the fand in its compofition, will become firmer after burning than it was before, and be in this ftate with more difficulty reduced to powder, which is the reverfe of what happens with limeftone.

Marle, therefore, is fit to act as a manure, without any other preparation than digging it from the pit, and fpreading it upon the ground ; whereas lime-ftone always requires to be reduced to a powder, either by burning or otherwife, before it can be of any ufe in that way.

But as lime-ftone is at once reduced into much fmaller parts by calcination than marle ever can be brought to at firft, a much fmaller proportion of lime may be equally fpread over an acre of ground, than of marle ; and therefore it will produce, in equal quantities, a much more fenfible effect.

§ 31.

The difcerning reader, who attends to thefe circumftances, will eafily perceive the reafons for all the peculiarities of practice that prevail with regard to the application of lime and marle, and be able, without embarraffment, to judge in what cafes it may be moft for his profit to employ the one or the other of thefe manures, when they are both within his power.

He may afcertain the proportion of calcareous matter contained in the marle, by the fame procefs already defcribed for trying lime-ftone, page 72, and thus compare the intrinfic value of the lime and marle in any cafe. For this is always in proportion to the calcareous matter contained in either.

He will eafily perceive, however, that the fame

quantity of calcareous matter in the state of *lime*, will produce a much greater effect than when it is in the state of *marle;* because it is divided into infinitely smaller particles, can be more equally spread upon the ground, and more intimately mixed with the soil.

Hence it universally happens, that a much larger quantity of marle is applied at one dressing, than of lime. From one to two hundred cart-loads of marle is a common dressing to an acre, that is, from three thousand to six thousand bushels; whereas, from thirty to three hundred bushels of lime is a common dressing for an acre of ground.

In these proportions, it is reasonable to think that the effects of the marle will continue to be longer felt than those of the lime: For, as the marle is gradually broken into smaller pieces every year, these will successively mix with the soil, and produce an effect nearly similar to what might be expected from an annual dressing of lime.

It may likewise be expected, that a full dressing of marle, in the proportions above named, will produce a more capital improvement upon light spungy grounds, than an ordinary dressing of lime;—because, independent of the calcareous matter, the large proportion of clay applied in this manner, may produce some alteration on the quality of the soil. This alteration, however, will be different, according to the nature of the extraneous matter contained in the marle.

But as all marles contain clay, it is natural to think that clay lands will not be benefitted at all by this circumstance, as in these cases the calcareous matter alone in the marle will be to such soils an useful addition. Hence light land will be in general more highly benefitted by this manure than clay land, which has given rise to the following vulgar rhyme:

> He that marles sand,
> Will soon buy land;
> But he that marles clay,
> Throws all away.

The

The truth, however, is, that clay is as highly benefitted by the calcareous matter in marle, as sand is; so that a rich marle will be nearly equally beneficial in both cases. But there are some kinds of clays that are very free from any mixture of sand, and assume the appearance of marle; and are so called, although they hardly contain almost any calcareous matter at all. These may perhaps, on some occasions, be an useful addition to light soils, and worth the expense of carrying to them when near, but could scarcely be of any use at all upon clayey soils. It has probably been some poor kind of marle of this sort that has given rise to the proverb above quoted.

§ 32.

I shall not pretend to prescribe positive rules for determining when the one or the other of these substances, *lime* or *marle*, ought to be preferred as a manure; as a decision in favour of the one or the other must, in a great measure, depend upon the situation of the place where they can be both obtained; the purity of either of them respectively; the price at which they may be purchased, and the expense of carriage: all these circumstances may be best ascertained by every individual for himself.

But I may be allowed to observe, that it argues a great want of knowledge of the real qualities of these substances, when a man prefers the one of these, and condemns the other, in all cases. For it is merely a matter of calculation, *when* the one, or *when* the other, may be most valuable to any particular person.

If the marle be tolerably rich, and can be obtained at little expense near the field in the proportions usually employed, it will be, in general, more advantageous to the possessor, who has a prospect of enjoying his farm for a long time, to use marle in preference to lime.

But when it must be brought from a distance, *lime*,
in

in all cafes, will be cheaper, and on that account better than *marle*.

If marle contains a great proportion of clay, it may be worth the expenfe of driving to a light foil on fome occafions, even where lime could be procured as cheap: But, on all occafions, if the fame quantity of calcareous matter in the ftate of lime can be obtained at the fame price, *that* will be a much more beneficial manure for clayey foils than marle. Impure marle is indeed feldom worth the expenfe of carting on a clayey foil.

Some readers will be much diffatisfied at reading this fhort account of the nature of marle, and its operation as a manure. For as they have been accuftomed to look upon this manure as poffeffing fome very fingular qualities peculiar to itfelf, and to think that it differed from lime in fome very effential refpects, and would produce effects upon the foil nowife fimilar to that which would be produced by lime in any cafe; they will feel a kind of uneafinefs at being obliged to ftrike this one off their lift of diftinct and feparate manures. But it is the bufinefs of true philofophy to eradicate that fpirit for myfterious credulity, which is fo apt to lull the reafoning faculty afleep, and make the mind reft fatisfied with the contemplation of ideal phantoms created by the fancy, inftead of real objects of ufeful knowledge.

§ 33.

Of Shell Marle.

Shell marle is always found in low places, that either are, or have been covered with water. It is a whitifh powder, that has been formed by the gradual decompofition of fhells, in the courfe of many ages. It is, therefore, a pure calcareous matter, without any other mixture than the mud and other fediments, that may have funk to the bottom of the water, in ponds where it has been formed. As

As the proportion of sediment that may have mixed with the shells, may be very different in different situations; this kind of marle, like all others, may be more or less pure, and, of consequence, of greater or smaller value to the farmer. Its purity may be determined by the mode prescribed, page 72, and its value thus ascertained with precision.

It is usually a light, spungy substance, very slightly coherent; and contains more calcareous matter in proportion to its weight, than the common sorts of lime. And as it admits of being spread as equally as lime, it may in general be carried with profit as far as lime.

But as it is more spungy than lime, perhaps a smaller quantity will fill the measure; on which account, the prime cost of the same quantity of marle ought to be a little below that of lime, to be equally profitable to the farmer.

Shell marle, however, cannot be carried so far with profit as shell lime of the best sort; as this last, in that state, wants a great proportion of its moisture, air, &c. which greatly diminishes its weight.

It is, nevertheless, a very great treasure to those who can discover it, as it is almost in all cases of equal value with lime, produces the same effect upon the soil, admits of being equally easily spread, and can for the most part be obtained, upon the spot, at a much smaller expense.

But, in situations where fuel is scarce and dear, it is of much greater value than the best lime-stone, and ought to be prized accordingly by every possessor of ground: nor ought any one, in such a situation, to omit searching diligently every place where there is the smallest probability of finding it.

§ 34.

§ 34.

Of Shelly Sand.

On many parts of the sea-coast, great beds of shells are to be found, which have been broken into such small parts as to assume the appearance of sand. This is a rich and valuable manure, that deserves to be highly prized by those who are within reach of it; but, it is too often neglected and unobserved, as this kind of sand has, on many occasions, very much the appearance of ordinary sand.

This may readily be discovered, by pouring a little aqua-fortis, or any other mineral acid,* upon the sand you wish to examine. If it contains shells, an effervescence will ensue; and the proportion of calcareous matter contained in any sort of sand, may be ascertained by the same process already so often referred to, p. 72. Nor ought this trial ever to be omitted before the sand is employed as a manure; because, a very small proportion of shells will make it effervesce violently, so that the degree of effervescence is no proof of its purity, and because the proportion of shells varies in all possible degrees.

If the shells are broken into very small fragments, and if the proportion of sand be inconsiderable, it will be nearly as valuable as lime, and may be driven to a great distance with profit. If the proportion of ordinary

---

* Many persons make this trial with *vinegar*, instead of the mineral acids; but this ought never to be done, as it often happens, that vinegar makes no sensible effervescence with calcareous substances. I would, therefore, advise every country gentleman, to keep a phial of aqua-fortis, or muriatic acid, always by him, for making trials of calcareous substances: the expense is next to nothing; and I am persuaded, from the want of it alone, many persons have failed to make discoveries of calcareous matters that might have been of high importance to themselves and families.

nary fand be very great, the expenfe in ufing it will be greater, as the quantity muft be confiderably increafed.

But, as it may, for the moft part, be procured at little expenfe, thofe who are poffeffed of it, are ufually able to employ it in great quantities; in which cafe, it will produce amazing effects, efpecially upon ftrong clay-land.

A much fmaller quantity of calcareous matter in this ftate, will produce a more fenfible effect, than when it is in any fort of earthy marle; becaufe it admits of being more equally fpread upon the ground, and more intimately mixed with the foil. Thofe, therefore, who are upon the fea-coaft, ought to fearch for it with care, as they will ufually obtain an invaluable treafure when they difcover it.

This fort of fand is much more common on the eaft coaft of Scotland, than is ufually imagined. All along the coaft of Fife, efpecially about St. Andrew's, the fand upon the fhore is richly impregnated with fhells;—but, it has never there been employed as a manure. On the north coaft of Aberdeenfhire, fhelly fand abounds, and has been of late employed as a manure, with the greateft fuccefs, by a gentleman diftinguifhed for his knowledge and public fpirit in that corner. It is likewife found in Banff-fhire, where it has been applied with the higheft fuccefs. And all along the coaft of Southerland and Caithnefs, the fands upon the fhore confift almoft entirely of fhells.

Thefe are treafures which will enrich pofterity, although they are at prefent, in a great meafure neglected. I mention them here, to induce my countrymen not to neglect a treafure of fuch ineftimable value. But on the weft coafts of Scotland, and among the iflands, fhelly-fand much more abounds, and its effects as a manure, are much more generally known than on the eaft coaft, fo that it is there univerfally employed as the moft efficacious manure with which they are acquainted. Its effects upon fome of their heathy

mofly

mossy soils, appears to be, in some cases, little short of enchantment.

The ingenious Mr. Craik, in Dumfriesshire, so well known for his judicious improvements in the drill husbandry, has, I am told, employed this manure for a longer time, and in greater quantities, than any other person in Scotland, and has been highly benefitted by it. I wish to produce such a respectable authority, with a view to induce others to follow his example.

§ 35.

Mr. Arthur Young, in one of his Tours, mentions a bed of shells near Colchester, in Essex, which the inhabitants distinguish by the name of *Cragg*, and employ as a manure, with great success. From his account of this substance, it would seem doubtful, whether it was a real calcareous matter or not. But he only tried it with vinegar, an acid too weak to produce any sensible effect on many sorts of calcareous matters, in certain circumstances. There is little room to doubt, but that, with a mineral acid, the effervescence would have been sufficiently violent.

§ 36.

In some places, there are found large beds of oyster-shells, almost entire. These are so large as to require to be broken into smaller fragments, before they can be profitably employed as a manure.—And as these may be easily calcined, they ought always to be reduced to the state of lime before they are used. Whoever finds a bed of these shells, finds a lime-quarry of the most valuable sort, and ought to value it accordingly.

It may be sometimes necessary to burn shelly sand into lime; and this may, on extraordinary emergencies, be practised, although it is rather a troublesome operation: For, as the incoherent sand always mixes with the fuel, and extinguishes the fire when in its native

tive state, it becomes necessary to reduce it first to some degree of consistency.—This may be effected by kneading the sand with a little clay, and moulding it into the form of bricks; which, when dried, will retain their form so long as to permit the fire to act upon the shells, and burn them to lime, which may be afterwards flaked and used. A manufacture of this kind was for some time carried on at the Duke of Bridgewater's great works, near Warrington, in Lancashire, as I am told, under the direction of the ingenious Mr. Brindley.

In situations where lime-stone cannot possibly be had, and where the carriage of *lime* would be extremely expensive, it may sometimes be advisable to burn some of this shelly sand into lime, for the *purpose of building* ;*—but if the lime is to be employed as a manure, it is a very idle and a useless process: For, the burning, in this case, can only be of use in dividing the calcareous matter into small parts, which has already been performed by Nature, when the shells were reduced to the state of fine sand.

§ 37.

Of Lime-Stone-Gravel.

This is a manure little known in Britain, although it is common in many parts of Ireland. It is a hard sort of marle, that assumes the appearance of small stones, or gravel, which, when spread upon the ground, and mixed with it, gradually falls into smaller pieces, and fertilizes the soil in proportion as it breaks down and mixes with it.

After what has already occurred, little needs be said as to the qualities or mode of applying this manure.

---

* The small quantity of clay that is introduced in this way, will not sensibly injure the power of the lime *as a cement* ; for, before the shells can be sufficiently calcined, the clay will be burnt to such a degree, as to render it impervious to moisture, like sand.

The reader will eafily be able to perceive, that if the pieces of which this gravel confifts are large, and diffolve but flowly, the quantity applied at one dreffing ought to be great, and the effects will be flow and lafting;—and, if the gravel is fmall, it will require a fmaller quantity, will operate more quickly, and laft for a fhorter time, like all other calcareous fubftances in the fame circumftances.

Thefe are all the varieties of calcareous matter that I have ever known to be ufed as a manure. They are all extremely ufeful in proper circumftances—perhaps equally fo, if thefe circumftances are duly attended to. To affift the farmer ftill farther, the following general Aphorifms relating to the application of calcareous matters, as a manure, may be of ufe:

§ 38.

APHORISM I.

There feems to be only one kind of calcareous matter; and all the varieties of calcareous fubftances that we meet with, are entirely occafioned by a diverfity in the nature of the extraneous bodies with which the calcareous matter is united, or a difference in the form it may appear in at the time.

* * * * * * * *

Confidered as a manure, thefe extraneous matters may be more or lefs beneficial, according to particular circumftances relating to the foil, &c. In all the foffil calcareous concretions, clay or fand feem to be the only extraneous matters worth attending to, neither of which can ever be of great confequence as a manure, although they may be more or lefs proper for different foils. In thofe calcareous fubftances that belong to the animal kingdom, the flefhy parts of the animals may be fometimes united with the calcareous, which will greatly promote their effects as a manure on every fort of foil whatever. This does not, however, feem to be the cafe, either with fhell-marle, or
fine

fine shelly sand; as, in both these cases, the animals which once inhabited these shells, have been so long dead that no part of the fleshy substance can remain. But the recent shells obtained from fishing towns, operate much more powerfully as an animal manure, than as a calcareous matter, when first applied.

It is not impossible but that man may in time fall upon some contrivance for obtaining this animal calcareous manure in much greater abundance and perfection than it has hitherto been obtained. There is a small species of fresh water *wilk*,—which increases so fast, as, in a surprisingly short time, to fill a considerable space with solid wilks, if a few of them have been placed in a proper receptacle for that purpose, and water duly administered to them. If then ponds were prepared for this purpose, and properly stocked with this animal, and if they were allowed to increase till a bed of them, of considerable thickness, was accumulated, might they not then be taken out in abundance to be employed as a manure? These, if bruised under a stone like a tanner's wheel, to reduce the shells to small fragments, would certainly form as rich and efficacious a manure as could possibly be devised: nor could there be any difficulty in disposing the ponds in such a manner as to afford a constant annual supply.

It has probably been by a natural process similar to this, that all those beds of shell-marle we now meet with, have been originally produced. This species of marle is generally found to consist of the shells of this sort of small wilk, more or less decomposed. The animals which inhabited these shells have been once nourished by the water contained in those hollow places where this sort of marle is always found, and have probably been entirely destroyed by some accidental drought, which deprived them of the water necessary for their existence, or to some other disastrous circumstance that it is impossible for us now to

point

point out; and the shells remaining behind, gradually mouldered down to the state in which we now find them.

§ 39.

APHORISM II.

The same quantity of calcareous matter, will, in all cases, operate equally powerful on soils of a similar quality, when in a similar state. But these effects may be accelerated or retarded,—be more uniform or unequal, according as the calcareous matter is more or less perfectly divided when it is first applied to the soil.

* * * * * * *

If the calcareous matter be divided into very small Particles, so as to admit of being equally spread over a very large surface, a small quantity of it will produce a much more sensible effect, than if the same quantity of calcareous matter had been applied in large lumps, which could, in that case, have operated only upon a very few particles of the soil:—Therefore, *lime, fine shelly sand, or shell marle*, if equally pure, may be applied, with profit, in much smaller quantities than any other class of calcareous manures.

Hence also it follows, that if equal quantities of calcareous matter are employed as a manure, that kind which admits of being most minutely divided, will produce the greatest effect at the beginning; because the separate particles will be at liberty to act on a much greater number of particles of the soil at once, than when it is less perfectly divided.

But if a sufficient quantity of calcareous matter has been applied, when in pretty large masses, so as to cover the ground pretty equally; and if these lumps continue to dissolve in the soil in all after-periods, the effect of this dressing will be much longer perceived, than that of a dressing of calcareous matter in fine powder, that should produce at first an effect equal to this.—Perhaps, in this case, the virtue of every particle

ticle of the calcareous matter will come, in time, to produce a full effect upon the soil, and benefit it nearly as much as an equal quantity of very finely powdered calcareous matter would have done, applied at different times. Stone and clay marles, therefore, are equally efficacious manures as powdered lime, although more slow in their operation.

But as lime that has been suffered to run into solid cakes before it is applied to the soil, can neither be properly spread upon it, nor has any chance of being dissolved by the action of the air afterwards, it never can be made to produce its full influence on the soil; and therefore this mode of applying calcareous matter is the most uneconomical that could ever be practised.

§ 40.

APHORISM III.

Calcareous matter, alone, is not capable of rearing plants to perfection: mould is necessary to be mixed with it, in certain proportions before it can form a proper soil. It remains, however, to be determined, what is the due proportion of these ingredients for forming a proper soil.

* * * * * *

We know, that neither chalk, nor marle, nor lime, can be made to nourish plants alone; and soils are sometimes found, that naturally abound with the two first of these to a faulty degree. But the proportion of calcareous matter in these is so much larger than could ever be produced by art, where the soil was naturally destitute of these substances, that there seems to be no danger of erring on that side. Probably, it would be much easier to correct the defects of those soils in which calcareous matters superabound, by driving earth upon them as a manure, than is generally imagined, as a very small proportion of it sometimes affords a very perfect soil. I shall illustrate my meaning by a few examples.

Near Sandside, in the county of Caithness, there is a pretty extensive plain on the sea-coast, endowed with a most singular degree of fertility. In all seasons, it produces a most luxuriant herbage, although it never got any manure since the creation, and has been for time immemorial subjected to the following course of crops:

1*st*, Bear, after once ploughing from grass, usually a good crop.

2*d*, Bear after once ploughing, a better crop than the first.

3*d*, Bear after once ploughing, a crop equal to the first.

4*th*, 5*th*, and 6*th*, Natural grass, as close and rich as could be imagined,—might be cut if the possessor so inclined, and would yield an extraordinary crop of hay each year.

After this, the same course of cropping is renewed. The soil that admits of this singular mode of farming, appears to be a pure incoherent sand, destitute of the smallest particle of vegetable mould;—but, upon examination, it is found to consist almost entirely of broken shells: the fine mould here, bears such a small proportion to the calcareous matter, as to be scarcely perceptible, and yet it forms the most fertile soil that ever I yet met with.

I have seen many other links (downs) upon the sea shore, which produced the most luxuriant herbage, and the closest and sweetest pile of grass, where they consisted of shelly sand, which, without doubt, derive their extraordinary fertility from that cause.

A very remarkable plain is found in the Island of *Tir-eye* or *Tyre-ty*, one of the Hebrides.—It has long been employed as a common, so that it has never been disturbed by the plough; and affords annually the most luxuriant crop of herbage, consisting of white clover, and other valuable pasture-grasses, that can be met with any where.—The soil consists of a very pure

shelly

shelly sand. And the finest crop of bear, without exception, I ever saw grow out of the earth, I found in the island of Barra, one of the Hebrides, growing upon a bed of shell-sand, in which, I could not perceive the smallest particle of earth. I do suppose, that the produce would have exceeded that of the best crop of barley I ever saw, by two quarters, at least, per acre.—It had been manured with sea ware.

From these examples, I think it is evident, that a very small proportion of vegetable mould, is sufficient to render calcareous matter a very rich soil. Perhaps, however, a larger proportion may be necessary when it is mixed with clay, than with sand; as poor chalky soils seem to be of the nature of that composition.

At any rate, however, from these examples, as well as from those that have occurred in the preceding parts of this Essay, I think we may be sufficiently authorised to conclude, that there is no danger of ever applying calcareous substances to any soil in an over-proportion, if that soil was not originally impregnated with some kind of calcareous matters, and if it shall be afterwards cropped in a judicious manner.

§ 41.

APHORISM IV.

Calcareous matters act as powerfully upon land that is naturally poor, as upon land that is more richly impregnated with those substances which tend to produce a luxuriant vegetation.

* * * * * * *

Writers on agriculture have been long in the custom of dividing manures into two classes, viz. *enriching* manures, or those that tended directly to render the soil more prolific, however sterile it may be,—among the foremost of which was reckoned *dung*,—and *exciting* manures, or those that were supposed to have a tendency to render the soil more prolific, merely by acting

ing upon those enriching manures that had been formerly in the soil, and giving them a new stimulus, so as to enable them to operate anew upon that soil which they had formerly fertilized. In which class of stimulating manures, *lime* was always allowed to hold the foremost rank.

In consequence of this theory, it would follow, that lime could only be of use as a manure when applied to rich soils, and, when applied to poor soils, would produce hardly any,—or even perhaps hurtful effects.

I will frankly acknowledge, that I myself, was so far imposed upon by the beauty of this theory, as to be hurried along with the general current of mankind, in the firm persuasion of the truth of this observation, and for many years did not sufficiently advert to those facts that were daily occurring to contradict this theory. I am now, however, firmly convinced, from repeated observations, that lime and other calcareous manures, produce a much greater *proportional* improvement upon poor soils, than on such as are richer: And that lime alone, upon a poor soil, will, in many cases, produce a much greater and more lasting degree of fertility, than dung alone.

In direct contradiction to the theory, I must add, that I never yet met with a poor soil in its natural state, which was not benefitted in a very great degree by calcareous matters, when administered in proper quantities. But I have met with several rich soils, that were fully impregnated with dung, and therefore exactly in that state in which the theory supposes that lime would produce the greatest effect; but, upon which, lime, applied in any quantities, produced not the smallest sensible effect.

As I concern myself little about theories, this discovery gave me much less uneasiness than it will give to some of my readers; on which account, I shall not be much surprised, if they withhold their assent to this proposition for a very long time. I do not desire any
one

one to agree to it, till their own obfervations extort affent,—which, I have no hefitation in faying, will fooner or later happen to every unprejudiced and attentive obferver.

§ 42.

I fhall conclude this very long Effay with a cautionary advice, that might, perhaps, have been more properly introduced before, if it had occurred at the time; but it is of too much importance to be omitted entirely. It is this:

When farmers employ a great deal of lime, it sometimes happens that their horfes' feet are burnt by it, which is extremely troublefome, and fometimes proves even fatal to the poor animals*; a method of preventing or remedying that inconvenience will therefore be of ufe.

The beft method of preventing any inconvenience of this fort, is to fpread the lime, when in its powdery ftate, upon the field, as evenly as poffible, and allow it to lie in that ftate for fome time, before you begin to plough it. If the lime has been in fine powder, it will have become perfectly *effette* in a week or fo; after which time it will be as little corrofive as any kind of common earth, fo that the horfes may work among it with perfect fafety. But if it has been fuffered to run into clods before it was fpread, thefe, if not broken fmall, will be longer in abforbing their air, and, of confequence, will remain longer in an acrid ftate, fo that the ploughing may, in that cafe, be deferred for a week or fo longer; nor will it be even then fo perfectly fafe as the other.

But if it becomes neceffary at any time to plough in the lime immediately after it is fpread,—take care to do it only when the foil is perfectly dry; and in leading

---

* I have known several horfes actually killed by this means, and others fo difabled as never to be perfectly well afterwards.

ing your horses to the plough, take care to prevent them from going through any wet place, so as to wet their hoofs or ankles; for lime acts not at all upon any dry substance,—but when it is in its acrid caustic state, it would corrode the hair and flesh in a moment, if it has access to water. As soon as the horses are unyoked, keep their feet dry till you have got them carefully brushed, so as to wipe away all the dry powdery lime that may adhere to them; and if the least shower should fall, unyoke your horses immediately and carry them off the field.

With these precautions, they may work among caustic lime for any length of time, without receiving any damage.

But in case of any accident, by which a horse or man that is working among lime should be scalded by it, it is always advisable for every farmer who has work of that kind going forward, to keep a tub of very sour milk or whey in some place ready to wash the part affected well with it, which will quickly destroy the poignancy of the lime, and prevent the mischief that would otherwise arise from it. The sourer the milk or whey is, the better it will be for this purpose; it ought therefore to be long kept. For want of this, vinegar will produce the same effect, or very stale urine will be of use; but, the milk or whey is the cheapest and best remedy, and ought to be always in readiness.

POSTSCRIPT.

POSTSCRIPT.

Directions for ascertaining the purity of Lime, and discovering the Nature of the Bodies that may be mixed with it.

§ 1.

In the preceding Essay, I have supposed that no other *absorbent** earth is ever mixed with the *calcareous* in any sort of lime-stone; because, in fact, if ever any of these are mixed with the calcareous in these substances, they are in such small proportion as not to be worth regarding. Those, however, who want to be critically exact in their analysis of lime-stone, may discover if there is any other sort of absorbent earth contained in it, by dropping into the filtred solution obtained by the process § 13, p. 72, a few drops of a clear solution of volatile alkali. If no turbidness ensue, the calcareous earth has been pure. If any precipitation takes place on adding the alkali, drop more, and more, till no turbidness arises: then filtre the whole: what remains in the filtre, is absorbent earth, that is not calcareous; for acids attract volatile alkali more strongly than any of the absorbent earths, except the calcareous class alone.

§ 2.

It may oftener happen, that a considerable proportion of *gypsum* may be united with lime-stone in the same quarry; and as this substance would greatly alter the nature of the lime as a cement (see p. 37) and would probably affect it as much as a manure, it is of more importance to inform the reader of the easiest way of discovering this substance when it is present in lime-stone. It

---

* Absorbent earths are all those that unite with acids, of which there are several varieties; calcareous earths being one of these.

It has been already faid, that *gypfum* is a compound, confifting of the vitriolic acid and calcareous earth ; and as the vitriolic acid attracts this earth more ftrongly than any of the other acids, this compofition is not in the leaft affected by either the nitrous or muriatic acids.

Hence it follows, that if *gypfum* fhall be contained in any calcareous mafs examined by the procefs defcribed § 13, p. 72, it will remain untouched by the acid, and be found in the filtre, after the calcareous earth diffolved in the acid fhall have paffed through it, forming a part of the *refiduum*.

Take this *refiduum*, therefore,—add to it nearly its weight of fixed alkali* previoufly diffolved in a confiderable quantity of water, and filtered ; digeft it in a warm bath, or even boil it for fome hours ; pour the whole into a filtre, while yet warm ; as the fluid paffes through the filtre, pour upon it more boiling water ; as that paffes off, continue to add more water, till it comes through the filtre quite infipid and pure, and then let it run off entirely.

By this procefs, the vitriolic acid leaves the calcareous earth to unite with the fixed alkali (to which it has a ftronger affinity) and with it forms a vitriolated tartar :—this vitriolated tartar, and the fuperfluous alkali, are diffolved by the water, and carried through the filtre along with it ; fo that what remains behind is the earthy part of the *gypfum*, and the heterogeneous matters contained in the original lime-ftone. By pouring upon this *refiduum*, therefore, fome nitrous or muriatic acid, and treating it as directed in § 13, page 72, the calcareous earth that was in the *gypfum* will be now entirely diffolved ; fo that when it is filtered and dry, the difference between the weight of this *refiduum*, and what it formerly was, is the real weight of the *gypfum* originally contained in the lime-ftone.

N. B.

* Potafh.

- N. B. If the alkali employed to decompofe the *gyp-fum* was in a *mild* ftate, the calcareous earth that remains will effervefce ftrongly when it is diffolving in the acid; but if a *cauftic* alkali has been employed, the folution will be effected without any effervefcence at all.

As vitriolated tartar is not readily foluble in water, a confiderable quantity of water requires to be employed, which ought always to be hot, that the folution may be effected the more readily.

§ 3.

It has alfo been faid, (§ 30, p. 52,) that the only extraneous matter contained in lime-ftone is fand. But although fand, in general does predominate fo much over the other extraneous matters in lime-ftone, as to authorife the expreffion *in general,* yet there are fome exceptions that ought to be taken notice of.

1ft, There are fome kinds of lime-ftone, that, when analyfed, are found to contain a *refiduum* confifting of a foft flimy-like fubftance. This is always in very fmall proportions, and has probably been formed by a fediment fubfiding from the water while the rock was forming. It feems probable, that this kind of lime would be lefs proper to be employed as a cement than as a manure.

2d, Although marle and lime-ftone are juftly enough diftinguifhed in the text (§ 5 ;) yet it happens, that clay and fand are found naturally mixed with one another, in fuch various proportions, and in thefe ftates joined with calcareous matter, that there is no poffibility of afcertaining the exact point where marle ends, and lime-ftone begins.

A very fmall proportion of clay is fufficient to make an exceedingly hard lime-ftone relent in time in the air, and fall to pieces; fo that there are many forts of ftone marle that confift chiefly of fand and calcareous earth, and only a very little clay.

These very hard kinds of marle may be easily burnt into lime, so that they may be indifferently called marle or lime-stone.

3*d*, The same may be said of the distinction between marle and chalk (§ 5. p. 9.) Many substances which have the appearance and distinguishing properties of chalk, contain clay in different proportions. These dissolve in the air, or *run*, as it is termed, more readily than the pure hard kinds of chalk, and feel more unctuous or fatty to the touch; from whence they are called *fat* chalks. These, however, may be converted into lime; so that they might indifferently be called *chalk, marle,* or *lime-stone*.

The lime that is made from any of those substances that contain clay in their composition, is more proper for manure than for cement; especially that made from those substances that may be made to *fall* after they have undergone only a small degree of heat in calcining them, as in *chalk*; because, in these cases, the clay will not be sufficiently burnt to prevent it from being affected by water, and rendered soft by it.

The proportion of clay and sand contained in any lime-stone or marle, may be ascertained, by diffusing in water the *residuum* obtained by the analysis, (§ 13, p. 72*) allowing it to subside a little, and gently pouring off the fluid parts from the coarser sediment that subsides to the bottom; for, as clay remains much longer suspended in water than sand, it may be thus separated from the sand entirely;—when the water comes off clear, after having been left to subside a little, the *residuum* may be evaporated to dryness, and the loss of weight it has sustained by this operation, denotes the quantity of clay.

This is rather a mechanical, than a chemical process, which is called *elutriation*. § 4.

---

* Observe, it is *unburnt* lime-stone, or marle only, that should be subjected to this trial.

§ 4.

It has been demonstrated above, § 35, p. 58, that the quality of lime, considered as a cement, is greatly altered, by being more or less perfectly calcined;—it may therefore be, on many occasions, of use to those who are concerned in building, to be able to ascertain what proportion of any particular kind of lime is really reduced to a caustic state.—This may be done as under:

Take a known quantity of the quick-lime, perfectly dry;—add to that its own weight, or more, of common crude sal-ammoniac,* previously dissolved in a large proportion of water, and filtered;—digest this nearly in a boiling heat for some hours, till no more smell of volatile alkali is found to arise from it, adding fresh water as it evaporates. When the volatile alkaline smell is no longer perceived, throw the whole into a filtre,—let that pass off,—add more hot water,—and more still, till it come through the filtre tasteless and pure;—then dry the *residuum*, and weigh it;—the difference between that and the weight of the original lime, denotes the proportion of pure caustic lime that was contained in the original mass.

For, as the muriatic acid attracts *caustic* calcareous earth more strongly than it does the volatile alkali, the acid of the sal-ammoniac,† during the process, quits the alkali, and unites with the lime, and the alkali is suffered to fly off in a pungent vapour. The new substance formed by the union of the quick-lime with the muriatic acid, is called *liquid shell;* and as this is readily soluble in water, it passes off, together with the remaining undecomposed ammoniacal salt, with the water through the filtre; while the uncaustic lime, as it was neither capable of acting upon the ammoniac, nor of being dissolved in the water, remains behind in its solid state.

* Observe, it is not volatile sal-ammoniac.

† Crude sal-ammoniac is a compound salt, consisting of the muriatic acid and the volatile alkali.

BOOKS
Lately published by J. NANCREDE,
No. 49, Marlboro'-Street, BOSTON.

"On the title page of its Laws, as well as on its standards, was written the motto of,
"*Havoc, and spoil, and ruin, are my gain.*"

JUST PUBLISHED,
Embellished with an Emblematical Plate,
THE HISTORY OF THE
DESTRUCTION
OF THE
HELVETIC UNION
AND
LIBERTY;
BY J. MALLET DU PAN.

"Its situation (Switzerland's) is correctly and energetically drawn in the picture of *Athens*, left us by a writer of the middle ages, after the invasion of *Alaric*, It is the empty and bloody skin of an immolated victim! She has nothing left but ROCKS, RUINS, and DEMAGOGUES!" *Preface, p. 5.*

☞ "IF it be true, that the AMERICAN UNION AND LIBERTY have been and are still *threatened* by *France*,——That a number of American Citizens still doubt it ;—and that it is equally their wish and their interest, to transmit both to their descendants, in all their integrity—surely there can be nothing more interesting, or more useful for them, at this time of danger, than to read the melancholy account of the annihilation of a people, who, being situated like them, but more credulous, and less energetic, in their exertions for defence, fell under the combined weight of foreign and domestic intrigue !——the most dreadful scourge against which the American Government has had to contend, ever since the beginning of the present European war !"

2.
POEMS on various Subjects, by ROBERT SOUTHEY, *Author of Joan of Arc.*
"It can scarcely be necessary for us formally to recommend this little volume to the notice of our poetical readers, and its author to their esteem. No one who possesses a true relish for Poetry, we conceive, will open with indifference, a volume by the author of *Joan of Arc.* Genius is a despotic power, and irresistibly commands homage." *Monthly Review.*

3.
JOAN OF ARC, an Epic Poem, by ROBERT SOUTHEY; with Notes.

"We do not hesitate to declare our opinion, that the poetical powers displayed in it are of a very superior kind.——Conceptions more lofty and daring, sentiments more commanding, and language more energetic, will not easily be found: nor does scarcely any part of it sink to langour, as the glow of feelings and genius animates the whole. The language is, for the most part, moddled on that of Milton; and not unfrequently, it has a strong relish of Shakespeare."

Monthly Review, vol. 19, p. 361.

4.
JUST PUBLISHED,

Price 20 Cents.

AN ABRIDGMENT OF L. MURRAY's ENGLISH GRAMMAR, with an Appendix, containing an exemplification of the parts of speech and exercises in syntax, designed for the use of the younger class of learners; by LINDLEY MURRAY. *Its Character.*

"Having already expressed our approbation of Mr. Murray's English Grammar, we have only, in announcing this Abridgment, to observe, that it appears to us to be made with great judgment, and *that we do not know a performance of this kind better fitted for the use of Children*."

Analytical Review, Oct. 1797.

5.
IN THE PRESS,
And speedily will be published,
AN INTRODUCTION TO THE KNOWLEDGE AND PRACTICE OF GARDENING, by CHARLES MARSHALL, *Vicar of Brixworth, Northamptonshire.*

"God Almighty first planted a *Garden*; and indeed it is the purest of human pleasures: It is the greatest refreshment to the spirits of Man; without which, buildings and palaces are but gross handy works." *Bacon's Essays.*

Character of Marshall's Gardening.

"We have examined this performance, and we are well satisfied that the respectable author has, as he professes, given to the public the result of his *experience*; delivered with that plainness and perspicuity, which cannot fail of rendering his work highly useful to every reader who shall consult it, either for pleasure, or instruction. We say with pleasure, because Mr. Marshall has not dryly written his book in the common didactic and unvaried style: His manner is his own; and he has occasionally, but not too frequently, enlivened his pre-

Books lately publifhed by J. Nancrede.

cepts by fhort poetic quotations from THOMSON, COWPER, and other moral bards, who often, with ufeful and delighttul effects, direct their readers to
" Look through nature up to nature's God."
6. *Monthly Review.*

THE STUDIES OF NATURE, tranflated from the French of J. H. B. de St. PIERRE, by H. HUNTER, D. D. 3 vols. 8 vo.—fine wove paper, embellifhed with plates.

⁂ This very ingenious, interefting, and inftructive work has, fince its firft publication, gone through four fucceffive impreffions, under the author's immediate infpection; befides a variety of pirated editions in different parts of the European continent.

" No book difplays a more fublime Theology, inculcates a purer morality, or breathes a more ardent and expanfive philanthropy. St. Pierre has enabled us to contemplate this univerfe with other eyes; has furnifhed new arguments to COMBAT ATHEISM; has eftablifhed, beyond the power of contradiction, the doctrine of a Univerfal Providence; has excited a warmer intereft in favour of fuffering humanity; and has difcovered fources, unknown before, of moral and intellectual enjoyment."

7.

THE only Work of the kind extant in any language, which is of the greateft utility to the Merchant—the Seaman—the Student—Schools, Academies, &c.—and recommended by the LORDS of the ADMIRALTY.

Lately publifhed, in two volumes, in 8vo. Price 6 Dolls. bound,

The NAVAL GAZETTEER;
Or, SEAMAN's COMPLETE GUIDE.

Comprifing a full and accurate account, alphabetically arranged, of the feveral Coafts of all the Countries and Iflands in the known world, fhewing their Latitude, Longitude, Soundings, Stations for Anchorage, &c.

With a particular defcription of the feveral

BAYS,	CURRENTS,	OCEANS,	SANDS,
CAPES,	GULPHS,	RACES,	SHOALS,
CHANNELS,	HARBOURS,	RIVERS,	SOUNDS,
COVES,	HAVENS,	ROADS,	STRAITS,
CREEKS,	LAKES,	ROCKS,.	TIDES,

VARIATION of the COMPASS, &c.
Together with a picturefque Defcription of the form and appearance at fea of the feveral Headlands, Ifthmuffes, Peninfulas, Points, Promontories, &c. With ample directions for failing into or out of the different Ports, Straits, and Harbours of the four Quarters of the Globe, and for avoiding Dangers on the various and extended coafts; in which more than 12,000 Names of Places, &c. are treated of and explained.

Illuftrated with 17 correct Charts, including a Whole Sheet Chart of the World, on Mercator's Projection.

BY JOHN MALHAM.
Author of Navigation made Eafy and Familiar, &c.

Books lately published by J. Nancrede.

Character of the NAVAL GAZETTEER.

"The Author has given Directions for avoiding Dangers, and all other information that he could collect necessary for Pilotage; and he has carefully consulted the Discoveries of modern Navigators. The whole bears the Mark of Diligence and Ability; and we are of opinion that the NAVAL GAZETTEER is a valuable Addition to the Seaman's Library."

MONTHLY REVIEW for July, 1797.

"We may venture to recommend the NAVAL GAZETTEER as an important Acquisition in the Study of maritime Affairs, and no less useful to the general Student than to the Merchant. The Charts are numerous, and distinctly delineated."

CRITICAL REVIEW for September 1798.

*** This Work has been found particularly improving to Youth, and is therefore a valuable and acceptable Present to Persons entering on a Sea-faring Life, or learning Navigation.

8.

A VINDICATION OF DIVINE PROVIDENCE, *derived from a moral and philosophical survey of nature and of man.* By the Author of *Studies of Nature.*—2 vols. 8vo. with plates.

9.

The same work abridged, in 1 vol. 8vo. plates.

10.

BOTANICAL HARMONY DELINEATED; or, Applications of some general Laws of Nature to Plants; by the Author of *Studies of Nature,* with three botanical plates, elegantly engraved, 1 vol. 8vo.

11.

THE ADVENTURES OF TELEMACHUS, Son of Ulysses, by M. SALIGNAC FENELON.

*** *Of Fenelon, the Monthly Reviewers said in March, 1796,* "The annals of time do not, perhaps, contain a name more revered, by the best and wisest friends of the human race, than that of Fenelon; and it is to be doubted, whether any production of human genius ever was so effectual in enlightening mankind, and in rendering them benevolent and just, as the beautiful philosophic poem of Telemachus. It contains a greater portion of political and moral wisdom, than, as we believe, is to be found in any preceding work."

12.

The same work is to be had in English, with the French text on the opposite page, with corrections, in two vols. 12mo.

13.

Also in French, separate.—For execution and accuracy, the above is superior to the late English edition.

www.ingramcontent.com/pod-product-compliance
Lightning Source LLC
Chambersburg PA
CBHW021357230426
43666CB00006B/560